CAVERNS MEASURELESS TO MAN

CAVERNS MEASURELESS TO MAN

Sheck Exley

CAVE BOOKS

Published by CAVE BOOKS, 756 Harvard Avenue,
St. Louis, MO 63130, U.S.A.

CAVE BOOKS is the publications affiliate of
The Cave Research Foundation.

Layout and typesetting by Karen Lindsley
Print production by Pete Lindsley

Library of Congress Cataloging-in-Publication Data

    Exley, Sheck
        Caverns measureless to man / Sheck Exley.
        Includes index.
        ISBN 0-939748-20-7 (boxed lim. ed.)
        ISBN 0-939748-33-9 (hb)
        ISBN 0-939748-25-8 (pbk.)
        GV200.63.E95   1994
        797.2'3—dc20   94-17149
                                            CIP

Printed in the United States of America

In Xanadu did Kubla Khan

A stately pleasure-dome decree:

Where Alph, the sacred river, ran

Through caverns measureless to man

Down to a sunless sea.

— Samuel Taylor Coleridge

Acknowledgements

The author would like to express his appreciation to the many persons who helped with this book. Ned DeLoach, Beth Exley Paulsen, Pat Carver, Paul DeLoach, and Mary Ellen Eckhoff, among others provided invaluable assistance with the manuscript. Also many photographers provided illustrations for the book: Ned DeLoach, Paul Heinerth, John Harper, Henry Nicholson, Dave Sweet, Rob Power, Joe Prosser, Bob Gatling, Franjorg Krieg, Paul Smith, Court Smith, Edward Exley, Yolanda Iliffe, Glenn Thompson, Lee Gilman, Karan Pribble, Carl Cowart, Lewis Holtzendorff, Mary Ellen Eckhoff, Dan Lenihan, and Barbara Hasenmayer.

A special word of thanks must go to my invaluable and very patient editor, Richard A. Watson.

Contents

(continued)

Maps

1

Another Man's Nightmare

Invisible fingers grasped mine and drew me relentlessly downward, away from the surface of the sea. A powerful whirlpool was sucking me into the bowels of the earth along with myriad jellyfish, shrimp, and snapper. The large, dark eyes of the fish darted frantically back and forth as they struggled to escape the vortex. The harsh rasp of my scuba regulator echoed metallically in my ears as I inhaled. My exhaust bubbles sank with me into the narrow, pitch–black crevice instead of floating upward to the surface.

The spinning torrent slammed me into a rocky vise. I was wedged in so tightly that I could barely expand my chest to breathe. The rushing water flooded my face mask as I twisted to back out of the squeeze. Then a cloud of liquid mud descended upon me, blotting out what little vision I had left.

I laughed, thinking that my predicament would make a great nightmare for most people. Wriggling backward out of the narrow slot, I cleared the water out of my mask, then relaxed while the natural escalator—the inflowing current—continued to carry me downward. In seconds, I was spewed from the narrow, muddy entrance into an underground room more than 100 feet wide and 25 feet high. The water was suddenly as clear as air and the powerful lights of my five companions completely illuminated the vast cavern in all directions. We looked like giant fireflies as we hovered weightlessly among hundreds of crystal stalactites that hung from the ceiling like giant icicles of stone.

We were very strange fireflies. Over our rubber wet suits we wore 150 pounds of complicated equipment. On each diver's back were two large steel cylinders of air, double tanks connected with two valves. On one of the valves was clamped a regulator with a small rubber hose leading to a mouthpiece that delivered air to the diver each time he inhaled. Clamped to the other valve was an identical regulator, its mouthpiece dangling from a strap in case of an emergency. The first regulator had two extra rubber hoses attached, one of which went to an air pressure gauge that showed how much air was in the double tanks. The other hose was used for inflating the diver's buoyancy compensator vest at the press of a button. This vest, called a B. C., was worn around the neck and on the diver's chest or was sandwiched between the tanks and his back. The diver released air into the B. C. vest to counteract the weight of his gear, enabling him to hover effortlessly above the bottom. Completing this array were several underwater lights, two guideline reels, a knife, a watch, and a depth gauge, all clipped on for easy removal and use.

Despite the high reliability of scuba diving equipment, each of us carried redundant gear so that every one of us could handle any emergency alone. Also we had been trained to help each other in the various courses of the Cave Diving Section of the National Speleological Society (NSSCDS), sponsor of this 1982 expedition to dive Giant Cave in Belize, Central America. Included in our team of NSSCDS instructors and officers were Paul Heinerth and Shannon Heinerth, the original discoverers of the cave and Bill Fehring, Sandy Fehring, Mary Ellen Eckhoff, and me.

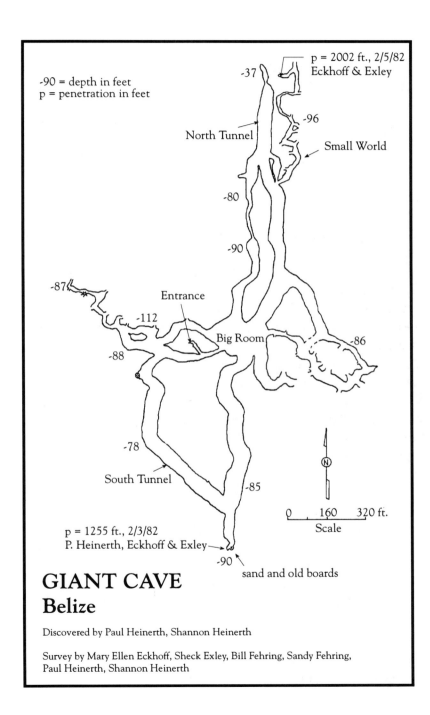

-90 = depth in feet
p = penetration in feet

-37

p = 2002 ft., 2/5/82
Eckhoff & Exley

-96

North Tunnel

Small World

-80

-90

-87

Entrance

-112

Big Room

-86

-88

-78

South Tunnel

-85

p = 1255 ft., 2/3/82
P. Heinerth, Eckhoff & Exley

-90

sand and old boards

0   160   320 ft.
Scale

N

GIANT CAVE
Belize

Discovered by Paul Heinerth, Shannon Heinerth

Survey by Mary Ellen Eckhoff, Sheck Exley, Bill Fehring, Sandy Fehring,
Paul Heinerth, Shannon Heinerth

Shannon Heinerth cruises through a forest of stalactites and stalagmites in Giant Cave, Belize. (*Photos by Paul Heinerth*)

Shannon Heinerth checks out a large stalagmite in Giant Cave. (*Photo by Paul Heinerth*)

I joined my companions in the huge room, put my hand in the light of my lamp for all to see, and signaled, "I'm OK." There was no sound except for periodic muted rumbles of our exhaust bubbles as we exhaled. I glanced at Mary Ellen to check on her and saw her blue eyes gleaming with excitement. She pivoted to lead us farther into the cave. We flapped our fins slowly to glide through a forest of huge calcite columns. The freedom from gravity was exhilarating, but each of us felt some slight unease from the realization that we were strangers in an environment where we could perish in an instant. Every few seconds we had to divert our attention from enjoyment of the cave to routine but grim matters of survival: gauge checks to see how much air was left, buddy checks to make sure our partners were OK, and line checks to verify our closeness to the guideline leading to the cave entrance.

As previously planned, Mary Ellen and I turned off into a side passage while the others continued down the main cavern to explore another tunnel. The side passage was considerably smaller than the main cavern's 100–foot–plus width. It was still an impressive tube with a diameter of 15 feet containing thousands of stalactites. We quickly reached the end of the old guideline, and Mary Ellen unhooked a fresh spool of 1/16 inch nylon twine. She tied it to the end of the line while hovering 10 feet above the cave floor, then turned around to confront the unknown.

Now we were going somewhere no one had ever been before, a rare privilege enjoyed by only a few explorers under the earth or the sea and on the moon. In one way, a cave explorer's thrill is greater than that of undersea explorers or astronauts: in this day of telescopes, space probes, sonic probes, and remote cameras, they can study where they are going ahead of time; cave explorers go into the unknown. Moreover, unlike an explorer of air–filled caves, a cave diver is rarely worried by the nagging suspicion that a torch–bearing prehistoric Indian might have been there before him: the technology for exploring underwater caves is scarcely three decades old.

As Mary Ellen led into the new cave area, she installed the guideline. This indicated our way back to the cave entrance if our lights failed or the water suddenly became cloudy from our carelessly stirring up mud by swimming too close to the floor. As we swam down the winding conduit, I wondered where it was going. Would it lead us for hundreds of feet eastward under a nearby island, or would we find a huge new cave area around the next bend? Suddenly, Mary Ellen turned and waved her light back and forth at me to get my attention. She pointed to a dim glow far ahead of us. Had we found a new entrance to the cave?

The mystery was solved when the glow gradually blossomed into the gleaming spotlights of our four companions. The tunnel they had explored and our side passage were connected as a loop several hundred feet long. After greeting each other and shaking hands, I checked my pressure gauge to find that I was down to nearly two–thirds of my starting air supply, the cave diver's turnaround point that I had established many years earlier. I gave everyone the thumbs–up hand signal, indicating that we should start out, and the six of us began our exit via the side passage Mary Ellen and I had explored. As we swam along I measured the distance, depth, and direction of the guideline and recorded it on an underwater slate so we could add this new section onto our map of Giant Cave.

By the time we had returned to the narrow entrance, nature's escalator had reversed. The current now swept us up and out of the crevice. This change in the direction of flow is caused by daily tidal changes in most caves that open into the sea. We could not let the current take us all the way to the surface, though. While our dive had lasted only an hour, we had been as deep as 90 feet at one point, so had to stop at 10 feet below the surface for several minutes to give the nitrogen in our blood time to adjust to reduced pressure. If we went up too soon, the nitrogen would form bubbles, causing the bends, which can cripple a person. We use submersible decompression tables to calculate the amount of time needed to stop; it increases with the time and depth of a dive.

Mary Ellen Eckhoff, Sheck Exley and Shannon Heinerth pause between dives. (*Photo by Franzjorg Krieg*)

A couple of hours later, I was savoring the last of a lobster dinner and was wiggling my toes in the soft sand floor of a thatched–roof hut on Caye Cawlker as I plotted the latest information onto our sprawling cave map. Paul swatted a mosquito in the warm night air, then leaned over to squint at the map.

"It looks like an octopus!" he said in his French Canadian accent.

The various tunnels of the cave extended in all directions from the narrow entrance like tentacles.

"Biggest octopus I ever saw," observed Bill, a marine biologist.

"And the biggest sea cave as well," I added as I finished totalling up the latest surveyed length of the cave.

"What?" All six of us hunched over my notes to verify my figures. Yes, we had passed Bermuda's Green Bay Cave system's one mile of passage, making Belize's Giant Cave the world's longest salt water cave. As a matter of fact, the total of the measured lengths of all the tentacles now approached 10,000 feet, nearly twice as long as the Green Bay System.

"You know, an octopus that big would have no trouble eating all six of us," Mary Ellen said, pointing at the map.

"Or a church," Paul added, opening a can of beer with his diver's knife.

"What do you mean?"

"Well, there's a story that many years ago a church on the beach disappeared during a hurricane."

"Probably blew out to sea."

"No, because even the foundation was gone. All they found was a hole in the ground, right about there," Paul said, pointing with his knife at an area on the map just beyond the loop we had completed earlier that day.

"But we didn't see any offshoots there," I protested. "Probably fell into a sinkhole that doesn't connect with the cave."

We divided into two three–diver teams the next day. Paul, Mary Ellen, and I selected as our objective the southern area of the cave near the loop we had completed the day before. Minutes after rolling into the water from Paul's inflatable rubber boat we were in the cave, gawking at a huge stalactite column fully ten feet in diameter, larger than any other dripstone pillar that had ever been found underwater. Just beyond the column I glimpsed a shadowy area in the wall. Was there an offshoot there after all?

Swimming over to investigate, we were amazed to see a

wide, low passage leading farther southward. Paul tied a new line onto a nearby rock and we followed the 20–foot–wide passage for a couple of hundred feet. The ceiling was only three feet high, so we progressed by pushing off from the ceiling with our fins to avoid disturbing the muddy floor with swimming strokes. As we rounded a bend in the tunnel, Paul's light picked out a huge mound of glistening white beach sand that reached to the cave ceiling. Seeking a way onward, Paul first ran the line to a deadend around the right side of the mound, then reeled in and tried the left side without success.

While Paul cut the line off his reel and prepared to tie it to a rock, I thought I spotted something in the mound. Reaching into the sand, I pulled it out and showed it to Paul: an ancient timber. We looked at each other and nodded. We had found the missing church.

Yet other mysteries remain in Giant Cave. On our last dive, Mary Ellen and I pushed a considerable distance into a tiny tunnel that she named Small World. It soon was obvious that Small World was small only in diameter: even with four tanks each we could not explore all of its seemingly endless succession of small grottoes that extend more than 2,000 feet from the cave entrance. How much farther does it go? Until a future expedition finishes exploring it, we just don't know how long the world's longest sea cave really is.

2

The Rock Melts

I have been caving since before I was born; my pregnant mother took the commercial tour of New Mexico's Carlsbad Cavern in 1948. Did some aspect of that magnificent cave register on my embryonic mind so that I was compelled to be a cave explorer? Or did my future preoccupation with the so—called world's most dangerous sport have something to do with my April Fool's Day birthdate?

The answer to both questions is probably no. I did not visit a cave again for a decade, when I returned to Carlsbad on a family vacation. It was not due to a lack of interest on my part, for my playmates and I frequently dug caves in the soft dirt around my Florida home to plot our mock battles in. Somehow I got the impression that caves were found only in mountainous areas such as New Mexico and Tennessee. It seemed that the most that I could hope for in the way of outdoor adventure in Florida was to play Tarzan in our many swamps.

It was armed with this misinformation that I first visited Florida's famous Silver Springs resort with my Boy Scout troop in 1959. Equipped with a dimestore mask and fins, I found the crystal clear water and plants and fish to be a fascinating paradise, though pain in my ears made it impossible for me to descend below a depth of 10 feet. One of the older scouts, Drew Conrad, knew the diver's trick of equalizing the pressure on his ears to prevent the pain. Jackknifing his body between tourist–crammed glass bottom boats, he quickly disappeared into the deep blue void where the half–billion–gallon–a–day Silver River originated. Moments later he surfaced gasping and yelled, "There's a cave down there!"

I was astounded. Caves underwater? And in mountain–less Florida? Impossible! I also could not understand why a full–blown river would suddenly appear in the middle of a subtropical swamp. "Where is the water coming from?" I asked when he had caught his breath.

"From the cave, naturally."

"Yes," I persisted, "but where does it come from at the back of the cave?"

"It comes out of the rock," he pronounced with finality, starting to swim away.

I caught his leg, still not satisfied. "Yes, but how does it do that?"

My older friend looked at me with a mixture of disdain and exasperation. "The rock melts, of course."

It was not until much later that I would learn what Frank DenBlykker and Charles McNabb had discovered at Silver Springs just six years before my visit: the spring cave was caused by rain water sinking into the ground, carrying weak acids that eventually dissolved the limestone, eating out vast rooms and long tunnels through which the water traveled back to the surface to form gin–clear pools such as Silver Springs. On their dive in January of 1953, they discovered that Silver Springs is the entrance to a large cave similar in many respects to the one that I had admired at Carlsbad Caverns. While much smaller than Carlsbad and lacking the beautiful stalactites found there, Silver was found to have a large room 60 feet deep and 100 feet in diameter. In the dim light the divers could barely make out house–sized boulders covered with what appeared to be huge bones. Surfacing excitedly, they talked the owner of the resort, Bill Ray, into returning with them for another look, and soon learned that the petrified remains were in fact the remnants of huge elephant–like mastodons.

Frank's and Charles' dive was the earliest known use of SCUBA (self–contained underwater breathing apparatus) in a cave in the United States with the sole exception of a solo excursion by an NSS (National Speleological Society) diver at nearby Jugg Hole about a year earlier. The NSS adventurer found no mastodons, but did recover two prehistoric alligator skulls for Dr. Auffenberg, a biologist the University of Florida. American divers had made earlier excursions into underwater caves, for example, the "hard hat" surface–air–supply dive of Walter S. Chamberlin at Nevada's Devil's Hole in 1947, some two years before I was born, and the thrilling breath–holding exploits of Abe Davis at Florida's Little River Springs prior to 1860. Chamberlin's cumbersome air hoses, which had to reach all the way to the surface, and Davis' limited air supply severely limited their exploration distance in caves, however.

It was not until Jacques–Yves Cousteau's World War II invention, the "aqua–lung", was imported into the United States in the early 1950's that American divers could begin to think seriously about venturing underground. This relatively recent date for the birth of cave diving in our country is somewhat surprising when one realizes that the Cave Diving Group, the British counterpart to America's NSS Cave Diving Section, had already been cave diving for a decade using oxygen rebreathing scuba similar to Cousteau's later invention. An article describing the British Group's activities had been published in the NSS Bulletin in 1947. The oxygen scuba never achieved any popularity among Americans, probably because of the frightening stories of divers going into convulsions from breathing pure oxygen and drowning.

While DenBlykker, McNabb, and various NSS divers were first venturing into the better–known springs and caves in California, Georgia, New Jersey, Texas, Virginia, and primarily Florida, I was busy growing up. I had all the heroes in sports and adventure that any red–blooded American boy had: Fran Tarkenton, Lou Gehrig, Lawrence of Arabia. But, I was probably not big enough or fast enough to consider emulating Tarkenton or Gehrig, and I was born too late to ride across the desert sands with Lawrence. Thanks to that and to the fact that school was fairly easy for me, I had spare time on my hands as I moved into my early teens.

My first love has always been the water. Like many native Floridians, I learned to swim at an age so early that I cannot remember the event. One of the most popular television programs of the day was Sea Hunt, an adventure series about scuba diving whose underwater scenes were shot primarily at my beloved Silver Springs. There just happened to be a scuba diving course at the local YMCA taught by Ken Brock, one of the first nationally certified instructors in the country. I decided to enroll.

The check–out dive for the course was set for Crystal River, a huge Florida spring on the Gulf of Mexico. It was a cold, rainy day in February, 1966, so I was not expecting much as our boats left the dock for the springs. Fighting fever and the sniffles from a head cold, I reflected as I shivered that this scuba diving was not as much fun in the water as it seemed to be on television. I momentarily considered quitting right then and there, but decided to wait until after the dive so I could at least get my diver certification.

"Sheck, this is Joe Prosser," Ken said when we anchored over the spring. "Why don't you two dive together?"

I turned to meet Prosser, the diver, and my worst fears were realized: my partner was a huge strapping guy who had the disturbing habit of glaring directly at you with big dark eyes under bushy black eyebrows. Throughout the six weeks dive

Joe Prosser before a dive at Zuber Sink. (*Photo by Sheck Exley*)

course, I had never seen him smile a single time! The dreary day did not invite conversation, so we quickly put on our tanks without a single word passing between us while I privately wondered why he was so hostile to the world. With a final miserable shiver I put on my face mask, nodded to Joe and jumped off the boat.

A split second later, I splashed into another world. My first sensation was one of unexpected warmth. Because the spring remains a constant 72° F all year, the contrast from the near–freezing air temperature above made the water feel like a warm bath. The most dramatic sensation, though, was visual. The water was literally as clear as air, and my plunge had taken me into a fascinating forest of billowing yellow–green hydrilla. Among its densely foliated branches swarmed numerous brightly–colored red, orange, and gold tropical fish from the nearby Gulf of Mexico. Off to my right, the forest gave way to a waving plain of dark–green eel grass over which meandered vast schools of striped trout, snapper, and red–breasted bream. Nearby a painted turtle blinked at me, then withdrew into the grass, showing me a glimpse of its vivid yellow underside, while in the far distance a file of large catfish snaked through the grass over a precipice into a deep blue void. Above me, a handful of boats bobbed on their anchor ropes like big balloons.

We were quickly drawn to the underwater precipice and the mysterious void beyond. On the way, I playfully swam through a large school of bream, which casually parted for me like a curtain, the scarlet–vested fish eyeing me without fear. I reached out to pet one of them, but it easily darted out of my grasp, its reflexes four times quicker than mine. As we cruised over the cliff, a vast panorama unfolded below us of deep, cream–colored canyons and high pinnacles of rock. I felt a brief moment of panic from an instinctive fear of heights, then relaxed because of an overwhelming sensation of weightlessness. Down here I was literally as free as a bird, able to hover effortlessly over a chasm scores of feet deep.

I dipped a shoulder and swooped into the submerged canyon, following the catfish down to a cascade of glistening white sand 30 feet below. The sand led deeper, under an immense span of limestone into the twilight of a cave beyond. So this is what Drew saw at Silver Springs! In the shadowy entrance I could see a dozen yard–long eels, which wiggled into crevices in the rocky floor as I approached. I had no flashlight, so had to interrupt my exploration while my eyes adjusted to the dim recesses of the cave. Fifteen feet above me, exhaust bubbles of my regulator struck the jagged ceiling, then spilled past it in a quicksilver torrent to shoot on up past the arch to the water surface. I idly wondered if the disturbance of my air bubbles would cause the rock to tumble down, crushing me in an engulfed tomb. I quickly dismissed my fears after reflecting that the labyrinth I was in was surely thousands of years old.

My greatest misgiving at this point was being alone (Joe and I had become separated while I was having trouble clearing my ears). For the first time in my young life I was utterly dependent on myself for survival, and the resultant feeling was one of exhilaration as well as trepidation. By now my eyes had adjusted, and I ventured onward into the cave, finally stopping at a gray rock wall where I could dimly read 60 feet on my depth gauge. At that moment I would have given anything to have had a light so I could see where the tunnel went from there. Did it get deeper? Were there big rooms? Or did the tunnel branch out into a confusing maze of passages, its floor littered with the fossil remains of huge prehistoric animals?

My musings were interrupted by the arrival of Ken, who had noticed me missing from the rest of the class, which was in the hydrilla forest, playing with two friendly manatees (large sea–dwelling mammals related to porpoises). Ken stabbed a finger toward me and authoritatively pointed me out of the cave, so I left reluctantly, glancing back once more to wonder at the silent, cathedral–like hallway.

Back in the boats, Ken seemed ready to reprimand me for wandering off alone, then he saw a gleam in my eye.

"You're hooked," he said.

3

Seconds To Live

The low limestone hill rose in rounded shelves from a dense subtropical jungle, where oaks and cypresses towered skyward in bright green vine–covered majesty. The jungle was cleft by a thin bright blue ribbon of water that boiled upward vigorously at the base of the hill. Brightly colored birds moved from branch to branch, calling to each other and occasionally dipping down to the water to catch fish. I could imagine how the Spanish explorers felt in the 1500's when they discovered this beautiful Ichetucknee River.

This was the first club dive for the "Aquacks", a group that Ken Brock had organized from some young graduates of his course, including Joe Prosser and me. By now Joe and I were talking to each other as well as diving together, and I quickly discovered that beneath the gruff exterior was a kindred spirit full of youthful enthusiasm for laughter and good times, including most especially cave diving. Once you got Joe started talking and smiling, there was no stopping him. Especially fun with Joe were joke contests and swapping insults, even though I never won:

"Sure was a lot of silt kicked up on that dive," I would venture to him in mock complaint.

"Yeah, and it was all behind you," he would retort without a moment's hesitation.

At Ichetucknee we had time to have only a half dozen such exchanges before we had all our equipment on and were hustling down the hill into the chilly 72° F water. Yes, 72° F, the same temperature as the warm bath at Crystal River a couple of months earlier. The difference was that spring had arrived, and the air temperature had zoomed up to 80° F, making the water feel cool by contrast. Swimming in single file, we followed the narrow ribbon of water downstream, pausing occasionally to check the sandy bottom for fossils and bones, and to admire the striking red color of the primrose plants that lined the banks underwater.

A quarter of a mile below the start of the river we suddenly encountered a much larger flow of water blasting in from the left. After a short but tiring pull up an eel grass—carpeted run we rested against some twisted cypress knees to admire the spectacle of nearly 100 cubic feet of water per second, gushing straight up through a five–foot–diameter hole in the river bottom, making a turbulent boil on the water surface that defied the efforts on any boat to anchor there. This was Jugg Hole, the same spring where the NSS diver had made the first American cave dive using SCUBA some 15 years earlier. Little had changed since then in cave diving equipment and procedures. We now used single hose regulators instead of the flimsy, less dependable double hose models, but that was about it as far as improvements went. A single tank, wet suit, weight belt, leg knife, depth gauge, dim underwater light, mask, snorkel, and fins completed my attire for my fourth cave dive ever.

As the name suggests, Jugg Hole is shaped like an upright jug, with the narrowest part, or the "neck," constituting the five–foot–diameter hole at the top. The crystal–clear stream of water enters the bottom of the jug from an opening that leads to a horizontal series of small rooms connected by narrow

Ichetucknee River at the headspring. (*Photo by Ned DeLoach*)

passageways, then spews upward through the neck.

I cruised over the river bottom toward the neck, then swooped upward slightly to plunge into the center of the hole feet first. After all, I reasoned, one did not jump out of trees head first, and if I was to plummet 35 feet to the base of the jug, I did not want to land on my head. Unfortunately, one has to learn a completely new set of rules for the underwater world, and the strong boil quickly shot me out of the water like a Polaris missile. Fortunately I instinctively remembered to exhale during the ascent to avoid the diver's malady known as air embolism, which is caused by air expanding in a diver's lungs as the water pressure outside his body decreases.

My next try, head first so that I could kick with my fins to propel myself downward, was somewhat more successful in that I was treated to a tantalizing glimpse of the sloping white sandy floor far below, but then I tired and once more the ferocious torrent pushed me away. While I was resting on the bottom nearby, trying to catch my breath, I finally watched another diver demonstrate the proper entry: headfirst, pulling one's way down the rock of the neck with one's hands like an upside-down mountain climber.

It still was not easy, but I did manage to make it down into the incredible stillness of the base of the jug. Here there was an almost total absence of water movement, and a dozen divers swam around with quiet ease in dramatic contrast to the violence in the five-foot diameter neck three stories above us. A broad, gleaming shaft of sunlight descended through the neck at an angle, providing us with more than ample light to explore the nooks and crannies in the limestone walls and to look for prehistoric bones in the floor, which I discovered was not sand at all but millions of tiny bleached shells from countless generations of snails that had lived in the spring. All too soon I felt a great deal of inhalation resistance from my regulator, indicating that my air was running low. I quickly pulled on the rod activating my small reserve air supply and prepared to ascend.

But now I hit upon a brilliant idea. Or so it seemed at the time. I would swim over to the opening leading to the horizontal series of rooms and ride the current emerging from it up the 30 feet and through the neck to the surface beyond. I was well within the depth and time limits that required a stop to avoid the bends, so why not use the water as my natural elevator?

Unfortunately, water seldom flows through caves in a straight line. As a result, rather than being gracefully funnelled toward the neck in an ever-more-rapidly ascending trajectory, I was viciously and repeatedly hurled against the rough rock walls, collecting a bump on the noggin each time. On the third and final time my snorkel caught on the wall and my facemask was partially knocked off my head, blinding me and forcing water up my nose. Finally I tumbled helplessly up out of the neck of the jug, a most comical sight for Joe and the other divers present.

What was not comical was that when my mask flooded I came uncomfortably close to panic. A novice with only four cave dives and a total of eight scuba dives of any sort under his belt is simply not mentally prepared to be pushed around helplessly by a strong current, rammed into a rock wall, blinded by water rushing into his mask, and gagged by water forced up his nose, all at the same time. Even though I may have never been in any real danger, for a few seconds I fancied I was, and this was all I needed to send me to the uncomfortable edge of frenzied, rock–clawing fear. And fear can kill, no matter how safe you may actually be.

By summer, Joe and I were diving every weekend, skipping lunches at high school to have money to keep our VW's gassed up for expeditions. We had purchased a diver's guidebook that listed a couple of dozen of the better–known cave diving sites and went "spring–hopping," crossing each of them off as we dived them. Some days we would dive six or eight or more different caves, an accomplishment that was fairly easy since our dives were short. A typical cave dive in 1966 was limited to a penetration (one–way swimming distance from the entrance) of 200 feet, a major dive was twice that, and the world record, set by John Harper at Hornsby Springs four years previously, was only a little over 1,000 feet. Somewhere along this way we passed from the novice stage to veteran diver, a transition most prominently marked by the ability to relax in the water and be so used to your equipment that it seems an extension of your own body. Many times in the crystal water of a spring I found myself feeling so at home that I actually imagined that I could take the regulator out of my mouth and breathe water.

One weekend in July, I was looking for Peacock Springs, a spot the description in the book made especially intriguing. With me was my brother Edward, who would eventually become an enthusiastic member of the Aquacks, but at this date he had not yet been hooked.

Edward Exley cools off in Blue Grotto in 1967. (*Photo by Sheck Exley*)

"Haven't we been down this road before?" he complained as our VW Beetle banged down still another pot hole–lined dirt trail.

"Maybe, but not from this direction. I don't remember seeing a rut this deep." Wham! Our abused little car suddenly made a whining sound and the atmosphere became noticeably hotter.

"Oh great, there goes the A/C, Slick." Edward always called me Slick as if saying the name Sheck hurt his mouth. Although he was more than three years younger than I, he was already over six feet tall and I no longer wrestled with him.

"Well, we're bound to find it. After all, the book did say follow the most used dirt road to the garbage dump and take a right, and you have to admit," I said, gritting my teeth as the car bottomed out on still another pot hole, "this road has seen a lot of use. I just can't understand why we haven't found the garbage dump."

"If you hit another bump like that last one, our car will be the garbage dump."

I slammed on the brakes as the road suddenly ended at the edge of a high sand bank that dropped precipitously to the tea–colored water of the Suwannee River. "Darn. Another dead end."

"Yeah, but what's that over to the right?"

In a hummock to the right was a small oval pool of clear blue water that flowed no more than a 100 feet to the river.

"What do you think, Slick?"

"Well," I said, the perspiration streaming off my body, "it sure ain't Peacock, but it's cold and wet..."

Minutes later I was below the surface. The spring basin was quite clear, but strangely devoid of underwater plants, probably washed out by frequent backflooding of the nearby Suwannee. Several large bass darted across the pool and peered at me from the security of submerged boulders. Not wishing to disturb my finny friends, I eased past the boulders upstream into a narrow channel that seemed to be emerging from the roots of a great live oak. Oh well. It was too much to hope that I had discovered a new cave. After all, most Florida springs are filled with gravel or sand or have openings too small to enter. Nevertheless, I pulled my way toward the roots just to make sure. Below the roots was a big block of purest white limestone, and below the block was...a cave!

The opening was a crack five feet long but only two feet wide, just big enough for me to enter with my single tank. It was surprisingly shallow, only six feet deep at the entrance, but I quickly dropped down a rubble slope to a small room at a depth of 15 feet. This was a whole new ball game, diving in a spring that was not in the guidebook or known by any of my friends, so I had absolutely no idea what to expect.

I spent several moments probing around with my flash-light and finally found the source of the water, a wide low crevice only a foot high that led on horizontally at a depth of 20 feet. For the first time I was in a place where no human being had ever been before, and felt that strange mixture of the excitement of discovery and the dread of the unknown. I hesitated briefly, but excitement overcame dread – just as it always has for me—and I tried to wiggle into the crevice, turning my body first one way, then the other. No go. I started to remove my tank so that I would be smaller, then the third voice of exploration made itself heard – prudence. Prudence dictated that if I went ahead I could very well get stuck, lose control of my tank in the current, or become disoriented since I had only one light and no guideline. So I turned to leave— but not before getting one last tantalizing glimpse of that unknown darkness beyond the crevice.

Not until a year later did I found out for certain that this cave, known as Running Springs, was indeed virgin before my dive. The knowledge gave me a strange and most satisfying pride. Satisfying because of the feeling of mystical possession and intimacy with the spring that I felt. Strange because the cave had existed for thousands of years before me, would exist for many years after me, and could care less about my intrusion, momentous as it was for me.

Two weeks later I finally made it to Peacock with Tommy Hawkins. Thin and bespectacled, Tommy was at once the smallest and the toughest member of our club. This seeming contradiction was explained by his knowledge of Shotokan karate, a pursuit in which he eventually interested Joe and me. As a matter of fact, all three of us soon tackled karate workouts with an enthusiasm exceeded only by our passion for diving, and earned black belts later in college. Karate training was of considerable benefit to our diving careers because it vastly improved our physical condition, willpower, and ability to concentrate.

Earlier that day Tommy and I made our deepest dive yet at nearby Orange Grove Sink, to a vertical depth of 132 feet. On that dive our 200 feet of guideline slid off the coffee can we had it wound around to become a frightening underwater spider web in our weightless environment. We managed to collect the line and surface without becoming dangerously ensnared, but because of our difficulties resolved not to use the line at Peacock. I switched to a fresh tank, but for our second dive Tommy had only the air remaining in the tank he had used at Orange Grove.

At Peacock we found azure water every bit as clear as that at Jugg Hole, without Jugg Hole's vigorous current. The lily pad–fringed pool looked much like a placid pond with a small amount of water running off down a sluggish mile–long slough to the Suwannee River. Only a deep blue slit below a limestone shelf along one bank hinted at what lay below.

Diving down the 15–foot deep slit, we found a horizontal crevice some 20 feet long, but less than three feet high. The silt–laden rubble floor of the crevice dropped away to a tilted kidney–shaped room roughly 60 feet across and 10 feet high that sloped to a narrow vertical chute at a depth of 50 feet. The entire chamber was filled with a dim glow from sunlight reflected from the entrance, giving it a sapphire hue. We named it the Blue Room. We dropped down the chute to the 65–foot level to find an impressive horizontal tunnel some 10 feet in diameter. By this point all natural light had faded away, so only our flashlight beams revealed the spaciousness of the tunnel.

At this point Tommy ran low on air, so he pulled the rod activating his reserve air supply and reluctantly turned back. I accompanied him to the entrance to make sure that he got out okay, then returned alone to the labyrinth at 65 feet. My only source of light was a three–watt sealed–beam model that I had been using for months without changing the battery. Dim as it was, it nevertheless enabled my gloom–adjusted eyes to see a considerable distance down the cream–colored tunnel, which lacked any sign of previous human traffic. The floor was a flat sea of soft brown silt which I noticed readily mixed with the water whenever I came too close to it, creating a dense cloud of mud that blinded me. Since the invention of B. C.

vests was years away, the only way that I was able to stay off the bottom was by swimming very rapidly with my head higher that my feet.

After a 100 feet of this I tired and plummeted back to the mud floor to rest. To my right an equally large passage doubled back, while before me the tunnel swerved to the left and split into three identical conduits. The pattern was further complicated by interconnections caused by frequent side passages which cut across the three main conduits at irregular intervals. With excitement I realized that this cave was very different from Crystal River, Jugg Hole, Running Springs, and the other spring caves I had visited, all of which seemed to end quickly or become too small to explore. Ignoring the obvious risk, I sped onward into the middle conduit, driven by the need to see what was around the next bend. At each intersection I paused briefly to glance back in an effort to memorize the way back. All too soon I was approximately 400 feet from the cave entrance, a distance which in those days seemed much farther and was in fact the longest penetration I had yet made.

Wrenching my mind away from the still–beckoning tunnels, I forced myself to turn around and head back. I quickly reached the first junction with an intersecting side passage and paused to remember which route that I had taken coming in. In the dim glow of my light both passages looked identical. I realized with a sudden burst of anxiety that in the excitement of exploration I had forgotten the correct way out. Adding to my growing sense of dread was the fact I had no idea how much air or light that I had left.

I picked the tunnel on the right and swam on to another confusing intersection, then another. Would this maze never end? Abruptly the passage that I was in did end, and I quickly looked up for the life–saving chute to the Blue Room that I had entered by. Instead my disbelieving eyes saw only a blank, uncaring rock ceiling. Now the full realization finally sank in: I was quite lost.

I backtracked to the first intersection and turned left, then left again, and—another dead end. Glancing upward I saw only another flat, featureless cave roof marred only by an an impossibly small crack. As I turned around my regulator started breathing hard, a certain indication that I had only a few minutes of life left, assuming that my reserve air was intact and had not been accidently activated by banging into a ceiling projection during my wanderings. Now I was firmly in the grasp of panic, which caused me to flip around in indecision in the tunnel, kicking up clouds of silt. I hopelessly prayed "Please don't let me die," and even made some sort of promise which I later conveniently forgot.

Somehow my mind cleared, perhaps from a blind surge of determination to get out but more probably from the calmness accompanying resignation to death. Rather than continue my frantic search for the correct route out I resolved to somehow ascend the impossible crack in the nearby ceiling.

As I squeezed upward into the crack I noticed with some hope that it did in fact extend upward out of sight. It quickly narrowed still more, however; and I was soon tightly wedged, having to squirm, wiggle and claw at the walls to make further progress. Now I was stuck so tight that I could not even expand my chest to get a full breath of air. The arm holding my light was pinned to my side so that I could not illuminate the continuation of the crack above. As I looked upward into the darkness I seemed to see a faint glow in the distance. Fueled by this new hope I struggled upward with a new surge of energy and burst into the Blue Room by a route entirely different from the one I had used going down

The following weekend Tommy and I selected Ginnie Springs from the guidebook for our next adventure. The directions took us down a sand trail to the floodplain of the Santa Fe River, a major tributary of the Suwannee. Since the floodplain was actually a dense cypress swamp, the sand road turned to a muddy quagmire at that point. VW Beetles are

David Fisk in Ginnie spring in 1973. (*Photo by Sheck Exley*)

hard to get stuck, but I paused nevertheless to survey the deep ruts ahead. Always serious, Tommy took that opportunity to remind me of the lesson learned the previous weekend.

"I guess we'll be taking the guideline this time, even if there is some chance of an entanglement," he ventured.

"You guessed right," I said. There was no way I was going to get lost in a cave again.

About that time we stopped moving as the car sank up to the floor pan in the mud. Fortunately, some other divers were at the spring ahead of us, and with the camaraderie common in those days, they picked my tiny car up and set it on sturdier ground.

We quickly suited up and plopped into the water to cool off. We were used to very clear water from our visits to other springs, but Ginnie seemed even clearer, with visibility that appeared unlimited. Moreover, the walls of the cave were bright white and reflected our light beams a considerable distance down the passage so we could see better than on any dive that we had made to that point. Tommy led the way from a small horizontal entrance at 15 feet down a sloping corridor to a domed chamber 40 feet in diameter called the Ballroom. Even from that point, at a depth of 65 feet, I could clearly see every detail of the blue–green eel grass outside the entrances, well over 100 feet away.

Beyond the Ballroom the white sand and rock floor continued to slope into an irregular tunnel, which leveled out at a depth of 75 feet. The tunnel quickly branched out into a three–foot–high maze of interconnecting passages that made me thankful for Tommy's line. Unfortunately, all too soon we were out of line, just as the cave began to be really intriguing. Ahead of us the winding three–foot–high by five–foot–wide tunnel had no fin prints in the clay floor nor scratch marks on the walls, a sure sign that few if any divers had been there before us.

Overcome by the beauty of the place, I motioned to Tommy to stay at the end of the line while I swam on a little bit. He was not overjoyed by this, but was as interested in what lie ahead of us as I was, so agreed. At least my near fatal experience at Peacock had made enough impression on me that I resolved not to stray past any confusing side passages. I also glanced back occasionally to make sure that the motion of my fins was not stirring up excessive amounts of the clay silt behind me. The guidebook warned about severe silting in the cave, so I began to worry about the visibility behind me even though the water seemed to remain acceptably clear. Accordingly, I turned back after proceeding only about 200 feet past the end of Tommy's line.

What I did not realize was that, in one of the many peculiarities of underground water flow, the slight silt I had been kicking up behind me had "bottlenecked" at a constricted area behind me, so the water became considerably muddier as I progressed out. Soon I could see only a few inches, far too short a distance for any sort of visual route–finding. I had to resort to feeling my way forward with my hands to avoid ramming my head unexpectedly into rock projections.

Suddenly my hands felt what my mind rejected as an impossibility: the only way onward was through a tiny rock window no more than a few inches in diameter. I could feel that the tunnel was larger beyond, with a flow of water from left to right, some sort of parallel passage to the one I was in. However, there was no way I could squeeze myself and my tank through it. A week earlier in my career and I might have balked at this predicament and perished, but this time I was more accustomed to adversity and without wasting time to reflect on my dire predicament, immediately set about digging with my hands to enlarge the window. Because of the narrowness of the rock wall separating the tunnels and the brittle, soft texture of the rock, I was able to enlarge the opening further by breaking off chunks of limestone.

Finally I broke through into the adjoining passageway and soon saw the welcome glow of Tommy's light ahead of me, considerably obscured by the silt in the water. After the dive, I joked about digging my own cave tunnel to get out, but Tommy did not laugh. He said that he had gotten so low on air that he would have soon been forced to leave the cave without me. I soberly realized how lucky I had been to get out alive. I had found a prehistoric bone in the entrance to the cave and I had narrowly escaped becoming still another pile of fossil bones in the cave.

Because of the scare at Ginnie, we decided to select a relatively mud–free cave for our second dive of the day, Little River Spring, where Abe Davis had pioneered American cave diving in the mid 1800's. Little River is probably one of the safest cave dives in Florida, but is well–known and located only a few feet from the end of a well–maintained paved road.

The net result of this high visibility and accessibility is that 31 divers have perished there over the years, none of them having been properly equipped or trained for cave diving.

On the way to Little River, Tommy and I stopped to replenish the tanks we had emptied at Ginnie and were informed that the shop owner was out. Being bull–headed teenagers we finally prevailed upon a lady from the restaurant next door to fill our single tanks. Arriving at the spring, we hurriedly unpacked our gear since it was already late in the day and we did not want to be late getting home. To save time, we skipped gauging our tanks before the dive since they had been filled only moments earlier and we had seen the compressor gauge at the shop.

Little River is only a 100 feet from the Suwannee, so is quickly covered by river water whenever the river rises. When we arrived in the late afternoon, the dark brown river water had backed up all the way to the edge of the cave opening, where only the force of the upwelling water kept it from being obscured completely. We submerged in the clear water over the 10–foot diameter entrance and paused while I tied off our line on a huge boulder at a depth of 15 feet. I glanced back up toward the surface and was greeted by an unusual sight: the late afternoon sunlight penetrating the tannic river water colored everything a weird shade of red: blood red.

Our route at Little River took us down a steeply sloping 10–foot–diameter tube to a depth of 60 feet. The floor of the tube was a series of ledges three to five feet high that looked like giant steps. We pulled our way along them against the strong current. At the 60 feet level the tube made a 90 degree turn to the left to enter a horizontal area over 100 feet wide, but only two to three feet high.

By following a silt–free path in the floor caused by diver traffic, I was able to continue 100 feet to the top of the Chimney, a scenic vertical shaft that abruptly drops from a depth of 80 feet to more than 100 feet, some 150 feet in from

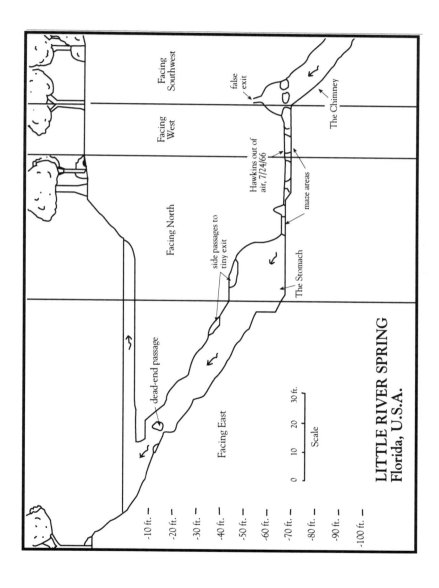

LITTLE RIVER SPRING
Florida, U.S.A.

the entrance to the cave.

Suddenly I noticed Tommy's light beam on the wall in front of me moving violently back and forth. When I turned, my disbelieving eyes were greeted by the hand signal for "need air." I dropped the coffee can and rushed to his side, fumbling to free the regulator neck strap so I could pass my mouthpiece to him. I finally got one of the snaps loose and thrust my regulator to him upside down. Because of this, his frantic efforts to get the mouthpiece into his gasping mouth pushed the exhaust tee of the regulator against his mask, flooding it and adding to his terror. The dangling neck strap also got in the way, so that each breath that he succeeded in getting was more water than air.

By now I badly needed air myself, so I got my regulator mouthpiece back for a couple of breaths. As I passed it back again, I became alarmed at my own situation. After all, our breathing rates were about the same and we had just had both our tanks filled at the same shop to the same pressure. Accordingly, I began to urge him toward the cave entrance.

That was all it took. Tommy's hand lunged for my regulator, jerking it out of my mouth and knocking my mask completely off my head. Now I could neither breathe nor see! I remember very little of the crazed struggle that followed. Somehow I got away from him, miraculously found my mask and got my mouthpiece back, Clearing the water out of my mask, I glanced back at my partner to see the horrible sight of his arms stabbing violently out in all directions, his fingernails frantically clawing the cold, uncaring rock.

I was terrified. In a blind panic, I bolted back up the tunnel toward the entrance, absolutely convinced that I was also going to die at any moment. Not until I could see sunlight streaming in from the entrance 75 feet away was I able to get a grip on myself. I remember thinking, "I'll be darned if I'm going to leave him there."

Returning, I found his maskless and apparently lifeless

body face down in the silt on the cave floor. Lifting him by the tank valve, I tried to shove my regulator into his mouth, but his teeth were clenched tightly shut. Quickly giving up that futile effort, I began moving him out of the cave as rapidly as possible, doing the best I could to protect him from the jagged, abrasive limestone. When we began our vertical ascent near the entrance, I remembered what Ken Brock had taught us about air embolism and pushed on my partner's diaphragm, forcing air out of his nose and mouth to prevent overexpansion of his lungs. (Such a rupture would have caused air bubbles to enter his blood stream and go to the brain, ensuring instant death.)

Popping to the surface, I immediately began administering mouth–to–mouth resuscitation while towing him to shore.

Joe Prosser in Little River in 1966 near where Tom Hawkins ran out of air. (*Photo by Bob Gatling*)

I barely noticed the yellowish vomit streaming out of his nose and mouth. When I got to shallow water some swimmers helped me remove his tank and get him on the beach while I continued resuscitation efforts. By now the vomit had turned to blood, and I immediately began thinking the worst: embolism! Like the bends, the only treatment for embolism is immediate recompression in a recompression chamber.

"Someone get an ambulance quick!" I yelled. By the time the ambulance had arrived, fate had smiled on our foolhardiness and Tommy was breathing for himself and was semi–conscious. He was in considerable pain. We took him to a nearby hospital where, to my dismay, the doctors had never heard of embolism and were not about to let themselves be instructed in diving medicine by a 17–year–old kid in a dripping rubber wet suit. In frustration I finally changed my diagnosis of the problem from embolism to the bends, which resulted in knowing nods and a low–flying trip to the nearest recompression chamber in Charleston, South Carolina. Fortunately, Tommy did not have an embolism or a related problem, and after a two–week stay in the hospital was soon diving again.

4

The Bottomless Holes

"Shore ah've heard of it," the old–timer said. "Jest foller the next dirt road and ya cain't miss it." He paused to spit a mouthful of tobacco juice, then added, "But be keerful, 'cause it ain't got no bottom."

By the summer of 1967, we had tired of spring hopping. Now we turned our attention to the bottomless holes of north Florida. Already we had visited several sites that were ru-mored by local residents to have no bottom simply because they had let out 200 feet of fishing line without getting any slack. At Devil's Sink, Edward and I had even been treated to a tale of how the comode–shaped sinkhole periodically flushed, sending its contents rushing through a natural limestone pipeline under a highway to spew up in a nearby lake. None of these stories had proven true, and only rarely did we find water more than 100 feet deep.

We found the road the old man had indicated and followed it in Tommy's station wagon to the top of a hill. With us were Joe and Edward. At the base of a hill was a broad expanse of clear blue water nearly a 100 yards across: Morrison Springs. Morrison had intrigued us ever since we had heard

Edward Exley grins before a 1967 dive in Devil's Sink, Florida. (*Photo by Sheck Exley*)

stories of dives there to over 270 foot depth by Jack Faver a few years earlier. The *Atlanta Constitution* had even quoted him as saying he had stopped in a vertical chasm that could be "1,000 feet deep," which was possible since test wells have encountered water–filled cavities in Florida at depths in excess of 8,000 feet.

We found a parking place halfway down the hill near a huge sign that notified us that eight divers had drowned there, which was more than any other cave diving site in the world at that time. The most ominous thing about the sign was that the death toll was shown by a interchangeable number hanging on a nail.

Dependable air pressure gauges were now available, so we could tell at all times during our dives how much air we had left. We had also started diving with double tanks to give us more air for deeper dives. The deeper you go, the faster you use up your air. For example, a tank of air lasts only half as long

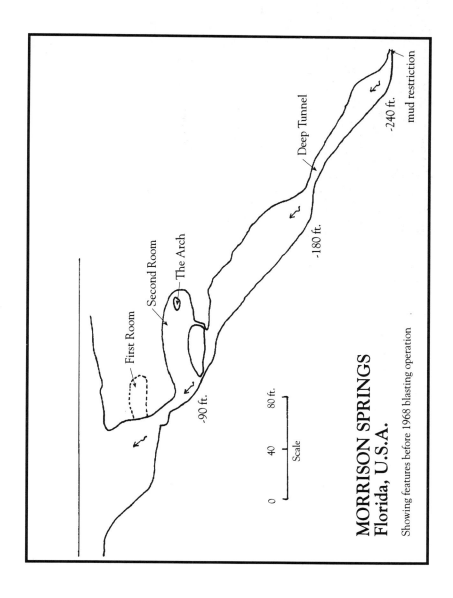

First Room

Second Room

The Arch

Deep Tunnel

-90 ft.

-180 ft.

-240 ft.

mud restriction

0   40   80 ft.

Scale

MORRISON SPRINGS
Florida, U.S.A.

Showing features before 1968 blasting operation

Edward Exley prepares to snorkel Morrison Spring. (*Photo by Sheck Exley*)

at 99 feet as it does at 33 feet. Another problem with deep diving is an increased likelihood of getting the bends. But the biggest concern is that compressed air becomes increasingly intoxicating and even toxic the deeper you go. This latter effect is known as narcosis and can affect one on dives as shallow as 100 feet. The U. S. Navy Diving Manual states that few divers can work effectively below 200 feet.

We swam out on the surface to an inner tube in the middle of the spring basin. A yellow polypropylene rope led from the tube to a log 50 feet below us. From that point we could swim into the horizontal first room to our right, or follow the sandy slope down against the current to enter the larger second room at a depth of 70 feet. We decided to go deep, and pulled our way into the oval second chamber, which opens to approximately 60 feet wide and 20 feet high. In the back of the second room was a broad arch of limestone that spanned 30 feet to connect two walls. The clear water and bone-white limestone reminded me of Ginnie Springs, except that Morrison is bigger.

After a brief search I discovered that the only way below the 100–foot level was to squeeze past a boulder as big as a small house that nearly plugged the tunnel leading from the second room to the third room. On three sides of the boulder, jets of water emerged from tiny cracks that looked too small to enter. From one of them, however, the tattered end of a guideline fluttered in the current.

We halted our ascent to confer in a large air pocket in the first room of the cave. The pocket was not natural; a dome of impermeable rock had trapped our ascending exhaust bubbles at a depth of 45 feet.

"What do you think?" Joe asked, pushing his mask back on his head.

I took my regulator out of my mouth. "Looks like the only way down is past that boulder."

"I don't like the looks of those restrictions," Tommy said. "I bet the only way anyone gets to the third room is by taking his tanks off, and I don't want any part of that."

"Well," I said, "why don't we do this. On the next dive, I'll wear a single and see if I can wiggle through a slot on the far side while the rest of you wait for me in case I have trouble."

"OK."

The next day I began the descent of the slot at 80 feet by scaring quite a few freshwater eels, which slithered past me into the darkness below. After spending a few minutes wriggling back and forth I finally made it to 100 feet. With a quick thrust of my legs I propelled myself into the large room beyond. Suddenly I felt something dragging me backward.

The guideline was caught around my tank valve and regulator first stage. I was afraid to cut the line since the current could blow the outer segment through the crevice I had descended, making it difficult to find my way back out. After a couple of anxious moments and almost dislocating my left shoulder, I managed to free myself.

Continuing into the cave, I looped my guideline around the tattered line leading to another opening, then turned in the other direction to follow it into the blue expanse beyond. This room was larger than either of the other two, a giant cylinder over 100 feet long and 20 feet in diameter, tilted at a 45–degree angle. At the bottom I paused to check my depth gauge: 170 feet. Ahead of me a horizontal tunnel beckoned, but because of the limited amount of air in my single tank, I turned back.

As I approached 100 feet, the current suddenly swept me into the crevice. I was stuck. Since I was now heading up instead of down, my body was in a different configuration and did not line up with the convolutions of the constriction as it had when I was pointed down. All I had to do to align my body properly was back down into the third room and come back up feet first. Unfortunately, the profile of a prone diver is like a wedge, making it easier to move forward than backward. When I tried to back, the base of my tank caught on a rock projection that prevented me moving any further. Now I could move neither forward nor backward and even lacked enough room to remove my tank to make myself smaller.

With desperate strength I tried once more to go back-ward, pressing my pelvis tightly against the bottom and push-ing with all my might. Finally I scraped through and quickly yanked open the quick–release straps of my tank to free it. I pushed it ahead of me into the crevice, carefully controlling the tank to keep the current from wrenching it from my grasp. I rejoined my anxious companions with only enough air left for my brief decompressions stops to avoid the bends. Joe said the management of the spring had already started to replace the "8" on the warning sign with a "9."

During the next two years, John Harper and Hal Watts led double–tank expeditions into the third room. Both groups found that the tunnel I saw at the 170–foot depth sloped to a fourth room with depths of 240 feet. Beyond that room was only a wide but very low slit with a nasty floor of fluffy red clay. George Krasle, who accompanied Jack Faver on his deepest dive, does not recall crossing such an area. Did they make a mistake with the inaccurate depth gauges of their day and over–estimate their depth? Or did John's and Hal's teams miss a side passage leading to Jack's bottomless chasm?

Unfortunately, before I could refine my own equipment and techniques to continue exploration at Morrison, tragedy struck. In 1968, a beginning diver with only a handful of cave dives to his credit perished in the third room (all previous drownings had occurred in the first two rooms). In one of the most difficult recoveries ever, David Desautels and Larry Briel somehow managed to extricate the body. Because of rigor mortis they almost had to break the victim's limbs to get him through the restriction at 100 feet.

Under heavy pressure to do something about the drownings, the local sheriff retained a local diver to dynamite the cave. When the charge went off it fractured the boulder, completely sealing the route I had used with my single tank and greatly narrowing the restriction with the guideline in it used by double tank divers. The blast also collapsed the arch in the second room onto the boulder, further obscuring the way to the third room.

Is Morrison Spring 1,000 feet deep? With tons of rubble blocking the way, we will probably never know.

Meanwhile the Aquacks fell apart as the more enthusiastic divers left for college. My enrolling at the University of Georgia gave me the opportunity to found the Dixie Cavern Kings, with members in several southern states. Like the Descenders in Georgia and the Cave Dwellers in Florida, the Dixie Cavern Kings was one of a new generation of scuba diving clubs—those specializing in cave diving instead of catering to diving in general. While I was D.C.K. president in 1969, I wrote America's first cave diving manual and orga-

Carl Fowler in Jugg Hole in 1970. (*Photo by Sheck Exley*)

nized a training program, forerunners of the textbooks and certified cave diving training courses of today.

My usual cave diving companion in the Dixie Cavern Kings was a fellow Georgia business student named Carl Fowler. Carl was about 5'8", with an average build except for huge shoulders which were ideal for throwing double tanks into my van. A rock fan, he wore his coarse auburn hair to his shoulders and his toothy grin from ear to ear. Except for music (I much preferred Rachmaninoff) we shared the same enthusiasms: little for college, a lot for cave diving. We arranged our class schedules so we were free from Thursday night until Monday night for 300–mile treks to north Florida's underwater caves. Sometimes I cut those classes too. Eventually Carl did me one better: he quit school completely to become the manager of Blue Grotto, a resort for cave divers in central Florida. While there he perfected his imitation cracker routine, a defense against the local rednecks (or crackers) who were suspicious of his long hair and subterranean excursions.

"Why fo' y'all go down in dem dark holes?" they would say.

"We heard there's Spanish gold down thar," he'd answer, a reason even a cracker could understand.

"Well, how far y'all goin' to git it?"

"Goin' miles and miles and hunnerts of feet deep."

"Ain't that dangerous?"

"Shootahreckon," and he would end the conversation by breaking into that wide grin of his, certain to melt the heart of any good ole boy.

On one of our trips, we stopped near Blue Grotto at Zuber Sink. The minute you pulled up to the huge oval basin you knew it was deep. The emerald–hued water extends more than 200 feet in diameter, a far cry from the 30–foot pools common in Florida sinks. On one side a sheer wall of limestone drops a dozen feet to the water and vanishes in the gloom below.

We had cut our deep diving teeth at Zuber, making our first 200–foot dives there. Over a series of dives we had gradually acclimatized ourselves to the numbing effects of narcosis, which has been known to cause divers to lose consciousness as shallow as 150 feet. Now we were ready to try to reach the bottom. Our improved equipment included the new octopus regulators, with redundant second stages for sharing air in an emergency, and backup lights in case our main lights went out. Also improved, was our dive planning—I had devised the third rule: reserve two-thirds of your air for the trip out.

I tied our guideline to a projection on the sheer rock wall and started down. Algae growth from the recent warm, rainy weather had clouded the water so that I could barely see Carl's powerful light from just a few feet away. At a depth of 40 feet we crossed a thermocline into noticeably cooler water and visibility increased dramatically to nearly 50 feet. Ahead of us the wall cut back under to enter the ceiling of an immense cavern. There was no sign of any walls or bottom.

Commercial guideline reels were now available, reducing the risk of line entanglement. I held mine with my thumb against the drum to keep the line taut, and paused to inflate my Clorox jug, blowing air into it from the exhaust of my regulator. The jug was tied to my tank valve and enabled me to control my buoyancy. This is especially important on deep dives, where a hard swim against negative buoyancy can cause you to black out from narcosis.

Carl had seen the cavern and was grinning so big I thought his mouthpiece would fall out. With excited gestures we agreed to continue our descent. The flat ceiling was nearly white, but was covered with huge embedded echinoids the size of dinner plates. With spokes radiating outward from the center, the flat fossils look vaguely like hubcaps plastered on the rock. After 50 feet the ceiling began to shelve downward at 45 degrees, and we quickly followed the glistening ledges downward.

At 150 feet, I stopped to hover near a chunk of rock jutting from the sloping cavern ceiling while Carl swam down to join me. Behind him was a dim green glow from the last of the sunlight penetrating through the depths. He signalled that he was still clear–headed, so we began a vertical descent from the limestone projection. The deepest part of the sink lay directly below us. We plummeted spread–eagle like sky divers into the green void.

Now that we had left the undercut cavern wall, we had absolutely no visual reference. In our near–weightless state only our rising exhaust bubbles told us which way was up. As we dropped, I was not sure whether I was still facing the wall or was spinning slowly to face the cavern entrance. The water rushed past my body as I fell, and I glanced at my depth gauge. The needle of the gauge moved with alarming speed to 200 feet, then beyond. I became conscious of a warm, fuzzy feeling

Sheck Exley emerges from Zuber Sink after a dive in 1967. (*Photo by Edward Exley*)

in my head, the first symptom of narcosis.

Suddenly the beam of my light picked out a spinning log beneath me. It took a few extra seconds for my numbed mind to realize that it was not the log but me that was spinning. I kicked a fin to stop the spin, then reached out with an arm to grab a limb of the log to keep from falling into the deep mud floor. In slow motion I went through the process of adding air to my jug to get the buoyancy needed to stay off the bottom: first grab the cord, then pull the jug down, then move the end over my regulator, then exhale into it.

Carl's regulator made a strange shrill sound as it moved the enormous volume of air needed to inflate his lungs at this depth. I looked at him and noticed that his grin was now replaced by a frown of total concentration. Since Carl is blind in one eye, he had developed a phobia about vast open spaces like this one in Zuber and had that problem to contend with as well as the narcosis.

Sheck Exley at Zuber Sink. (*Photo by Joe Prosser*). The photo on the right shows Hal Watts, the first diver to bottom Zuber Sink. (*Photo by John Harper*)

In a couple of minutes we adjusted our equipment, looked carefully at the dark muck floor to determine its slope, then set out from the log. After a 100 feet the slight downward slope ceased and started to creep upward. I turned and flashed my light at Carl, who nodded knowingly: "We're here!" I settled gently to the floor and plunged my arm downward at the deepest point. The depth gauge on my wrist read 253 feet. We exuberantly shook hands, then burst into laughter for no real reason except perhaps the giddiness of narcosis. Thumbs up. Time to head back.

In minutes we ascended to 40 feet, where we paused to take out decompression tables to calculate our schedule of stops to avoid the bends. I checked my watch and was surprised to discover that we had been submerged only 25 minutes. An hour later we surfaced, cold and tired but happy.

While Hal Watts had been to the bottom of Zuber at least three years earlier, our duplication of his feat was very satisfying. I turned to Carl and commented, "Now that was an OK dive."

Carl broke into one of his patented wide grins. "Shootahreckon."

The toughest cave dive in Florida in the 1960's was Eagle's Nest, also known as Lost Sink. Hornsby was longer, and Zuber was nearly as deep, but Eagle's Nest was long and deep. Cave dives into the northwest passage there were considered suicidal. Yet at the same time many divers considered a dive in its spacious entrance room their biggest underwater thrill. Only the fact that it lay in a remote and largely inaccessible swamp kept it from accumulating a death toll that would have dwarfed Little River and Morrison.

After conquering Zuber, I was ready for a new challenge. I had been intrigued by Eagle's Nest ever since Joe Prosser and I had first dived it in 1966. The following year I met Tom Mount, who had made more cave dives than anyone else in the world. Tom quickly targeted the Nest as Florida's top deep cave dive: "That tunnel goes just as deep as you want to go."

There was just one problem. I could not get anyone to go with me. Carl and my other friends in the Dixie Cavern Kings lacked the depth experience. The divers who were qualified to go on the dive—John Harper, Hal Watts, and Frank Martz, who had made more deep dives in the Nest than anyone —did not know me. You do not cave dive casually with strangers, regardless of their credentials, much less try to add length to the permanent exploration line in the Nest. Furthermore, if they did dive with me and something happened, they could be sued: I was only twenty years old, still legally a child.

Early on May 11, 1969, after fighting my way two miles down the deeply rutted swamp trail that led from the nearest paved road, I pulled up alone at the Nest. Fortunately the weather had been very dry, so all of the puddles in the trail were gone except the one where someone had dynamited the road to discourage divers. As I methodically unpacked my gear I was unusually aware of the Chassahowitzka Swamp around me. Awakening songbirds eagerly called to one another in the bright green cypress and bay trees lining the sink. A break in the tall sawgrass revealed the silvery surface of the 200–foot diameter surface pool, smooth as glass before the morning winds started. As I watched, a great blue heron honked in the grass and leaped up to flap its way slowly across the pond. Even the musky smell of the soft black swamp mud seemed new and exciting to me.

A small alligator swam past as I submerged, watching me from a safe distance while its graceful tail cut a shimmering wake in the pond. I followed a pine log on the bottom to a depth of 20 feet near the center of the pool, then fanned away a small school of bream so I could tie off my guideline on a branch. Below, the bottom sloped precipitously to a cluster of three dark holes at a depth of 50 feet. I dropped down the largest hole, which was four feet in diameter and cylindrical enough to appear man–made. At 70 feet, I abruptly dropped into a black void without apparent bottom or walls despite the superb visibility. The entrance room had a perfectly flat ceiling, from which plunged shimmering beams of sunlight through the three holes.

After dropping another 30 feet, I could see a mountain of sand and rock far below me. I followed its slope northwest 150 feet to a wall of the 300–foot–wide room at a depth of 200 feet. My eyes had now become accustomed to the gloom, so I was able to enjoy the ghostly spectacle of the 85–foot–high mountain illuminated by three beams of sunlight. The boulders in the huge mound looked like tombstones sticking out of the white sand.

Turning back to the wall, I quickly found the left edge of the notorious northwest passage where three fatal accidents had occurred. The entrance to the passage was 105 feet wide

Frank Martz, John Harper and Randy Hylton prepare to dive Eagle's Nest, Florida. (*Photo by John Harper*)

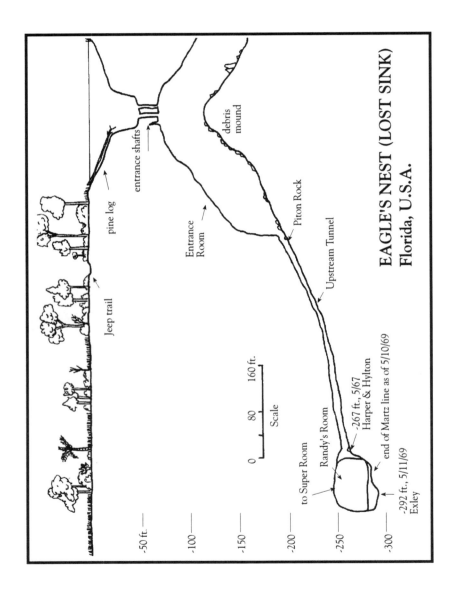

EAGLE'S NEST (LOST SINK)
Florida, U.S.A.

but only 10 feet high, with a floor of deep mud. I snapped my guideline reel to a piton in a rock where the permanent exploratory line began. After a brief rest on the rock, I followed the slight mud slope into the passage. One hundred feet further, the passage narrowed to only 35 feet wide and five feet high at a depth of 235 feet. Past that point it widened again, but the slope was so gradual that it actually appeared horizontal to my narcosis–numbed eyes. My depth gauge, however, continued to indicate increasing depth. In contrast to the spectacular entrance room, this passage was dark and dull in the dim beam of my three–watt light. The regular sound of my exhalations started monotonous chords of organ music in my head, most appropriate for a place that looked like a tomb.

After another 300 feet, I reached a 20–foot–wide boulder that stuck up out of the mud like a dozing dinosaur. My depth gauge read 260 feet. Now the line bent slightly to the right and dropped sharply. I had stopped here the previous day. I followed it until suddenly the line disappeared into the black mud floor. I reached into the slimy ooze, felt something in the mud at the end of the line and pulled it up. A small plexiglas spool came up on a metal hub, the mud falling away from it in a brown cloud. Ahead I could see a shallow depression and deeper water. The spool still had some unused line on it from Frank Martz' previous dives, so I continued onward perhaps 20 feet horizontally to the deepest point before jamming it back into the mud. As I did so, I caught a glimpse of my depth gauge: 283 feet! Since the gauge was adjusted for denser sea water, my actual depth in the fresh water of the Nest was 292 feet.

My exit proceeded without incident to the dinosaur–sized boulder at 260 feet, when a concussion jolted me and everything went black. In my befuddled state, it took me a couple of seconds to realize what had happened. The immense pressure of the water at this depth—nearly 150 pounds per square inch—had imploded the sealed beam of my light and sent the glass spewing over the floor of the cave. When I fumbled for my backup light and hastily switched it on, the tiny glass fragments sparkled like diamonds on the floor.

Now came the long, nearly horizontal swim back to the rock at 200 feet. Mindful of my rapidly diminishing air supply and of the greatly lengthening decompression stop required for every minute I spent at this depth, I had a strong tendency to speed up at this point. I forced myself to slow down, however, to avoid the exertion–enhanced narcosis that had caused three other divers to black out and drown in this same passage.

Finally the rock and my reel came into view. After nearly half an hour of near–darkness my eyes had adapted so well that the dim sunlight reaching that depth illuminated the entire 105–foot–wide passage. Moments later I was on the ceiling of the entrance room at 70 feet. I began my two and a half hours of decompression stops to avoid the bends. I was exhilarated. My 700–foot penetration at the Nest had been further than I had ever been in an underwater cave. It was also the deepest cave dive ever made in the eastern United States, and possibly the entire Western Hemisphere. At the time unaware of slightly deeper dives in Nevada and Africa, the Florida cave diving community thought it was a world record.

5

Deeper and Deeper

"Help! Help! Help!" the diver bleated from the surface of
the sinkhole, his eyes wide with fear. It was something that
experienced divers fear even more than drowning: the total
loss of reasoning ability through the mind–numbing onslaught
of panic. Yet, under the right conditions, any of us can fall prey
to the same paralyzing terror. The diver now floating in the
water was unable to do anything for himself other than breathe
and scream the same word over and over.

But there is something we fear even more than panic and
drowning—the searing pain of explosive decompression sickness, as dissolved gas comes boiling out of solution in every cell
of the body, disintegrating the tissue in its path. Almost all
cases of decompression sickness, or bends, occur after minor
decompression errors, or direct ascents to the surface after
short, shallow dives. They usually result in minor symptoms
such as skin rash and joint pain, earning the diver a trip to a
recompression chamber for treatment. Sometimes the symptoms are more serious: sensory disturbances, numbness, and
even paralysis. But the rare explosive decompression sickness,
possible only after a very deep or long dive followed by a very

rapid ascent with major omission of decompression stops, is almost always excruciatingly fatal. Imagine every nerve cell in the body simultaneously set to maximum pain. Compared to that, the drowning experienced (and survived by) Tommy Hawkins, and most other ways of dying, are nothing. The only possible relief is if the diver becomes paralyzed or lapses into a coma. Yet now I had deliberately chosen this form of death rather than abandon the helpless diver, my dive partner and friend.

As I swam toward the quivering, pale form of my buddy, I could not help wishing that I could somehow go into "rewind", and change the foolish actions that had brought us to the brink of agonizing death.

᪣

My fascination with depth had not ended with my record dive to 292 feet in Eagle's Nest on May 11, 1969. After diving in Hornsby Sink with John Harper (best cave diver of the 1960's) and Hal Watts (then the world's best deep diver) at a cave diving conference a couple of weeks later, I had naively confided to my companions, of whom I was still a little in awe, the results of my dive.

"Gee, that's neat," John said, with his usual friendly, boyish enthusiasm. "Let's tell Frank. That was his line you added on to."

"Well, I dunno." I mumbled reluctantly. I did not like to brag, and did not want to offend anyone. "Will it make him mad?" Like my companions, Frank had started cave diving a couple of years before me. What I did not know was that, because of the many dives he had made there, Frank considered Eagle's Nest "his place", a connotation that was as inviolate to a cave diver as marriage.

"Naw, he'll be interested in hearing about it. C'mon."

After we took off our twin tanks, John marched me over to where Frank, a short, wiry man in his mid–thirties with reddish–brown hair, was brandishing his newest underwater light before a crowd of admirers. One diver lifted a camera to photograph Martz Underwater Engineering's latest creation. Frank stepped between the dive light and the camera and glared up at the offender. "You want a picture, you buy it first," he asserted feistily in his high–pitched midwest twang.

"Hey Frank," John interjected gleefully, "here's a guy who just added onto your line in the Nest."

Frank swiveled his gaze to me. In his eyes I was a 20–year–old kid, poorly equipped (even by the standards of that day) with primitive 3–watt lantern lights instead of his infinitely brighter and more reliable 30–watt deluxe nicad systems. How could this punk have added line in the toughest cave in the world? "Oh yeah? What did you find?" he demanded skeptically after a few moments.

Conscious of the intent eyes of the many divers around me, I quickly stammered out the details of the cave, spool, and line. At the end of my recital, Frank lifted his chin and shook his head. "I'm sorry" he said, dismissing my dive as sheer fantasy.

I stood there in shock for a few seconds while everyone heard the older man and accepted expert call me a liar. In the embarrassed silence, John Harper finally tried to come to my rescue. "C'mon, Frank, wasn't that the spool I saw you putting line on before the dive?"

"Nope," Martz shot back, turning away to fiddle with his light.

I have never been very good at verbal confrontations. I am one of those folks who ever afterward is always tormented by the thought, "I wish I had said..." I had plenty of advice from friends. Lawrence Huff, a student of mine in the University of Georgia Karate Club (and future heavyweight national champion), advocated the direct approach: "A roundhouse kick upside his head would bring him around." Like most martial artists, however, I abhor violence. Jim Lockwood said I should have challenged Frank to dive with me at the Nest so that I could show him what he had so conveniently forgotten. But I had already learned the hard way, through accidents to Tommy Hawkins and my brother, that challenging other divers in even a more indirect fashion was a good way to get them seriously hurt. Hundreds of divers, including all of our best cave divers at the time, had dived the same tunnel in Eagle's Nest, but had been stopped by the incapacitating effects of nitrogen narcosis. What if Frank blacked out before reaching the end of the line? I was angry with Frank for the way he had treated me, but did not want him physically harmed.

But I could still be personally challenged, and the memory of the confrontation with Frank stung. Added to my natural desire to excel, it goaded me to prove for once and all that I was the best cave diver ever. It is painful for me to admit this now, an attitude that I have long since learned to despise, but that is what I was thinking as a 20–year–old college kid. Before the year was out, I became the youngest certified scuba instructor in the country, and published America's first cave diving manual. As 1970 rolled around, the Dixie Cavern Kings helped me set a new distance record for cave diving with a 2,099–foot penetration at Blue Springs near Madison, Florida, using a technique I had invented of carrying extra tanks called "stage diving". Before this, cave divers had been limited to the air they could carry on their backs. At Blue, we added 120 feet to a line left by Tom Mount and Dick Williams by carrying extra bottles slung beneath our bodies, some of which were installed in the cave on previous dives. Nevertheless, distance measurements at the time were very imprecise (we then thought my dive was nearly 3,000 feet, for example), so one–upmanship in terms of penetration length was difficult. On the other hand, the new depth gauges being sold by Scubapro

Sheck Exley pauses outside the entrance of a Florida spring. (*Photo by Ned DeLoach*)

reliably measured depths in excess of 300 feet.

Even though Frank was loath to admit it, I had already been deeper in a cave than anyone, at least in Florida. Now I resolved to go still deeper. But where? Zuber and Eagle's Nest were believed to go no deeper, Morrison had been dynamited shut below 100 feet, and Wakulla, site of reputed dives to 250 feet, was closed to all diving and was carefully guarded.

In the Caribbean are numerous inland sinkholes, some of which had been sounded to depths in excess of 300 feet. In one of these, we discovered in the summer of 1970 that the walls cut back under even more dramatically than at Zuber. At last I had a site with world record potential! I phoned a close friend who was also one of the top deep cave divers of the day, and arranged a joint trip.

We made a warm–up dive to 283 feet, then made the final preparations for our record attempt. We had acquired a lot of new equipment. For better buoyancy control, we had the compensator vests just introduced by Nemrod, a design that was destined to replace chlorox jugs in the cave diving community. I was also using a 30–watt neck light I had made with a motorcycle battery, a popular configuration in those days that was much cheaper than, yet as bright as, Frank's fancy commercial models. I did, however, have a Martz Underwater Engineering guideline reel. I also carried a net bag and a small hammer to collect rock samples for a geologist friend of mine. Still another item carried was the SOS decompression meter.

On the afternoon of the dive, we reviewed our plans in shallow water at the edge of the sink before submerging, starting with a gear check. Then we read our air content gauges and used the "Third Rule" to establish a safe air turnaround. Despite the fact that I had devised the procedure nearly two years earlier, it was meeting a lot of resistance. Part of the problem was that cave divers, used to using nearly half their air (in some cases even more) to swim into the cave, did not want to limit their penetration to only a third. The whole idea of reserving twice as much air for the trip out of the cave was so that two divers could share the air of one in the unlikely event that the other lost his total air supply at maximum penetration. At the time, successful air–sharing cave rescues were virtually unknown, so many divers wondered, why bother? Others reasoned that they could "skip–breathe" out in such an emergency, reducing their air consumption by holding each breath. No one actually tested that hypothesis, however, and it was further invalidated by the fact that most of us skip–breathed into the cave, making further reduction of air consumption for an emergency exit impossible. Nevertheless, my partners and I insisted on reserving two–thirds of our starting air for the trip out of the cave. If we wanted to penetrate farther without skip–breathing or violating our reserve, we simply used the tank staging procedure. While this dive would be extremely deep, our bottom time would be very short, so we decided not to encumber ourselves with stage bottles.

Finally, we were ready. My partner spat into his mask and rinsed it out. "How long is it going to take you to get the rock samples?"

I paused before answering. Time is of the essence on deep dives, since we breathed ten times as much air at 300 feet as near the surface, and decompression stops would increase enormously for each additional minute on the bottom. "Well, if we still have plenty of air and our time is less than 10 minutes, I'll take a minute to get one. Otherwise, we'll skip the sample."

"Sounds good to me."

We submerged slowly in the murky water, carefully keeping track of each other. Since other divers were present, bouncing to the bottom in open water, I decided to start our guideline underwater, away from the entry point, despite the poor visibility. I tied off on a nice tree root at a depth of about 10 feet, then followed the sloping muddy bottom toward the center of the sink. Visibility was less than five feet down to the narrowest part of the sink at a depth of 60 feet, and was made even worse by the silt and debris raining down from other divers entering the sink.

Fortunately, below that level the side walls cut back sharply, at an angle of perhaps 30 degrees from the vertical, enabling us to swim out of the debris zone. There was no surface light, so only the powerful beams of our lights cut through the darkness. Periodically I stopped and turned to check on my partner, each time receiving a reassuring "OK" signal with his joined forefinger and thumb.

At 150 feet, the visibility increased to over 50 feet, but the overhanging wall we were following became even more of a ceiling, the angle increasing to 45 degrees. Nevertheless, our rate of descent increased, and we quickly passed the 200–foot level. Now we felt the first warm buzz of nitrogen narcosis, a slightly numbing effect accompanied by a sort of relaxing exhilaration. I idly wondered if this were the same part of the sink that we had dived two days previously, but could see no sign of our exhaust bubbles on the ceiling.

We continued checking each other. The narcosis, which gradually increases with depth, seemed well under control. The cream–colored, smoothly–sculptured walls of the sink began to show a dark brown, almost black deposit that I knew our geologist friend would find interesting. I paused and checked my depth gauge: 280 feet. I flashed my light at my partner and signaled to him. His eyes were still clear and alert, and he gave a thumb down response.

I turned and picked out a likely–looking ledge below us that I estimated would be at the magic depth of 300 feet. We quickly dropped to the targeted rock projection, and I wrapped the guideline around the handle of my reel to stop it. I glanced upward to check on my partner, then checked my depth gauge before unhooking my net bag for the rock sample. I was amazed to see that we were well below 300 feet. I still felt okay, but the excessive depth and the fact that we were already more than 10 minutes into the dive made me decide to skip the sample collection and start up. Below us was nothing but ledge upon ledge, ever growing dimmer until at last the wall vanished into the black void of unknown depths.

After exchanging thumbs up signals with my partner, I unwrapped the guideline and started reeling it in as we as-cended. I noticed that my partner was having difficulty staying off the ceiling ahead of me. We stopped, and he signaled that he was having trouble with his new buoyancy vest. Air was not venting from the overinflation valve or the inflation hose. Since the trapped air expanded as we rose, his buoyancy was increasing dramatically. It had worsened to the point that he was now effectively plastered to the ceiling, unable to move without great effort. With our bottom time climbing beyond

15 minutes and our air dwindling rapidly, he decided to ditch the vest, calmly removing his neck light, then unsnapping the straps holding the vest. The neck opening of the vest had narrowed due to the inflation, forcing him to remove his mask and his regulator mouthpiece to finish slipping the vest over his head.

I suppose that at this point, those unwanted but persistent voices started to make themselves heard in his head: "You can't see...your nose is in the water...your mouthpiece is out of your mouth, so you can't breathe...you are ditching your vest, will you be able to swim up...you have just been deeper in a cave than anyone else...it's mighty cold and dark down here...you are running out of air...you need to get out of here FAST...above all, DON'T PANIC, PANIC KILLS!" So the power of negative thinking started taking control.

I watched him fumble around for a few seconds, then he agitatedly signaled me by waving his light back and forth. Since he was virtually blind without his mask on, I took the mouthpiece out of my mouth, pushed it against his lips, and pressed the external purge button, releasing a big bubble of air. He frantically seized it with one hand while I found my spare mouthpiece. Next, I found his dangling regulator mouthpiece and breathed on it to make sure it was okay. Then I handed him back his own mouthpiece and finally got him to accept it as he regained some mental control. There was no sign of his mask, so I grabbed him by the shoulder and tried to force him toward the surface before our air ran out. There was no time to check a depth gauge, but I am sure we were still well over 250 feet deep.

Suddenly he began fighting me hysterically as panic took total control. It was like the accident with Tommy at Little River all over again, only this time the victim had plenty of air to fight me with. I broke away from him and felt something binding my feet. Glancing down, I saw that our guideline, which had gone slack during our struggles, had been snagged by both my fins and was wrapped around them. I tightened the line with the reel, reached down and freed my fins, then turned to check on my partner. As soon as my light shone on him, he swam frenziedly upward toward me, homing in on my beam like a moth. When he got close, I pushed away from him, turned my light away, and reeled up a few feet. Then I shined my light at him to activate his clawing flight again.

Our retreat to shallower water was a series of similar cycles, as I led him upward using my light as a lure. Each time I managed to elude his grasp, but at least three times one or the other of us became momentarily entangled in the line, forcing me to cut us free. At a depth of 150 feet, we reentered the silty water, then at 130 feet his tank valve and his fins snagged in the line simultaneously. I quickly cut the line above and below him, and he bolted to the surface.

I chased him as rapidly as I could, hoping that he would miraculously get a grip on himself and stop to decompress before surfacing. Before ascending into the zero visibility layer above 60 feet, I stole a glance at my decompression meter. The instrument, now known to be very unreliable with dangerously shallow stops, gave a first stop depth of 35 feet. Today's decompression tables would have called for our stops to begin at 120 feet. Skipping the 120-foot stop meant that theoretically we should get decompression sickness. Skipping the next, or 110-foot, stop, meant that bends was even more likely, and so forth. We had skipped all of our stops.

On the surface, I found him as described at the start of this chapter, screaming for help over and over, yet curiously without inflection or expression to his voice. It was as if his brain had become nothing more than a endless loop of audio tape, containing only one frantic monosyllable. I swam over to him on the surface, while part of my mind imagined that my body was becoming a giant Alka–Seltzer, fizzing violently with painful, tissue–rupturing nitrogen bubbles. Each second that I spent up here made it that much more likely that I would die, and each movement of my body made things even worse. On the other hand, if I did not help, my partner had no chance at all.

I grabbed him by his tank valve, and towed him about 50 feet to the entry area, where he managed to grasp the steps. He was still incoherent, his eyes huge with fear. In the back of my mind, the stopwatch of death from the bends ticked louder than ever. I squeezed his shoulder and stuck my face in his. "You need to go back down and decompress!" I commanded

He eyes narrowed, and he shook his head as if awakening from a dream. "What? What?"

"Where is your mask?" I demanded. He simply stared at me. I was not getting anywhere. "Here!" I said, putting my mask on his head. "Put this on and go back down." I helped him secure it, then placed his hand on a decompression line. "I'll be right behind you."

There was, of course, no way that I was going back underwater without a mask to decompress with a madman. But at least *he* now had a chance of surviving our ordeal. Lucky for me, there were some divers standing on the shore next to me. "Can I borrow a mask to decompress?" I asked them. The ticks of death's stopwatch now seemed deafening.

I grabbed the proffered mask and followed the line down to my partner, moving him to a depth of 30 feet instead of the 25 feet now indicated by our decompression meters, which had been decompressing while we were struggling on the surface. That meant that they were now totally inaccurate as far as our decompression requirements went. So we had to wing it. I decided to go five feet deeper than indicated by the meter, and remain at the final level (10 feet) for an extra half hour.

Meanwhile, my partner gradually returned to normal while we cringed, waiting for the first symptoms of what we felt were inevitable cases of the bends. Miraculously, they did not come, and several hours after surfacing, we finally relaxed, confident that somehow we had cheated the grim reaper. As a matter of fact, about the only interesting thing about our long decompression was that, after an hour or so, my partner sheepishly showed me what he had carried in one hand all the way up from over 250 feet: his face mask. Such is the power of panic.

You may be wondering where the preceding dive was made and who my partner was. I have chosen not to reveal that information. It is a sad commentary on our activity that there is a stigma that is attached to anyone who panics. It is as if cave divers, confronted by perhaps the most hostile environment known, are supposed to be fearless heroes or something. Yet all of us know that, under the right conditions, any of us can panic. Millions of years of evolution have programmed us to get a sudden surge of adrenalin when we perceive danger, sending us into a blind, unreasoning frenzy to escape from the situation through fight or flight. Unfortunately, in cave diving, that natural reaction all too often results in death. Survival depends on being able to suppress anxiety and replace it with calm, clear, quick, and correct reasoning.

But that is not the response we are born with, and certainly is not taught in school. I learned it by accident, through the miracle of surviving the incidents described in the previous chapters. I was even luckier in that the most harrowing of the incidents was preceded by easier escapes, where I was gradually able to discover and reinforce the fact that cool, focused reasoning is the key to survival rather than panic. For example, if I had become lost at Peacock on my third cave dive (when I nearly panicked at Jugg Spring from hitting my head on the ceiling and accidentally flooding my mask) instead of on my twenty-fifth dive, I would never have been able to continue searching for the exit to the cave. In the final analysis, the only difference between my partner and me on our 300-foot-plus deep dive is that I had been stupid enough to get myself into the situations in the previous chapters and he had not.

Nowadays, we have certified cave diving courses and books detailing the safety procedures for our activity, so there is no longer any need for new divers to discover safe cave diving techniques as I did, through trial and error. But how do we teach divers not to panic?

Ironically, our hard–won depth record lasted only a few weeks, until we made a dive to a depth of 325 feet in a similar cave at Mystery Sink in Orlando. This time my partner was my original cave diving buddy, Joe Prosser. From our many years of diving together, I knew that Joe could keep as levelheaded as anyone in emergency situations. Perhaps the most supreme irony of all is that, many years later, we learned from Martyn Farr that both dives were only American cave depth records. Four British divers had made a mixed–gas dive to 335 feet in Sinoia Caves, Zimbabwe (then Rhodesia) the previous year.

"Every sport must have its champion. I want to be the champion of scuba diving." Those words were used by Jean Clarke–Samazen to explain his motivation for setting the world depth record for scuba diving on compressed air of 350 feet in 1954. The record lasted more than a dozen years, an incredibly long time for a diving record. According to *Dive* magazine, two men died trying to break it, including Florida attorney Hope Root.

"My old dive shop partner just set the world record of 355 feet," Ken Brock proudly reported to us at the September, 1966 meeting of the Aquacks Dive Club. There was no need to explain *which* record. The depth record for scuba diving was *the* record to all divers, occupying a special niche above the cave diving records, the breathhold diving records, the distance records of Fred Baldasare, and even the depth records of mixed–gas "lockout" divers such as Hannes Keller, despite their greater depth. To us, the lockout diving records were largely set by machines—the special deep submarines used to transport the divers to and from their lockout depth in dry comfort and security—rather than by people. To give a record to Keller seemed to make as much sense as giving horse racing's Triple Crown to the jockey instead of Secretariat.

On the other hand, the scuba diving record was a record set by human beings. And the man of the hour was Hal Watts, who had made my instructor and original scuba diving hero, Ken Brock, a junior partner in his Orlando dive shop. With Ken's announcement, Hal immediately became the person most admired by the teenaged members of our dive club. Like Ken, Hal was a genuine hero engaged in pushing back frontiers in the sea, rather than the relatively senseless pursuits of organized professional sports, or worse, the imitation heroics of actors like our beloved "Mike Nelson" on the popular *Sea Hunt* television series. More than that, Hal was one of us — a Florida cave diver—which seemed to confirm what more and more people were saying: cave divers were simply the world's best divers, period.

Since no decompression tables existed for scuba diving on the exotic helium gas mixtures used by the submarine-assisted lockout divers, compressed air was the only gas that could be breathed on such a dive. Compressed air is cheap and universally available, but its principal components, nitrogen and oxygen, become narcotic or even toxic below 130 feet. Breathing air at such depths can cause divers to black out with little or no warning or even convulse and drown. The problem becomes progressively worse with increased depth and time. Through years of diving at Forty Fathom Grotto, Hal had discovered several narcosis management techniques including acclimation through a series of progressively deeper dives at relatively short intervals. These techniques were of benefit to the entire diving community, helping us all make safer dives.

That is not to say that Hal's exploits were not controversial. Some diving organizations and publications called his 355–foot dive with Herb Johnson and his 390–foot record dive with A. J. Muns the following year, "suicidal." They vilified him for setting a record that could cost imitators their lives.

Hal's detractors had only to point to the 1947 death of Cousteau's top diver, Maurice Fargues, and the others mentioned earlier in the chapter, to find ammunition for their claims. While there was some genuine concern, many of us were able to see that much of the controversy was caused by jealousy: when you are at the top, you are a very good target. Also, Hal was not helped by the fact that he was closely associated with one particular line of diving equipment and one scuba training organization. That provided a financial reason as well for others to criticize him.

Nevertheless, when Canadians Archie Forfar and Anne Gunderson began planning their record attempt in early 1971, one of their first concerns was whether or not they would lose their scuba instructor ratings. Since both of them made their living operating Archie's Andros Reef Inn dive resort, such worries were significant. The regional manager of their instructional organization assured Anne, however, that they would not be expelled.

By 1971, the official record for scuba diving was 437 feet, set by two of Hal's former students, Neal Watson and John Gruener. We had heard that they had been lowered while attached to a platform, had completely lost consciousness and could not remember the details of the dive. Some divers suggested that the two had blacked out shallower and were lowered in a senseless state, which would be a silly way to set a record. An intriguing "unofficial" 460–foot dive had been claimed several years earlier by Dick Birch of the neighboring Small Hope Bay Lodge, Archie's closest competitor for tourist divers. I have never paid much attention to whether or not a record is "official," a rather meaningless term that seems to apply only to entries in the Guinness book. The only relevant question is, did the dive happen? In the case of Birch's dive, however, most of the diving community seemed to think that inaccurate measuring methods were used and that the dive was actually much shallower. Regardless of the validity of their claims, I personally admired all of them—Watson, Gruener, and Birch—for trying to find ways to increase our limits.

Anne Gunderson was a short blonde in her twenties. She unsuccessfully tried to hide her beauty with a serious disposition and wire frame glasses. I had first learned of her when I overheard a YMCA scuba instructor institute staff discussing my time for the bailout. The bailout is a procedure where the aspiring scuba instructor jumps into deep water holding all of his equipment (including even facemask and tank) in his hand, then puts it on and returns to the surface. Several of the staff thought my time was a world record.

"Heck, a *girl* has beaten Sheck's time," an instructor interjected. "Anne Gunderson did it in 12 seconds at her institute."

Nowadays, after the exploits of Mary Ellen Eckhoff, India Fuller, Sylvia Earle, Marty Dunwoody, Angela Bandini, Ann Kristovich, and others, female expertise at diving is not surprising. But in the early 1970's, scuba diving was very much a male-dominated sport.

Archie hired Anne to work for him as a divemaster and instructor, and they became lovers. They met Jim Lockwood while he was diving neighboring "blue holes" as part of George Benjamin's expeditions. A fellow Canadian and friend of Archie's, George had pioneered exploration in many of the underwater caves of the Bahamas, known locally as blue holes (see chapter 7), and published a popular article on the subject in *National Geographic*. George was also quite an innovator, coming up with the safer "dual valve" design for manifolding twin tanks at about the same time as South Carolina cave diver Ed Dixon. But George, limited by his age (over 60) and his technique, could not safely penetrate the caves more than a couple of hundred feet. So he invited our best-known cave diver, Tom Mount, to organize teams of Floridians to push further. Through Tom, George became aware of our procedures such as the third rule, as well as the lights and guideline reels manufactured by Frank Martz. Naturally, Frank was invited along, with his favorite diving partner, Jim Lockwood.

Respected for an exceptionally low breathing rate and good head at depth, Jim became notorious when in the space of 12 months, three diving partners died while diving with him. In none of the three incidents was Jim primarily to blame, and he attempted rescues each time at considerable personal risk. But some questioned whether Jim had lured divers of lesser ability into dangerous situations, and a few of the more ignorant actually called him "Killer Lockwood". Archie and Anne realized that such accusations were groundless, however, and Archie once paid Jim the supreme compliment: "Jim, you're the only deep diver I ever met that wasn't crazy."

Jim had actually begun practicing for a record dive the previous year at Hal Watts' Mystery Sink, Florida. While Joe Prosser and I were setting our 325–foot cave depth record there, Jim told me that he had gone even deeper than Hal in the open water section, all the way to 375 feet. Jim realized that Archie and Anne's proximity to the "wall" of Andros Island, a nearly–vertical cliff that drops from a depth of 150 feet to approximately 1000 feet, was the ideal situation for him to attain his dream of setting a new record.

During the summer of 1970, Jim also helped Frank Martz add onto my line in Eagle's Nest. They discovered a large section they named the "Super Room." I heard about their discovery, however, and on August 29, 1971, Chuck Stevens and I continued exploration to find the end of the Super Room. By that time, Frank's abrasive personality had caused a split with Jim, and my Dixie Cavern Kings partners had pretty much quit cave diving, so both of us were in need of new dive partners. Jim called me up, eager to see what we had found, and soon the two of us were pushing both ends of Eagle's Nest nearly every weekend.

Meanwhile, on Andros Island, preparations for the record attempt were progressing rapidly. Using Hal's technique of depth acclimation, the three had gradually built up to dives of 400 feet and even deeper, encountering bizarre symptoms of severe narcosis: total blindness, temporary and permanent amnesia, and even total loss of consciousness. In the latter event, the diver would suddenly appear to go to sleep with his eyes open, and if not helped would lie on the bottom continuing to breathe until his air was gone. Fortunately, using drop-away weights in conjunction with the new buoyancy compensator vests and Frank Martz' automatic injection system, Archie had designed a foolproof method of surviving such a depth blackout. When one of the three blacked out, the weights would drop and the diver would float up to a depth where consciousness would be regained.

One danger remained, however: the possibility that the diver would not awaken until above the first decompression stop necessary to avoid the bends. A support team was needed to catch the deep divers on their ascent. Archie did not want to repeat the mistakes of Hannes Keller, where two relatively inexperienced divers were invited along for publicity reasons and perished. He wanted the best deep divers available, period. My Eagle's Nest dive buddy was kind enough to recommend me.

I was flown over the next weekend for an all–expenses-paid look at their project. I knew Jim was the best deep diving partner I had dived with up to that time, and soon developed a high regard for Archie and Anne and the safety preparations for the dive. I still had some concerns, however, which I voiced to Archie.

"You know, I believe in what you are trying to do," I began, while the lanky, bearded Canadian quietly regarded me. "But I'm also aware of the hell that Hal Watts was put through for his dives. I would hope that this is going to be kept quiet, with publicity at a minimum."

Archie responded in his ever–calm, quiet manner. He never spoke more than was absolutely necessary, and when he did speak, it was so softly that you had to strain sometimes to hear him. "Don't worry, we don't want publicity either." And he smiled, one of the few times I ever saw him do so.

The next day the four of us went to the wall on Archie's boat. As always, I got violently seasick in the 4-foot seas despite liberal doses of the anti-seasickness drug marezine. Jim was eager to show me how much easier deep diving was in open water than in a cave like Eagle's Nest. "When we dive," he said between my stomach spasms, "don't look at your depth gauge until I ask you to."

"Okay," I croaked weakly, scooping up seawater to wash my face.

Finally we were in the water below the violently churning surface. My stomach settled, and we swam down the anchor line to where it was hooked in the edge of the wall at 150 feet. I had dived a similar wall at the north end of Grand Cayman with Rick Frehsee, but this wall seemed to be more colorful and exciting, with many more fish and greater variety of brightly-colored coral, sponges, and gorgonians. I was not surprised that they had found several of the exceedingly rare slit shells there, selling each for thousands of dollars. There were also great trees of valuable black coral protruding from the wall. But I had barely time to spare them a glance as we plummeted rapidly downward. Because of the limited air supply in our twin tanks and the need to keep our decompression to a minimum, it was important to descend as quickly as possible.

I resisted the temptation to look at my depth gauge, diving instead on how I felt as Jim had requested. I used my martial arts training in meditation, concentration, and body awareness to monitor myself for symptoms of nitrogen narcosis, oxygen toxicity, or carbon dioxide excess. Only four minutes after we started down the wall, Jim paused and looked up at me, grinning like a Cheshire cat. When I joined him, he pointed at his depth gauge. I still felt clear-headed, so hesitated, wanting to waste no time in getting to the 280 to 300 foot level that we were used to in Eagle's Nest. Jim insisted, though, so I reluctantly peeked at his gauge. It read 400 feet.

Disbelieving, I immediately compared it to my own. I had recently taught myself the difficult technique of talking underwater, so shouted at Jim, "I can't believe it's so easy!" I had just become only the sixth scuba diver in history to attain that depth.

Our dive plan called for an ascent to 300 feet, where the four of us would pause for a half hour of acclimation. I chose to swim up with my fins to that level instead of relaxing and using the buoyancy of my compensator. I knew that working the big muscles in my legs would generate large amounts of carbon dioxide and possibly trigger narcosis and oxygen toxicity, but was not worried due to the ease of my descent.

Suddenly the video camera of my eyes and mind became a series of still shots in rapid succession. When I looked at Jim, it was as if there were three of him, one above the other. In all my deep dives I had never experienced symptoms like these. I prudently stopped kicking and inflated my compensator for the rest of the trip up.

Nevertheless, I soon grew bored while the others were sitting on a ledge at 300 feet, and amused myself by swimming back and forth at the level, exploring the wall. Unfortunately, once more my exertion triggered a problem, as I abruptly became nauseated from oxygen toxicity. I knew that oxygen toxicity meant an imminent convulsion and certain death, so I signaled to the others and ascended until the cramps eased. This time I used my vest to avoid making my condition worse by swimming.

Our decompression was unusual, a first stop at the un-heard-of depth (then) of 100 feet. A few months later, a supposed expert diver from the midwest, working with Randy Hylton on a major government saturation diving project, proudly proclaimed to everyone that he had just made his first

100–foot dive. Ever long on honesty and short on tolerance for charlatans, Randy immediately boomed "Hell, I've made dives where we *decompressed* deeper than that!"

During the 40–foot stop, a huge remora-a type of scavenger fish that attaches itself to the belly of sharks and feeds on the host animal's leftovers-amused us by trying to attach itself to Jim's fanny. Jim was not amused, however, and repeatedly kicked at the persistent varmint to keep it away. I also stopped laughing when I reflected that: (1) I had never heard of a remora this large, (2) I had never seen a remora without its host shark, so (3) the host was probably nearby, and (4) a huge remora had to have a huge host shark.

I forgot all about Mr. Shark, however, during the 20–foot stop. By then we were into the fringe of the surge from the surface, and I grew so seasick that I was forced to throw up underwater. I was not sure whether it was safer to throw up in my regulator and risk clogging the exhaust valve with debris, causing it to leak water, or to remove the mouthpiece and vomit directly into the ocean, risking drowning if I involuntarily gasped for air in the middle of a spasm. By the end of the stop, it was a moot question: sick as a dog, I had repeatedly heaved both ways. Then I looked up and realized that I had a 56–minute 10–foot stop ahead of me, in even more violent water. It was one of the most miserable feelings of my life.

That night, after my stomach had miraculously recovered and I had feasted on Bahamian peas and rice, Archie held council in his office. He had been impressed with the ease with which I had dived to 400 feet, and of course had been already impressed with Jim. Were all Florida cave divers like us? If so, a new world record would not last long! Jim and I went to considerable lengths to allay his fears. After all, we needed two more divers for the 300–foot support team.

"Do you think John and Randy could come?" Archie asked Jim.

Jim occasionally joined John Harper and his long–time

partner Randy Hylton on their dives. "Well, they were the deep support for Hal's last record dive," he began. "Randy would probably come, but John hasn't been any good at depth since getting bent at the Nest a couple of years ago."

"What about Hal?" I asked.

"He probably wouldn't come. Besides, he might want to steal the show."

"Well, we need one more diver on Sheck's team besides Randy," Archie observed. "Could Tom Mount dive to 300 feet?"

Tom was one of my fellow directors in NACD, and had recently told me about his deepest dive, when he dropped all the way to 340 feet to rescue an unconscious partner. "Sure," I said.

"But Tom's dive officer position with the University of Miami is too political," Jim added. "He's afraid he could lose his job. Bill Wiggins would be a good choice."

"Who is he?"

"He's a diver from Lakeland who has gone with Jim and me on some of our dives in the Nest," I responded. "He's got an excellent deep head."

The next day I watched Archie dive to 450 feet with the drop–away weight system. Jim had to drop his weight early, so stopped at 440 feet. Even though I lacked the safety of the weight system, I wanted to join them, but Anne aborted her dive at 300 feet and asked me to stay with her.

The record attempt was set for a month later, on December 11, 1971. Jim and I flew over on the 9th with Randy and Bill so we could do a rehearsal dive on the 10th. Unfortunately, it was not a "full–dress" rehearsal because the 600–foot–long stainless steel cable for measuring the depth had arrived only the day before and was still packed in cosmoline. Worse, the clips that the three record divers were to slide down the cable were 1/8 inch too small. So our rehearsal dive was made without the cable. Diving with the drop–away weights, all three unofficially broke Watson and Gruener's record:

Anne to 440 feet, and Archie and Jim to 450 feet. I stopped at 420 feet because I lacked the fail-safe weight system.

Meanwhile, Bill and Randy were having problems. They had been paired together since neither had been deeper than 320 feet. At 360 feet, Bill completely lost consciousness. Randy quickly went to his aid, grabbing the inert diver's tank valve manifold to haul him up to safety. Unfortunately, the exertion of doing that knocked him out, also. With incredible luck, by that time they had ascended enough for Bill to recover, so he was able to rescue his rescuer.

Their experience scared all of us. At our final meeting that night, Archie insisted: "Under no circumstances will anyone go below 300 feet except Anne, Jim, and me."

"What if someone blacks out?"

"Just wait at 300 feet for us to float up."

"Well, how deep do you plan on going?" Randy asked.

"We're going to shoot for 480," Archie replied. "That way we beat the official record and also answer any questions there might be about the possibility that Dick Birch might have gone to 460."

"What about the clips being too small for the cable?"

"Well, if we clean the grease off the cable, they ought to work fine."

The next morning was dismal, the sky overcast and the strong offshore wind was kicking up whitecaps on the waves. One look at that roiling sea, and I decided to skip breakfast and to take double the recommended dosage of marezine. My best regulator was free-flowing (leaking air) a little, so I switched to a harder-breathing one to avoid wasting air. I knew that the increased respiratory effort, like the increased dosage of anti-seasickness pills, would limit my ability to dive deep, but we had agreed with Archie not to dive below 300 feet. After all, I had been to 420 feet the previous day with no significant problems.

Three Bahamian government officials got on the boat.

"They're needed as official witnesses," Archie reassured us.

"What about the reporter?" The Associated Press had flown a man in the night before.

Archie just shrugged. I suppose it was naive of us to expect that the dive would go totally unnoticed. What I was most concerned about now was the psychological pressure. Archie had invested a lot of time, effort, and money to get all of us, including the government witnesses and the press, together for the dive on this particular day. Canceling the event and rescheduling for another day would have been very difficult. But all of the practice dives had gone by without a hitch. To all of us, beating Watson and Gruener's record seemed a foregone conclusion. It was only a matter of how much deeper could we go?

By 11:00 AM, we had fought our way through the churning waves to a point above the wall and anchored there. Bill, Randy, and I jumped in the water first to assist with the cable, clips, drop weights, and decompression tanks. The 300–pound engine block used to anchor the measured cable momentarily fouled on the boat's rear diving platform, but Randy, an extraordinarily powerful diver, somehow wrestled it loose. Meanwhile, the record divers hyperventilated and cooled their faces with ice packs to slow their hearts and reduce their air consumption.

At 11:13 AM, the six of us began our descent. Two underwater photographers from Ed Farmer's boat, Ross Ellis and Bob Knowles, accompanied us to the edge of the wall at 150 feet and stopped. As we continued down, I noticed that Archie, Anne, and Jim were having a lot of trouble sliding their clips down the cable. Nevertheless, we quickly reached 300 feet, where Randy, Bill, and I halted. The three record divers vanished below us into the deep blue amid a rising swirl of silvery exhaust bubbles.

To avoid having to use the extra bottles for decompression, because they might be needed by the record divers, I started skip breathing to conserve my air. Normally this technique of slowing respiration, which greatly increases carbon dioxide retention, thereby triggering narcosis and oxygen toxicity, is strictly avoided, but I was confident that I was sufficiently acclimated to handle it at 300 feet. My air tasted a little peculiar, as it had the day before. Bill suspected that the compressor oil was breaking down, but did not seem overly concerned about the possibility of dangerous impurities in our air.

It seemed to be taking a long time for our three friends to come back up. Some of the bubbles were now rising away from us, toward deeper water. Nine minutes after the dive started, I suddenly saw Jim float up under us through the veil of his bubbles, prone but face down, his body completely limp. I caught him and grabbed him by the shoulder, getting no response from his blank, staring eyes. He was obviously completely unconscious. Randy grabbed his tank valve manifold and hauled him on up, while Bill and I remained to wait for the others.

At 230 feet, Jim recovered enough to give Randy a feeble "OK" signal with forefinger and thumb, so Randy let him go and returned to 300 feet to help us. Three minutes after I had caught Jim, there was still no sign of Archie or Anne. Even with my skip breathing, my air was starting to get dangerously low. Archie and Anne, deeper and breathing normally, had to be using up their air at a much faster rate. Something had to be wrong.

I decided at once to break our promise to Archie to stay at 300 feet. It was not a decision made lightly. I keep promises, and probably carry more details of secret dives that others have made than anyone else. I signaled to Bill and Randy to wait at 300 while I dropped a short distance to see what the delay was all about. To my dismay, Randy started down, too. Sensing that he was going to try to reach Archie and Anne even if they were on the bottom, I grabbed him by the shoulder and told him, "Don't be an idiot!"

Randy shrugged me off, yelled something unintelligible, and continued down. Glancing up, I saw that Bill was starting to slide down the cable, also. Now I had to be concerned about them as well as Archie and Anne. I quickly passed Bill, then at 360 feet Randy slowed his descent and I passed him, too.

When I reached 400 feet, I saw Archie and Anne far below me, outlined against the silver–white background of the wall. They were exhaling bubbles, and at first I thought that they were upright and headed for the surface. I looked up at Randy, pointed at them, and signaled "OK". Oddly, Randy did not signal back, despite the fact that he seemed to be looking straight at me.

My main concern, however, was Archie and Anne. As I watched them, I finally realized that they were not moving up, so I renewed my descent. Below 380 feet the wall changed from strictly vertical to a steep slope of about 45 degrees, and the cable curved with it. That meant I had to risk the exertion of swimming a little as I went down, but two lives were in the balance.

At about 420 feet, I was able to see them better, Archie face down against the engine block, his legs kicking slowly as if he were trying to go deeper. Anne was about ten feet to his left, slightly farther out and face down, with no discernible movement. Both divers were still exhaling bubbles from their regulators. With the exception of Bill and Randy's mutual rescue from 360 feet the day before, no one had ever rescued a depth blackout victim from deeper than Tom Mount's 340–footer (I saved Dana Turner from 360 feet at Grand Bahama Island two years later). In the back of my mind I knew that I had no chance of saving even one, much less both of them, but with them clearly in sight and only 60 feet away, I had to try.

At about 440 feet I started having trouble with my distance vision, everything beyond about ten feet degenerating into a silver–gray blur of pale light and dim shadows. A little deeper, and the tunnel vision began, a certain sign of oxygen toxicity. As I continued down, the tunnel quickly tightened, and a sparkling spot like a burning fuse appeared in the lower part of the porthole. Blackout and/or a convulsion was seconds away. I quickly opened the valve of my buoyancy compensator inflator fully and tried to read my depth gauge so I could plan my decompression should I live that long. It seemed yards away in the tunnel of my vision, but clearly showed 460 feet. That meant that the tips of my fins were hanging down at 465 feet plus, only 15–20 feet away from my friends. But it might as well have been a mile.

Now it was a race to get up before I blacked out from narcosis or convulsed from oxygen toxicity. Either way, I would drown. I did not think I would make it, but once more called on my training in concentration and was able to avoid losing consciousness. By the time I had ascended to 280 feet, the tunnel vision had dilated and I could forget about dying from narcosis or oxygen toxicity.

At about 200 feet, I slowed my ascent and started to swim back and forth along the wall as I continued up, trying to locate the cable, divers, anchor line, or boats above me. My problem was that the diagonal route of the cable below 380 feet had placed my vertical ascent from 465 feet far from the vertical route to the boat. I knew that Archie and Anne were dead, and feared the same for Randy and Bill and possibly Jim as well. As far as I knew, I was the only survivor of the six divers who had set out that morning to 300 feet, and it did not look as though I would survive for long: I was down to only 900 psig in my twin 70's (about a third of my starting air), far too little to decompress from such a dive to avoid the bends. As I continued my searching ascent, I began to weigh the alterna- tives: drowning or the agony of explosive decompression (bends). Drowning was certainly faster and less painful: Tommy Hawkins had told me that after I revived him at Little River. The least painful way of all was the way Archie and Anne had died, blacking out at depth. Unfortunately, I had eliminated that alternative with the miraculous ascent I had just completed. I no longer had enough air to return to sufficient depth to black out.

Suddenly I felt something grab one of my fins violently. Shark? I quickly turned and was almost overcome with relief when I saw Randy: he was alive! He led me to the cable, and now I knew that I would probably live if our experimental decompression tables worked for my 15–minute dive to 465 feet. The tables were designed for only 10 minutes at 450 feet.

We joined Jim at the 90 foot stop, but there was still no sign of Bill Wiggins. Jim seemed to be in a daze. When he finally started coming around, it was obvious that he was very upset. His "Killer Lockwood" critics could now count five partners who had died in a little over a year, six if you counted Bill. Meanwhile, the crew on the boat above us, loaded with shocked and seasick Bahamians, started winching up the cable so they could go in to shore.

Ed Farmer led us to the decompression lines tied to his boat, where we were overjoyed to find Bill quietly decompressing. During the 10–foot stop, Jim reported some possible bends pain, but the pain subsided and he surfaced at 1:38 PM. Randy got out 15 minutes later, and I, seasick as usual, surfaced a couple of minutes after that. I was a little bit worried, but developed no recognizable symptoms of decompression sickness after the dive. I had a right to be worried: two decades later, modern decompression tables would have me decompress a total of 370 minutes, starting at a depth of 180 feet. I had actually decompressed for only 162 minutes, starting at 110 feet.

It was a very somber and quiet boat ride back to the Inn. Not until supper did we feel relaxed enough to compare notes. Despite giving Randy an OK signal, Jim did not remember a thing until Ed Farmer grabbed him at 80 feet, saving him from the bends. On our hopeless rescue attempt, Bill had halted after descending only a short distance and returned to 300 feet, certain that he would have the Herculean task of catching possibly as many as four divers as they came floating up. Randy did not respond to my signals at 400 feet because he was totally blind at that point. He yelled at me and immediately used his vest to go up.

What had happened to Archie's fail–safe system of drop–away weights? Jim reported that the diagonal route of the cable below 380 feet made sliding the undersized clips too difficult. Feeling pressure to complete the dive on this day, the trio had made the fatal decision to drop the weights prematurely, deflate their compensators, and swim the clips down the cable. Jim told us he started to black out at 400 feet, and remembered opening the inflator on his vest before losing consciousness. It was probably a good thing that he had not been able to go below 400 feet. If he had done so, he would have come up like I did, far from where we were waiting for him. I might not have seen him or been able to catch him, and he might have ascended to dangerously shallow depths to die of the bends.

Meanwhile I had my own private demons to wrestle with. To have come so close to Archie and Anne, probably less than 20 feet. What if I had been prepared for a deep dive? What if I had not overdosed on marezine? What if I had used a good regulator? What if I had not skip–breathed? What if my bottom time had been only five minutes instead of 15? Any one of those factors could have enabled me to reach and save one of them; eliminate all of the factors and maybe I could have saved both. It was bitter consolation to know that no one besides me had ever descended to 465 feet on compressed air and lived to tell about it (more than two decades later, no one else has), much less rescued anyone from that depth. But the what–if's still haunt me.

The next day the special deep submersible Alvin, stationed at a nearby test facility on Andros Island, made a special dive to look for the two drowned divers. The bodies had apparently slid down the slope, for the crew reported finding them at 1,000 feet. No recovery was possible because the mechanical arms used to retrieve objects at that extreme depth were not attached to the submersible.

Not long afterward, Lewis Holtzendorff, arguably our best cave diver of the early 1970's, asked me about the dive. "You know," he said, puffing on his pipe, "when you look at the conditions of your dive, it was probably equivalent to making a prepared dive on compressed air to well over 500 feet. Why don't you go back and make your record 'official' for the Guinness people?"

At the time, all I could do was think about Archie Forfar and Anne Gunderson.

"You've got to be kidding," was all I could say.

6

The Ten–Thousand–Year–Old Brain

The camera was whirring. Four underwater archaeolo-gists and I were seated around a table on the bank of Warm Mineral Springs, a popular health resort near Sarasota. Our script called for us to plan a dive using a map I had helped prepare. The area had been cordoned off to keep hundreds of curious tourists out of the range of our camera.

In the background, a nearly deaf, 75–year–old man waded by, oblivious to what we were doing. While the five of us were busy hamming it up for the camera, he slowly took a deep breath, then lay in the water face down. As the minutes passed, each of us became gradually aware that the man had gone without breathing for much longer than any of us, the oldest of whom was less than half his age, could have done. Had the old codger died on camera? In short order our well-planned discussion became forced and artificial, then fell off altogether as we turned to watch the water with alarm, Finally, just as we were rushing from our seats to see if anything could be done, Col. William Royal stood up casually, totally un-aware that he had made a complete shambles of our film. He was not even breathing hard!

That was my introduction to Bill Royal, the man who had first alerted the world to the bizarre nature of two springs in southwest Florida—Warm Mineral Springs and Little Salt Spring. Bill discovered that the springs have chemistry, temperature, mineral deposits, and ecology quite different from any other Florida caves, most of which lie far to the north. Perhaps their most intriguing aspect, however, is their archaeology: they have been the site of some of the most significant discoveries ever made. After years of calling attention to the potential of the springs and even attempting some excavation himself, Bill finally convinced archaeologists to take a look.

The first major expedition took place at Little Salt Spring in December, 1971. Carl Clausen, head of the Florida Underwater Archaeological Research Section, a state agency, was in charge of the investigation. His problem was how to keep a bunch of folks who were excellent scientists but marginal divers from killing themselves in a low–visibility spring at least 210 feet deep and containing hidden ledges and silty cave passages. With sensation–hungry wire–service and network television crews on site, Carl knew that the slightest accident would result in a tremendous amount of negative publicity that would cause his project to be cancelled.

The solution was to seek the help of cave divers with deep diving experience to serve as safety divers. Bob Friedman, a professional cave diving instructor from Miami who had been to 300 feet was hired to assemble and direct the team. He and I were both charter directors of the newly formed National Association for Cave Diving (NACD), so he knew I had set American records for both cave diving depth (325 feet) and penetration (2099 feet) the previous year. Also selected were Paul Therien and Bob's wife, Sue Friedman.

On the surface, Little Salt looks much like scores of other ponds amid the pines and palms flanking the Mykka River: circular, approximately 200 feet in diameter and surrounded by a low, muddy swamp. Underwater is quite different. Since

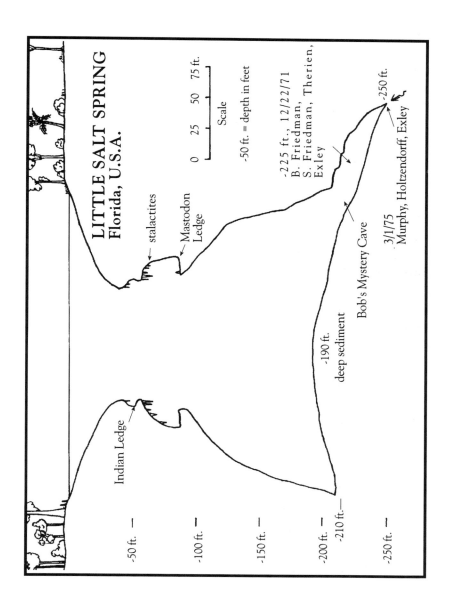

LITTLE SALT SPRING
Florida, U.S.A.

stalactites

Mastodon
Ledge

Scale

0   25   50   75 ft.

-50 ft. = depth in feet

-225 ft., 12/22/71
B. Friedman,
S. Friedman, Therien,
Exley

Bob's Mystery Cave

3/1/75
Murphy, Holtzendorff, Exley

-250 ft.

Indian Ledge

-190 ft.
deep sediment

-50 ft. —

-100 ft. —

-150 ft. —

-200 ft. —
-210 ft. —

-250 ft. —

Bob Friedman and Tom Mount before a deep cave dive at Eagle's Nest. (*Photo by Sheck Exley*)

The stalactites in Warm Mineral are partially redissolved. (*Photo by Paul Heinerth*)

the spring is one of the few sites in the eastern United States that is geothermally heated by the earth's interior to a temperature substantially above that of other springs, the December chill was quickly relieved by 82° F water. The water was tinged an eerie yellow brown, the color of fine Kentucky bourbon or weak iced tea. As we filmed for CBS, I noticed blind tarpon swimming by, their eyes apparently destroyed by the high mineral content of the water. The bottom was covered with a thick layer of black ooze that spilled over the walls of an 80–foot–diameter cavity in the center at a depth of 40 feet. The slimy ooze looked and felt disgusting, but it was the primary target of the expedition. Mired in its tarry grasp were suspected to be Indian remains thousands of years old, preserved by the oxygen–free water. The reason for the unusual lack of oxygen was believed to be the presence of an anaerobic bacteria which Carl morbidly dubbed "Anaero–bosaurus" since he figured the depths of the cavity was the perfect place for a monster to hide.

Suddenly the journalist that I was with freaked out, signalling to me that he had vertigo similar to that occasionally caused by narcosis at depths in excess of 130 feet. He had lost his sense of direction, including which way was up, and everything around him was spinning madly. Puzzled by the fact that we were only 20 feet deep, I grabbed him securely by his tank valve and wrestled him to the surface. While he gasped for breath I towed him to the shore.

"What happened?" Bob demanded, his long black beard and slender build making him look like the prophet Elijah.

I helped the journalist struggle ashore. "Anaerobosaurus almost got him," I replied.

"Anaerobosaurus?" the journalist turned to me his eyes still bulging.

"Yeah. That's a monster Carl found in the spring that gobbles up air bubbles and divers."

Everyone laughed, but the seriousness of the incident was

not lost upon us. If an experienced diver like the journalist had trouble at 20 feet, what could happen at greater depths to some of the scientists on the team who were novice divers? We were all thankful for Bob's safety precautions: no dives were to be made below 90 feet during the project, and all teams were to be accompanied by at least one safety diver. A command post was established on a dock, and the excavating archaeologist furnished with a sophisticated helmet that enabled him to maintain continuous voice communication with the post on the surface.

First, we helped Carl run heavy dredge pipes across the spring. They were held by floating 55–gallon drums, and were connected to a pump. Then we settled into a routine. On each dive, one of the four support divers would swim out with Carl or Gordon Watts to the excavation area staked out in the ooze in 20–40 feet of water. There the archaeologist would photo-graph the site with a stereoscopic camera, take core samples, or excavate by slowly fanning the ooze into the dredge pipe. We furnished an extra set of hands to help, and we kept track of the team's air supply, bottom time, etc.

On one dive, I watched Carl carefully pull a prehistoric skull out of the muck. It turned out to be that of a young girl who had lived nearly 10,000 years ago. The skull still con-tained a considerable amount of brain tissue – preservation of a sort almost unheard of. Did she and the other Indians found drown there, either accidentally or as part of a sacrificial ceremony? Or were their dead bodies pushed out from shore to partially decay and sink to the bottom?

The archaeology was fascinating, but my explorer's heart yearned for a chance to investigate the deep cavity. On one of our dives we were permitted to check it out, and Bob showed me scores of stalactites hanging from the walls of the pit at depths as great as 90 feet. The icicle–like rock formations can be formed only by dripping water in the air, so were proof that the water level in the spring was once at least 90 feet lower.

One ledge directly beneath our excavation area was particularly interesting in that it contained the bones of large prehistoric mammals from the Pleistocene epoch. How did they get there?

The next day I was back with Carl in the shallow excavation area. Suddenly I saw him wrestling with the dredge pipe as it dragged him backward. Anaerobosaurus had struck again! Carl dug in his heels in an effort to keep the pipe from moving further, but to no avail. His heels left twin furrows in the ooze as the pipe dragged us out over the 210–foot–deep chasm. Just as the pipe coiled like a giant grey python, ready to plunge to the bottom far below, somehow we got it stopped.

Already loaded with nitrogen from his repetitive dives, Carl drastically increased his need for decompression stops to avoid the bends by dropping down to 80 feet to check on a sagging portion of the pipe. Next, he exasperated me by shooting directly to the surface to shout directions to his surface crew. Preoccupied by his scientific pursuit and the urgency of saving his dredge equipment, only much too late did he realize that he also had a potential decompression problem. Sure enough, he soon began complaining of minor joint pain. Such pain is common after the body has been subjected to a cold and wet environment—such as on a dive— but it could also be an early symptom of the bends.

Ever a stickler for safety, Bob was taking no chances: back down we went with oxygen to perform the U. S. Navy Omitted Decompression Schedule. If additional symptoms showed up or the problem persisted after the dive, Carl would have to be sent to the nearest recompression chamber regardless of the publicity. It is better to have your project cancelled than to suffer permanent injury or death from the bends. Fortunately, after 75 minutes, Carl and I surfaced without any symptoms and the media never knew a thing.

Bob prescribed a day of rest for Carl, then we were back in the water again. This time we were excavating at 40 feet at the

Randy Hylton hoists a fossil tusk found in a Florida spring. (*Photo by John Harper*)

edge of the precipice, where there was a strange vertical groove in the rock. After a few minutes the dredge revealed an ancient hickory stake, then another one next to it—driven into the top of the pit. Hickory has not grown in this part of Florida since the last ice age. Directly below us was the mysterious ledge where we had found the bones of the extinct prehistoric mammals. Now we had evidence that thousand of years earlier, when water levels were lower, the Indians had used the stakes to anchor a vine they had climbed down, to dine on meat taken from the animals they had slain. The groove in the soft pit wall was worn by the vines rubbing against the rock.

Sonar mapping of the spring walls had indicated that on one side they overhung considerably and possibly descended below the reported maximum depth of 210 feet. This greatly excited the four safety divers, so on the next to last day of the expedition we descended to investigate. I elected to use the new double 100–cubic–foot tanks instead of my old double 70's, so that I would have more air. By now I had also discarded my Clorox jug in favor of a buoyancy compensator vest, and had replaced the dim three–watt light that had served me so faithfully for four years with a much brighter 30–watt version. The new light was especially valuable since our visibility was only 20 feet, and below 90 feet all surface light was lost.

Within a few minutes we had reeled down to 210 feet on the overhanging side, expecting to hit a bottom of black ooze. The bottom was not there! Instead we saw the overhang flatten into a bonafide cave ceiling that cut back horizontally out of sight. In a few minutes we were at 225 feet, still on the ceiling and squinting hard downward without seeing bottom. We headed back from that point, but three years later Larry Murphy, Lewis Holtzendorff, and I returned to find the bottom at 250 feet. A clear jet of warm water issued from a tiny opening at the deepest point.

The occasion of the latter dive was the next investigation by the state in the area. The 1975 expedition was based at Warm Mineral Springs and was headed by Dr. Sonny Cockrell, Carl Clausen having moved to Texas. That year I was learning the family car business, and had accepted the presidencies of both of America's national cave diving organizations, NACD and the much larger NSS Cave Diving Section. I was also vice–chairman of the World Cave Diving Organization, the International Union of Speleology Cave Diving Commission. This was all very prestigious. I am the only person ever to serve in more than one of those positions—much less all three at the same time—but it was a lot of work. Nevertheless, I put all that aside for a few days for the chance to dive with Sonny at Warm Mineral.

When I arrived, Sonny and Larry Murphy had just surfaced from a dive, surrounded by the elderly patrons of the spring, whom they affectionately called dinosaurs. Endlessly curious, the dinosaurs flocked around and asked questions not too different from those poised by the media at Little Salt in 1971: (1) How long did it take the Indians to dig the spring? (2) Have you found bottom yet? (3) Why are you doing this? (4) Would you please look for my wife's contact lens? Stock answers were: (1) A long time. (2) I'm standing on it. (3) To prove myself as a man (or woman). (4) Was it the left or right one? Left? Sorry, we found a right one.

Sonny squinted at me through his wire–rimmed glasses, then grinned. Water was still dripping onto his tall, slender frame from his long blond hair and beard. Larry spoke first, a huge, black–haired behemoth who looked as if he would be as much at home playing nose guard in the NFL as he was contemplating the mysteries of antiquity. "Well, Sheck, we got us one today," he said with a grin.

"One what?"

"It seems the dinosaurs congregate above our air bubbles while we take our decompression stops," Sonny explained. "Probably think it enhances the therapeutic properties of the spring like a whirlpool bath."

"Well, I surfaced fiddling with my camera," Larry continued, "and didn't see this one guy floating directly over me. His doctor will have a tough time getting my strobe out." We all laughed.

"We want to make a video of the deep cave, but I'm worried about what the dinosaurs will do with that 220–volt power cable."

"Or what it will do with them."

"Why don't we do it tomorrow night? It's going to be dark in the cave anyway. Besides, the water will be clearer."

"Clearer?" I asked, puzzled.

"Yeah. Kelly Brooks says the minerals in the spring water are photosensitive. It gets cloudy when exposed to sunlight."

I already knew that the water of the spring tarnished metal and turned yellow tanks a beautiful shade of green. At this latest information, I could only shake my head. Dr. Brooks was the project's geologist, and his discovery about the spring was just another one of the many unique aspects of Warm Mineral that set it apart from all other springs.

The following evening was cool and clear. A bright full moon dominated the sky and spilled silver over the tops of the palms fringing the 250–foot–wide spring pool. A giant plume of fog rose straight up into the sky from the water surface for 1,000 feet like steam from a volcano. A large alligator flashed his red eyes at us, then submerged noisily. There was no other sound in the still night except the clanking of the heavy equipment we were wearing. Added to our double hundreds now were dual valve manifolds, which permitted us to use two complete regulators in case one failed, and one of the regulators now had a five–foot hose to facilitate sharing air in an emergency. As I bent over to rest, it occurred to me that every equipment improvement we made over the years wound up adding weight. We were now easily up to 150 pounds of gear. I took a drink of water from a fountain, then spat the repugnant liquid out.

"This water tastes like crap!"

Larry laughed. "It should." He pointed at a sign on the water fountain: "Natural Spring Water—Has Mild Laxative Effect."

"That's why we call it "Warm Enema Springs," he said.

I had been warned about the temperature of the water, but it was still a pleasant surprise to have the 87° F water seeping into my wet suit. The water was a clear green with visibility of 40 feet. While a surface crew directed by Sonny fed the power cable down to us using the tug signals of commercial divers (one tug = more cable, two tugs = stop), I enjoyed the view. Larry had a 250–watt light on the video unit on the end of the cable that brightly illuminated the ledges where they had excavated Indian remains nearly 11,000 years old. They had also found an even older extinct saber tooth tiger, as well as stalactites as big as tree trunks that dwarfed those at Little Salt. Below 60 feet there were no more ledges or stalactites, but the walls cut back in a massive overhang reminiscent of Zuber.

Soon we were at 180 feet, and I hit a thermocline. You would expect the water to get colder below. But sticking my hand down into the lower layer of water, I was thrilled to feel a hot 92° F, by far the warmest water any of us had ever dived in. Easing down into it, I noticed that the visibility increased enormously also, to nearly 200 feet. It was nearly midnight. Was I dreaming? This had to be what cave diver's heaven is like.

As had been carefully planned on the surface, Larry and Dan Lenihan, an underwater archaeologist and veteran cave

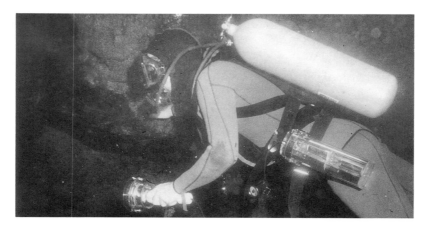

Dan Lenihan checks a ledge for artifacts. (*Photo by Sheck Exley*)

diving instructor with the National Park Service, and a former student of mine, Barry Kerley, proceeded into the small cave passage at 210 feet while Lewis Holtzendorff and I fed the cable to them from 200 feet and Bob Johnson fed it to us from 180 feet. Everything was proceeding remarkably smoothly for the deepest attempt ever to film an underwater cave. I felt three tugs on the cable from Dan and Larry, and Lewis and I started hauling out the cable.

Suddenly Bob Johnson's light flashed at us. Turning, I saw an exasperated Bob, covered with coils of heavy power cord, slowly sinking into the muck floor of the spring. The surface crew had felt only the first tug of Bob's signal and continued to send cable down long after Dan and Larry had stopped going into the cave.

We eventually got the error corrected, and within minutes were up to our moonlit decompression stops at 20 feet, which we made on pure oxygen since this eliminates nitrogen from your body more rapidly and reduces the likelihood of bends. I amused myself during our long stops by taking backup lights from Barry and snapping them on unsuspecting Lewis' belt. The friendly tussle that followed Barry's discovery of the theft was highly entertaining, so I did the same with all of the other divers except Larry. He blinded me with his 250–watt light as I approached and was too big to mess with anyway.

It is now known that Warm Mineral is the oldest burial site east of the Mississippi River. It may be the oldest in all of North America. Sonny is pushing for state acquisition of the spring, and he and his wife Barbara Cockrell and their assistant, Skip Wood, are planning to excavate the mound on the floor of the spring below 120 feet. Since the sea level never dropped below the top of the mound, it has always been anaerobic. Anything buried in the mound will be preserved even better than on the ledges at 45–60 feet.

Warm Mineral and Little Salt may be the most significant of the United States underwater caves as far as archaeology is concerned, but there are many other examples of significant finds, from dugout canoes at Missouri's Cave Spring to Civil War cannon at Florida's Natural Bridge Spring, and prehistoric cave paintings in once–dry caves now flooded by the Amistad Reservoir between Texas and Mexico. As early as 1930, divers from the Smithsonian Institution recovered the nearly complete fossilized skeleton of a Columbian mammoth from the limpid depths of Florida's Wakulla Spring, and even before that date the search was on for Spanish treasure at nearby Ponce de Leon Springs.

Speaking of treasure, several Florida springs and caves have been rumored to contain pirate gold, including Little Copper Spring on the Suwannee River and an unnamed 'gator cave near Ponte Vedra. Will any gold doubloons ever be found? Maybe they already have been. Florida's strict antiquities laws and insistence on taking 25% off the top do not encourage reporting such finds. Gold and precious gems have been recovered from cenotes and other underwater caves in Mexico. On NSS expeditions to Mexico's Yucatan Peninsula and to the giant springs of the Sierra Madre, I have seen scores of priceless pre–Columbian artifacts that are literally worth their weight in gold.

It is most important to remember that the removal of anything from a cave without scientific supervision destroys its scientific value forever. This applies to mineral formations and life forms—many of which are extremely rare and fragile —as well as to fossils and artifacts. It even extends to things that may seem to be trash, but in actuality could be extremely significant to a cave–diving archaeologist. The NSS insists that all of its members – cave divers and dry cavers alike – observe its famous motto at all times: take nothing but pictures, leave nothing but footprints, kill nothing but time.

Only in that way can we ensure that the caves we love will be there for future generations to enjoy and learn from.

7

The Mysterious Blue Holes

The rising sun spilled liquid gold across the South Bight, a wide salt water channel that completely bisects Andros Island, the largest of the Bahamian chain. The dawn brought a welcome breeze, brisk with the clean smell of salt, that drove away the mosquitoes and the oppressive heat of July, 1977. A couple of seagulls swooped overhead and squawked at us while a school of silvery bait fish jumped and splashed about the fringes of a violent whirlpool only a score of feet from our dory.

I paused to check my equipment one more time before rolling off the boat. I was preparing to make a dive to over 300 feet in Blue Hole #4, one of the two largest submarine caves, and should have felt exhilarated. Instead I felt a strange sense of dread. My uneasy feeling was not due to the depth—the day before Frank Fogarty, Terry More, and I had set a world depth record for cave diving with a descent to 340 feet in nearby Boiling Hole, and I had been to 465 feet in the open sea off this same island, also a record. The discomfort I felt was due to a memory of something that had happened six years earlier.

A small, wiry man arrived broke in Tampa on the back of a motorcycle in the early sixties. Beneath his short auburn hair, deep premature frown lines and an eternally serious expression belied the fact that he was only 30 years old. His no–nonsense midwestern twang was the result of a hard life in Missouri: his gunsmith business had gone bankrupt, he had buried a wife, and he felt alienated from the rest of his family. His name was Frank Martz.

Frank Martz and his blue van. (Photo by John Harper)

A friend of John Harper's named Pete Gaddy took Frank under his wing and started him cave diving in 1965. Pete took him to nearby Eagle's Nest, and like me, Frank fell in love with the huge entrance room and challenging deep tunnels. In the next six years he made more than 200 dives there, seeing places that no one had seen before and losing two partners and almost his own life in the process. Once he was trying to see how deep he could go holding his breath and blacked out before reaching the surface. He fell through one of the entrance shafts at 50 feet, landing on the back of a surprised diver at 125 feet. He towed Frank to the surface and revived him with mouth–to–mouth resuscitation. Frank crawled into his van and left without thanking him. As Randy Hylton later observed, "He didn't deserve the honor of saving my life." Nevertheless, due to his dedication, Eagle's Nest soon became known as "Frank's place."

Frank soon became our first professional cave diver, using his talent as a gunsmith to build cave diving lights based on John Harper's design that were much better than any commer-

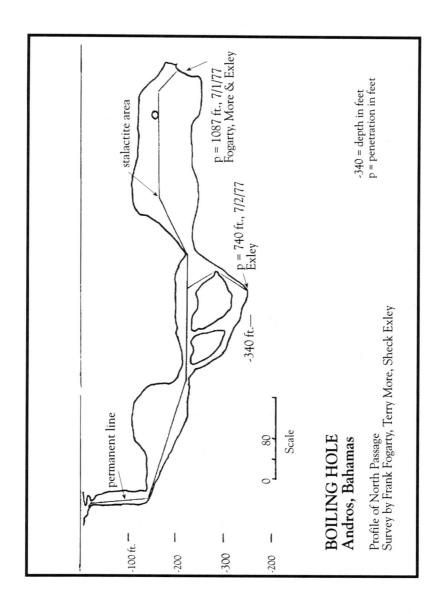

permanent line

stalactite area

p = 1087 ft., 7/1/77
Fogarty, More & Exley

p = 740 ft., 7/2/77
Exley

-340 ft.—

-100 ft.

-200

-300

-200

-340 = depth in feet
p = penetration in feet

BOILING HOLE
Andros, Bahamas

Profile of North Passage
Survey by Frank Fogarty, Terry More, Sheck Exley

0   80
Scale

cial lamp. "Martz Underwater Engineering" revolutionized cave diving with safety equipment such as the forearm knife and the quartz halogen light. Frank was also the first to use clear plexiglass in constructing reels and lights so that divers could look inside and see what was wrong in the event of a malfunction. Frank's perfectionist nature, however, made such malfunctions extremely rare.

Frank's passion for cave diving also had its bizarre aspects. One of these was his mystical obsession with the color blue. In the late sixties he moved into a blue house, drove a blue VW van, and used blue cave diving equipment. He even wore blue clothes, from his blue banlon short–sleeved shirt and trousers to blue shoes, for heaven's sake. The cave diving community privately wondered if Frank wore the same shirt seven days a week, but a friend put that speculation to rest when he spotted a stack of banlon shirts in his bedroom four feet high! If you think that is strange, consider this: Frank was even known to dine on blueberry pancakes before a dive.

Large bodies of pure water will generally have a blue tint. Frank surrounded himself with the color of water because he felt that it would help his spirit to relate better to underwater caves. He enhanced this spiritual communion by frequently decompressing for hours with his mask off his face, exhaling through his nose because he found it relaxing. Frank loved the big blue water caves with their pristine white walls. A perfect example of this was Eagle's Nest. Another was Blue Hole #4.

Dr. George Benjamin, a wealthy Canadian, was the first to dive many of the Bahamian blue holes, submarine caves whose currents reverse direction with tidal changes. He discovered that the violent whirlpools that periodically formed over the holes are caused not by the evil presence of the octopus–like monster "lusca" (as believed by native fishermen who had watched boats being sucked down, never to return) but simply by the reversing currents at high–tide stage. He learned how to time his dives to coincide with the brief "slack" periods

Shannon Heinerth swims past a stalactite in a blue hole. (Photo by Paul Heinerth)

between tidal changes so that his exploration teams would not join the fishermen's boats or be spewed out of the cave at low tide like human cannonballs.

When George's cave diving career began he was already past the age of 50. He knew that exploration of the unusually long and deep blue holes at Andros Island would have to be continued by younger and more able divers. He invited Tom Mount, who impressed him by making several important discoveries, including the first stalactites in George's favorite cave, which he designated Blue Hole #4. Tom also impressed George with his equipment, manufactured by Frank, and soon an invitation and a large order for lights was sent to the blue house in Tampa. George and Tom helped Cousteau make a film in #4 for his television series, and by the end of summer of 1971 had explored nearly 1,000 feet of passage there including areas over 250 feet deep.

The summer of 1971 was especially noteworthy in Florida. A tiny amoeba had infested the water of many lakes and ponds in central Florida. It had been reported as far north as Pasco County, a few miles south of Eagle's Nest, and especially liked warm, cloudy water. That summer the visibility in the Nest was the worst that I have ever seen it, the water so murky that the sun was invisible below 10 feet even at high noon. It is reasonable to assume that the amoeba was also present in the Nest.

If the amoeba infects a swimmer or diver, as it did several in Florida that year, it is 100% fatal. It causes encephalitis, swelling the human brain so that severe headaches are felt in the early stages. Later comes high fever and death a few short weeks after the initial infection. It gets into the brain through the nasal passages. Frank had spent countless hours decompressing with his nose in the water at Eagle's Nest.

Frank and I did not hit it off right away. He was especially hard to get to know, and on our second meeting at a cave diving conference in 1969, I had offended him when, unaware that the Nest was "Frank's place," I had told him that I had added on to his line there. By 1971, we had buried the hatchet, and after I ordered one of his lights, he gave me his unlisted phone number, an honor reserved for only a handful of his closest friends. To cement our new relationship, I suggested we make a dive together, which he eagerly accepted. When I offered to drive to his beloved Eagle's Nest for a dive—a cave familiar to both of us and quite handy to the blue house in Tampa—I got quite a shock when he responded with, "I'm not going to dive in the Nest any more until the water clears up this fall." As a result we wound up diving on August 4 in John Harper's new discovery at Devil's Eye, many times farther away from Frank's home than the Nest.

As Labor Day approached, another blue hole expedition was arranged, and Frank found his way to Miami, where he stopped off to visit Bob Friedman before going to see Tom Mount at the University of Miami. Frank took much longer to reach Tom's place than he should have. At Andros, divers soon noticed Frank acting strangely. He seemed unusually moody and depressed, and was intent on doing dives that were especially hazardous.

Finally, on the morning of September 4, a dive was planned in Blue Hole #4. Frank insisted on returning to the deepest known point, a canyon just past the grotto of stalactites that Tom had previously discovered some 500 feet back. With him went one of my regular diving partners, Jim Lockwood, who had been to 300 feet in caves in Florida. The other divers, less experienced at depth, headed into the shallower South Tunnel of the cave.

In the canyon, Frank led the way down through a narrow restriction at 280 feet that his partner described as shaped like a corkscrew. Because of the large amount of silt and the constricted passage, Frank's partner waited there while he continued his descent alone. When several minutes had passed and Frank had not returned, his partner became anxious and squeezed through the silty restriction, finding only a safety line dangling down into a seemingly bottomless blue void at 325 feet. Frank Martz was never seen again.

Frank's disappearance shocked the American cave diving community like nothing before or since. Although more than 100 cave divers had drowned in Florida's caves by then, all of them were what Frank sneeringly described as squirrels, divers with no training or experience in cave diving. Yet Frank was much more than merely a trained and experienced cave diver. He was one of our best divers and a cave diving instructor and a director of NACD. He even went so far as to tell the rest of us that he was invincible.

What happened? Frank had been impressed by my use of the new large–volume, twin 100–cubic foot tanks on our Devil's Eye dive together, and had taken a set along to the Bahamas. One drawback to the use of those tanks is that they are much heavier in the water than conventional gear, and the diver must be prepared to counteract that by using his vest and the buoyancy of his wet suit. The fatal dive was Frank's first dive with these tanks, and a photo taken while he was seated on the edge of the boat just before the dive shows that he was wearing only a wet suit top rather than the customary full suit which is more buoyant. The photo also shows that he was wearing a knife on his lower leg instead of the more accessible forearm knife he had invented and was accustomed to.

Did Frank cut the line in preparation for tying it off, then drop the unfamiliar knife or guideline reel or both, then dive down in an attempt to catch them? If so, the exertion of having to ascend with the heavy tanks could have caused him to black out. After all, despite more than 200 dives at Eagle's Nest, he had never been deeper than 300 feet, and the cut line was reportedly dangling at 325. The same thing might have happened if he was simply entangled in the guideline and had to struggle to free himself.

Or had Frank been having severe headaches? Did he stop

by a doctor's office on the way to Tom's place in Miami and become convinced he had incurable encephalitis? A terminally ill cave diver with no close family ties could scarcely pick a better way to commit suicide—in one of the world's most spectacular underwater caves—at a depth great enough to ensure that his death would be rendered painless by narcosis and would make it very unlikely that his body would ever be found.

Now I was going to see for myself the section of the cave where Frank had died.

Staccato splashes fractured the morning stillness as the three of us rolled off the dory into the gin–clear water. Underwater, my discomfort rapidly diminished as I watched swirling schools of red snapper and striped snook cavort over the shallow sandy bottom. Just beyond them a deep blue area formed an oasis in the desert of the bight: the 30–foot–wide entrance to the hole. Broad ribbons of golden fire coral cascaded over the rim, punctuated by red and orange clusters of gaping sea anemones, while forests of blue and purple gorgonians and sea fans swayed hungrily in the current, catching the nutrients brought by the last of the inflow. The continuous clickings of the myriad creatures inhabiting the hole assaulted our ears while a gaily–colored sea slug slowly made its way toward a horizontal opening at 30 feet, leaving a wake in the sandy floor of the pit.

Once inside the shadowy opening, we switched on our powerful Martz lights, revealing a rainbow scene of bright sponges and corals coating the walls. A large crayfish scurried down the steeply–sloping corridor into a crevice guarded by a heap of sinister–looking sea urchins, confident that their long black spines would keep him from becoming our lunch. After swimming 100 feet we reached a depth of 80 feet. At this point the entrance corridor joined the wall of the immense canyon that formed the major passage of the cave. We turned north.

A hundred feet further and we were over the first deep area of the canyon where John Crusell had died at 250 feet two weeks before Frank. Then our torches picked out a stirring sight ahead of us, a huge block of limestone wedged in the canyon and covered with a score of stalagmites and columns: Benjamin's Grotto. Already at 150 feet, I paused briefly to examine the largest of the formations, the three–foot–high Roman Gate, then continued down the canyon.

From our previous dives we knew that continuing horizontally down the canyon would eventually bring us to the end of the cave, nearly 1,000 feet from the entrance. Just past the grotto my light picked out a slender strand of white nylon plummeting down out of sight: the exploratory line left by Frank on his fatal dive. We had learned not to trust those old lines because they were heavily encrusted by marine organisms that substantially weakened the fibers. I unsnapped my Martz reel and started a new line.

At 260 feet, I paused to negotiate a silty restriction, carefully avoiding the old line, which was slack at this point. I had been acclimatized by our previous dives, so my mind was clear and I wiggled through the narrow chute with ease. But the old dread returned in force: were the skeletal remains of my lost friend awaiting me? None of the other search parties had gone this far.

At 280 feet I was surprised to see the cut end of the line hanging limply against a ledge of the canyon wall. Twenty–five feet more and I was on the floor of the canyon, spinning around slowly to look for evidence of Frank or his equipment. One side ascended to the 260–foot restriction and the grotto above me. The other side dipped slightly to perhaps 325 feet, then soared back up to the back of the cave. In contrast to the pristine white deeper sections of nearby Boiling Hole, this passage was dark and dull, the bottom shrouded in deep silt. There was no sign of Frank.

By now the current in the cave had reversed, so I could ride a gentle flow back to the entrance. On the way I thought about what I had found. Was what little that remained of Frank buried in the deep silt? Frank's partner seemed so certain of his description of the scene of the accident, which differed from what I had found. Even the depth and shape of the restriction was different. Perhaps the corkscrew restriction was in the canyon floor and had subsequently collapsed, sealing Frank in forever.

Like Frank, I have Tom Mount to thank for my first experience in blue hole diving. A big blond Tennessean with blue eyes, Tom was a charismatic leader in the diving community who had been hired as the diving safety officer for the University of Miami. We had worked together on a text, Safe Cave Diving, and by 1973, I had passed him in number of dives to become the first person to log 1,000 cave dives. The same year, Tom had to furnish divers to carry out research during the Hydrolab saturation project in the Bahamas, where aquanauts lived in an underwater habitat for days at a time. Saturation diving, where one cannot swim to the surface in an emergency for fear of the bends, is similar to cave diving, where a rock ceiling confines the diver. So Tom recruited experienced cave divers whenever possible. Added to the prestige of being an aquanaut was the pay of $100 a day plus expenses, which was not bad at all for someone like me who was fresh out of college and broke. As if I were not interested enough already, Tom dangled the added possibility of some blue hole diving.

Our team leader was Zidi Mount, a petite redhead who was an excellent cave diver and an experienced saturation diver. She was also a terrific leader, who easily managed the difficult task of keeping four highly individualistic divers working together smoothly in crowded and difficult conditions. We certainly kept things interesting for her during our eight–day mission. The first day, a team member ran low on air and I had to give him my extra mouthpiece to get him back to our base. Then Rick Frehsee, a champion spearfisher turned award–

winning photographer, harassed a giant nurse shark so he
could get some thrilling shots.   Finally, Tom decided to
surprise me by sending down an ice cream cake complete with
candles, for my twenty-fourth birthday.

Hydrolab's land base was at the Underwater Explorers
Club at Freeport. There we learned from Dick Clarke that one
of the resort divers, Ben Rose, had discovered a fascinating
inland blue hole nearby. Dick also had a photograph of the
most beautiful stalactites I had ever seen. A far cry from the
marine growth–encrusted, dull grey rock icicles of Andros and
Little Salt Springs, these stalactites were glistening white and
so pure that we could see right through the thinner ones. The
larger ones were as big as a truck!

The entrance to Ben's Cave involved a tricky 15–foot
climb down the roots of a tree to a mound of boulders in the
middle of a large room partially filled with water.   After
lowering our tanks, Rick tested his camera strobe, clearly
lighting the ghostly forms of immense underwater stalactites.
Tom led the way in as Rick's flashes went off almost continu-
ously in the beautiful underwater vista. Leading from the 200–
foot–wide entrance room was a large passage 20 feet high and
more than 60 feet wide, filled with fresh water so clear that the
roots we had climbed down in the entrance were plainly
visible nearly 300 feet away. The white walls of the passage
were made of a bizarre fossil coral that looked like frozen
tangles of spaghetti. Hanging from the walls and ceiling were
clusters of giant stalactites more than a dozen feet long. The
bottom of the passage was obscured with a layer of tannic sea
water. Rising through this layer were immense flat–topped
formations caused by the fall of the heavier stalactites from the
ceiling.

Dipping down into the salt layer, we discovered that the
halocline separating it from the fresh water caused images of
the cave above us to distort and blur. In remarkable contrast
to the pristine whiteness above us, everything in the salt water

was covered with a dull brown deposit. Longer stalactites that extended through both layers changed from white to mahogany as soon as they hit the top of the salt water at a depth of 30 feet. After 300 feet, the ceiling shelved down into the rather ominous salt layer, so we tied off our guideline and ascended.

Later that summer, I returned with Lewis Holtzendorff, Court Smith, and Dana Turner, three of the world's best cave divers, but could manage to add only about 150 feet in the salt layer. The tunnel narrowed considerably and we noticed that it headed toward a nearby cave called Jane's Cave (after Dick Clarke's wife). There was a strong outflow and leaves on the bottom, suggesting a connection to another opening. At this time no blue hole in the world had been connected to another by divers, and the longest penetration in a submarine cave until 1978 was 1,087 feet in Boiling Hole by our 1977 Andros expedition. We also knew that light objects such as leaves could be carried a considerable distance by cave water, so departed confident that we had effectively completed exploration of another small cave in the Bahamas.

In the late 1970's, a NASA engineer decided to stay in the Bahamas after the Apollo program was completed. With a broad forehead, compelling gaze, and deep, resonant voice, Dennis Williams was a natural leader who served as chairman of the NSS Cave Diving Section in 1981. He and Jill Yager, a biologist teaching school in Freeport, became interested in blue holes in general and Ben's Cave in particular after NSS instructors Gene Melton and Mary Brooks taught them to cave dive. Soon the four of them were meeting regularly at Dennis and Jill's place at Lucaya near Ben's Cave to explore the blue holes in the area. With Gene's custom cave diving equipment and phenomenal breathing rate and Mary's experience (no woman in the world except India Fuller had more cave dives), the four made a formidable team.

They began their explorations by entering Jane's Cave,

which had been renamed Lucayan Burial Ground after the prehistoric remains of Arawak Indians were found there. Fearlessly sinking into the dirty brown salt water that had daunted us, they took a right turn at 45 feet, then pulled their way through a passage less than three feet high. It was nearly filled with a soft reddish–brown algae that they nicknamed mung. After squirming through the mung for only 50 feet they saw a brown–stained cord by the right wall: the end of my Ben's Cave line.

Their success in connecting the Burial Ground to Ben's Cave did more than provide the world with its first multi–entrance blue hole, it also proved that the mung–filled salt water zone could provide access to considerably more cave passage. Later they turned left at the Lucayan junction and ascended into a fresh–water–filled room whose walls were covered with thick cascades of crystalline flowstone. They named it Wedding Hall. A 15–foot–wide breakdown tunnel, Avalanche Alley, continued at an upper level beyond Wedding Hall. Two hundred feet further, a side passage plunged back into the mung layer to enter a spacious bedding plane without apparent walls that they named Gene's Garden. The only ceiling support seemed to be a forest of thousands of rust–colored stalactite columns!

Now I was invited to inspect the "small" cave I had first entered five years earlier. "Dennis," I said, trying to hide my excitement, "what did you feed the cave to make it grow?"

Gene Melton and Bud Dillon before a 1977 dive (*Photo by Paul Smith*)

My companions were highly organized. Our transportation was in BHEV II (for Blue Hole Expedition Vehicle), a van that Dennis had customized for cave diving. A sturdy aluminum ladder now replaced the roots that we had struggled down in 1973. The cave itself was now known as Lucayan Caverns, and a wall of Dennis' study was covered with a large sheet of paper that was the beginning of a map of the cave.

The cool shadows of Ben's Cave were a welcome relief from the voracious yellow flies and sweltering heat of the Bahamian summer. Once underwater, I greeted each of the familiar glistening formations in turn while Dennis, Gene, and Mary led the way. Mary turned to me with a mischievous grin and pointed with glee as we passed the end of my line. I hung my head and shrugged sheepishly.

We surfaced briefly at the Burial Ground to confer, then continued to Wedding Hall. As we ascended from the warm sea water toward the cool blue fresh layer, I saw a surrealistic landscape of ice castles and glaciers through the blurring fog of the halocline. An instant later I was hovering in a fairyland drenched in the light of our four powerful lamps. Ahead loomed a massive flowstone wall which cascaded from ledge to ledge like a frozen waterfall. Each tier was liberally spiked with scores of small candle–like stalagmites. The overall impression was one of an incredibly elaborate wedding cake 30 feet high!

Gene flashed his light at me and I reluctantly left the spectacle to follow him up a shallow collapse route to the left of the flowstone wall. Avalanche Alley looked sufficiently precarious to me that I involuntarily held my breath as we scooted along over huge blocks of freshly–fallen white rock. I hoped the force of my rising bubbles would not cause another cave–in. The boulders were larger than BHEV II. In a few minutes more we passed the drop to Gene's Garden and reached our objective: the end of the exploration line in Avalanche Alley. With a grin, Gene graciously handed me his exploratory reel, fat with fresh line.

I tied off the line I wished I had installed five years earlier and led the way onward over an expanding vista of angular boulder–strewn passage. Beyond one pile lay another drop to a brown saline area, but I continued above it to a large chamber 50 feet wide and 100 feet long, where the Alley ended in impenetrable collapse. As I tied off our line, I caught a tell–tale glimmer in the ceiling off to one side: air. I was puzzled. I had seen thousands of similar air pockets before, caused by the rising exhalations of divers. Yet my companions had assured me that this area was virgin.

Ascending to investigate, I checked my depth gauge, then hastily dropped back down. My gauge had read "0". No wonder there was air! Since we had been down to 60 feet for more than an hour already, I was already required to make decompression stops. I could not tarry above 10 feet without risking the bends, but did linger long enough to observe tree roots growing down through a crack in the ceiling, a subtle reminder that there was only 20 feet of brittle, badly fractured rock over our heads. The four of us tried not to exhale as we quickly left the room.

On the way out I could not resist dropping into the saline pit we had discovered. Easing into a mung–festooned passage at the bottom, my heart leapt as I shined my light into a stalactite–studded bedding plane identical to Gene's Garden. The area was only three feet high but so wide that the far wall was not visible in the perfectly clear water. Many of the formations were soda straws, delicate crystal tubes only a fraction of an inch wide. Checking behind me, I felt like a bull in a china shop as I carefully ventured onward to the left past the most heavily decorated area I have ever seen in a cave. My painfully slow, cautious progress was rewarded by the discovery of a higher area at 60 feet where the bedding plane seemed to be changing to a vast tunnel.

After we had returned to Ben's Cave, I filled my smiling

companions' ears with every superlative I could think of. After I had covered an entire page of the BHEV log with my awed blitherings, Dennis turned to me, obviously pleased with my reaction to their discovery. "So you like this small cave that grew while you were gone?"

"Yes," I paused. "Especially since it's still growing."

Lucayan Caverns did not grow much that afternoon, since our long dive earlier precluded any extended pushes until the residual nitrogen had cleared out of our bodies. Gene and I had to be content with a short dive, which was nevertheless rewarding in that we found a new and more direct route between the Burial Ground and Ben's Cave entrances.

That evening we relaxed in a quiet Bahamian pub, feeling a warm glow of satisfaction caused by an exhilarating day of diving. "Just one thing bothers me," I said.

"What's that?"

"Whenever we drop into the salt layer we find current, and the water is warm, like the sea. Seems like we ought to be able to connect to a marine blue hole."

Dennis and Gene exchanged glances. "Well," Dennis intoned, "when I flew over the area the other day we did spot one nearby."

I sat up quickly. "Can we get to it?"

"No. It's not in the ocean but at the head of Gold Rock Creek. We tried to get a boat over it once but the mangroves were too thick." He paused. "It's a real shame, though. Gene has a tunnel on the south side of Ben's Cave that heads toward it."

I had been looking forward to a return to the new bedding plane we had discovered, now named "Sheck's Garden" over my feeble protests, but this sounded even better. "Why don't we take a look?"

Within minutes we were piling gear into BHEV II for a nocturnal push toward the coast. In the water, Gene led me southward around the breakdown in the entrance room of

Ben's Cave, to a saline tunnel at 50 feet. It branched off to the left from the connection that we had pioneered to the Burial Ground the previous day, and was carrying quite a bit of flow toward the sea. As we finned down the 10–foot–diameter passage, succulent stone crabs scurried off to the side, unaware that we would never consider them for a meal since they were inside the cave. Still, their presence raised our hopes for a connection to the sea. They were not cave–adapted, so were not permanent residents.

Soon we did spot a permanent resident: the rare blind cave fish Lucifuga. Pale and translucent, it reminded me of similar fish I had seen in the Gulf, a sink hole in Missouri. At several inches in length, Lucifuga was larger than its fresh water cousins. It hesitated, sensing vibrations in the water, then shot away with amazing speed, its fins rippling gracefully.

Lucifuga's lair was a large circular room whose floor was at less than 30 feet. The seaward–rushing current was picking up pieces of mung, limiting visibility to only 30 feet, so it took us a while to realize the full extent of the room. It turned out to be more than 60 feet wide. I swam up to check the ceiling, wondering what had happened to our 30–foot–deep fresh–water layer at Ben's Cave. I broke into cool, clear blue water at 15 feet, confirming that the island's fresh water aquifer was lens shaped. As we approached the coast we could expect it to get thinner and thinner until finally it disappeared. Now we knew we were headed in the right direction.

I spun around once, enjoying the complete view of the top of the room in the crystal water, then rejoined Gene in the warm mung–laden layer below me. The route beyond the room was confusing. The first two passages we tried ended in small rooms after only a couple of hundred feet. Finally we followed the current into a large passage, which my compass showed was heading due south, straight toward Gold Rock Blue Hole.

We ran out of line after reaching a point 800 feet from

Ben's, and I tied it off on a small
Glancing upward, I noticed a long,
ceiling that Gene immediately wantea
became too narrow and silty so we heade
crevice was very long, however, and para.
course. After 40 feet it seemed to widen to p.
sions, so I signalled to Gene and looped my spli
around the main line.

I squirmed upward through a rain of mud causec
exhaust bubbles loosening silt from the ledge above me. .
progressing 10 feet I reached the top of the crack, with gi
matted against the ceiling, presumably washed in from an exit.
I was puzzled because there was no grass around the known
entrances of Lucayan Caverns or Gold Rock Blue Hole. The
depth of the ceiling was only 10 feet, so I kept an eye on the
grass–covered roof as I eased down the crevice to my right.
Suddenly I spotted a small hole in the grass with the tell–tale
glisten of an air surface above it. With my light I could even
see the outline of mangrove trees in the night air above me!
Charging upward through the grass and roots, I rammed an
opening to the surface big enough for a diver. In seconds I was
sitting in a tiny 3–foot–diameter pond in the middle of a
sawgrass marsh, staring face to face with some sort of darn
Bahamian bird that was undoubtedly scared out of its wits.

Poor Gene! He had to wait below in the zero visibility
caused by my enlarging the opening, not knowing whether I
had made it to the surface or had simply gone totally mad and
wedged myself into a slimy no–exit crevice. Uncomfortably
aware of his plight, I hurriedly wiggled my way onto the soft
bank while slapping at hungry mosquitoes. Finally I made it
out, the bird squawked and left, and Gene was soon up and
blinking at our surroundings.

"Where the hell are we?"

Good question. We had plenty of air to swim back
underground to Ben's but the new entrance we had found

d be a desirable point for future entries. The trouble was, w do you identify a 3–foot–wide birdbath in the middle of featureless sawgrass marsh? There was only one solution: we ad to slog back to civilization on the surface, twin tanks, steaming hot wet suits and all, laying the remnants of line on my splice spool as we went to mark our path.

It could not be far, we had penetrated only 800 feet, obviously not in a perfectly straight line. By using our diver's compasses, we had merely to walk north and we were bound to hit the paved highway to Lucaya that paralleled the coast. Nevertheless, a vision of spending a miserable sweltering night swatting mosquitos and sand flies while lost in a sawgrass marsh fleetingly crossed my mind. Fortunately, Gene's un-canny sense of direction led us directly to our parked van. His path was so straight out that I later accused him of knowing about the existence of the new entrance (which we named "Taco" after its shape) all along, and of simply pretending to let me discover it to make me feel good.

Labor Day weekend I returned with Gene for another look. By this time the others had discovered another opening in the marsh near Taco that they dubbed Taco II. Unfortunately, neither opening was large enough to consider for a starting point for our dives, so we began our push at Ben's Cave. After a 20–minute swim, we passed the Taco entrances and Gene and I continued into a section that Dennis and Jill had explored with Glen Taylor. We started a new line and began a gradual ascent. When we reached a depth of 10 feet we entered a very bizarre area when the ceiling appeared to be nothing more than caked mud and mangrove roots. Our continued progress was marked by a trail of liquid mud as our bubble loosened the black sludge and brought it hailing down on us.

We passed through a 100 feet of mud–roofed pseudocave, then another 100 feet. Rounding a bend to the left, I saw a dim green glow in the distance. As we quickened our pace, the glow expanded to become the 30–foot–wide main entrance of Gold Rock Blue Hole. We had done it: the world's first connection of an inland, fresh water cave with a marine blue hole. We surfaced briefly to shake hands, then resubmerged for the 1,250–foot trip back to Ben's, unwilling to consider another epic trek back through the salt marsh.

That evening we phoned to tell Dennis our news. He was in the States on business. Naturally, he was disappointed that he had missed the big connection, but he graciously consented to let us take another look at Sheck's Garden. The four of them exploring in similar Gene's Garden had found a broad maze–like area that eventually looped back around to the main tunnel of Ben's Cave near the end of my five–year–old line. Would this new area prove equally vast?

As soon as Dennis hung up the phone, we threw our gear back into BHEV II and were on our way. In the cool clear water of Ben's Cave we sped past the familiar Burial Mound, Wedding Hall, and Avalanche Alley, scarcely noticing their splendors in our haste to reach the end of the Sheck's Garden line. At 46 feet, we sank into the salt layer, 16 feet deeper than the halocline at Ben's, indicating that we were now further inland, since the fresh water lens was thicker. Thirty minutes after the start of our dive we arrived at the end of the line at a depth of 60 feet.

Ahead of us stretched a vast horizontal bedding plane without any apparent walls or support for its 3–foot–high ceiling except thousands of thin stalactite columns. Seldom exceeding an inch in diameter, their brittle white tubes were in such profusion that in several directions they posed an impenetrable barrier. With no defined cave walls to guide us, our progress became a matter of doing the best we could to head north without damaging any of the formations. We were aided by the superb visibility. Apparently the mung in this area of relatively little current had settled out of the water completely, coating the ceiling and soft floor. Behind us, however, our rising exhaust bubbles dislodged the mung, changing the water to a brown mess where visibility was nil. Fortunately, most of the mung settled out quickly and in 20 minutes the way out would once more be clear.

After half an hour, we had laid all the line on our reels without finding any end. We were 1,800 feet from the nearest entrance, the longest dive made in the cave, yet the stalactite–studded bedding plane still extended beyond sight in every direction of the compass. With a feeling of awe I realized that in the past 30 minutes I had seen more dripstone formations than I had in all my previous years of caving, including fabulous Carlsbad Cavern.

To save bottom time, we entered at the Burial Ground, which allowed us to reach the end of the line at 1,800 feet in less than 40 minutes. After a couple of hundred feet, a few rock partitions started appearing behind the dense forest of stalac- tites, presenting us with better–defined routes to choose from. We chose to bend eastward, but the passage ended after a 100 feet. Backtracking, we selected a northward–trending passage on the right. After a 100 feet it was still going, but we were out of line and had to turn back.

Near the end of our line, I noticed a small dome in the ceiling with the azure tint of fresh water. If we had succeeded in progressing further into the interior of Grand Bahama Island, the depth of the top of the salt water would be greater than the 46 feet we measured at the start of Sheck's Garden. I checked the level of the halocline with my depth gauge: 51 feet.

On the way out, I surveyed our find for Dennis' map, using techniques I had developed and described in *Mapping Under- water Caves*, a book written with Bob Friedman in 1973. Normally this procedure includes noting all potential side leads on my slate. After progressing only a couple of hundred feet I gave that up, my slate being already half–covered with notes. Promising side passages zoomed off through the stalactites everywhere I looked. When would this cave ever stop?

More than five years later it still has not stopped. No more entrances have been discovered, but Dennis and Gene have pushed 1,600 feet past the end of our line. They have found that the side passages that were too numerous to note inter-connect in an incredible maze at 60 feet. They insist that "the whole damn island is hollow." The discovery in 1979 of a similar cave system by Dennis, Paul DeLoach, and me at Owl Cave several miles away supports that view.

In 1981, Lucayan Caverns surpassed the four–mile length of Florida's Peacock Springs Cave System, where I had orga-nized a surveying effort in the early 1970's. That made it the world's longest known underwater cave. Since that time the cave, now a national park, has grown to more than 30,000 feet of total passage.

The biggest discovery in Lucayan, however, might be its biology. In 1980, Dennis and Jill found a small animal that looks like a swimming centipede. A new species is big news in the world of Biospeleology. As Jill worked with the blind, white crustacean, she discovered that the creature is not only a new species, but is also of an entirely new genus, family, order, and class! She named the new class *Remipedia* and the animal itself *speleonectes* (cave swimmer).

Who knows? Maybe Grand Bahama Island is hollow and *speleonectes* outnumbers the humans there.

8

Blue Holes Across the World

I t looked like a dinosaur that should have died 26 million
years ago. Yet here it was, with a muscular tail that could
break a man's leg, sharp claws that could disembowel him,
and powerful teeth–studded jaws that could crush his cranium
like an eggshell. The eight–foot alligator arrogantly stared at
us, confident in his role as proprietor of the 80–foot–diameter
sinkhole.

"What the hell do we do now?" demanded Lewis
Holtzendorff, nervously running his hand through his straw–
colored hair. That year there were seven 'gator attacks on
humans in Florida, several of them fatal.

I looked from the 'gator to the beautiful clear blue water,
then back to the 'gator. "Well there's four divers." I began.

"Yeah, but 'four to one' doesn't mean much when the 'one'
is a quarter–ton, hungry–looking reptile!"

"Then look at it this way," I continued reasonably. "The
gator can't possibly eat us all at once, so the chance that you'll
be dinner is only 25 percent." The chances were even less than
that. Our unfortunate guide, Bill Bond, did not have on a wet
suit like the rest of us, so undoubtedly would be selected as the
most tender morsel. On the other hand, most attacks were by

alligators that had lost their fear of humans by being hand fed. Had anyone been feeding this one?

While Lewis and I argued, Court Smith was silently unloading our gear from the van. Still young enough to be confident of his own immortality, the powerfully built blond Georgian was not about to let an overgrown water lizard get between him and a beautiful virgin sinkhole. Finally he straightened up and drawled to us, "Y'all gonna take all day?"

The banks of Knight's Sink were covered with dense subtropical foliage, so the only access to the water was a narrow sandy ravine. At the base of the ravine we paused briefly to push out of the way some small white objects that looked like mushy ping–pong balls. Once below 10 feet I relaxed, since crocodillians cannot tolerate the pressure at greater depths. All around us the walls of the sink receded sharply, creating an enormous jug–shaped room. The bottom was a huge mound of dark silt and white sand, its peak at 60 feet covered with huge logs. On the southeast and northwest sides, the slopes of the mound plunged into a blue void. Southeast was toward the inky water of nearby Lake Tarpon Sink, so we headed northwest instead.

At 100 feet, my light picked out what appeared to be a perfectly flat, black floor. Continuing down, we discovered that it was not a floor, but a very thick accumulation of the poisonous chemical, hydrogen sulfide. I knew that it heralded the top of the salt water layer. I paused to enjoy the bizarre view of my companions, whose faces blurred and took on a ghastly shade of yellow as light rays wiggled through the strange medium. Then I remembered that at least one diver had died from hydrogen sulfide being absorbed through the pores of his skin, and hastily renewed my descent.

At 200 feet, we broke through the bottom of the hydrogen sulfide into crystal–clear salt water. Ahead of us stretched a large horizontal passage 60 feet wide with a floor at 210 feet, its ceiling obscured by the dark chemical. I laid another 200

Lewis Holtzendorff suits up for a dive. (*Photo by Court Smith*)

feet of line, then turned back when I noticed Bill shivering from the cool 74° F water.

None of us wanted to decompress with the alligator, so our 10–foot stop was unusually deep. It was also unusually long. Arranged back–to–back in a four–man phalanx like an underwater version of Custer's last stand, each of us waited patiently for one of the other cowards to make a break for the surface and 'gator land. Not having the luxury of a wet suit, Bill finally had to make the choice between the possibility of being 'gator food and the probability of succumbing to hypothermia. The minute Bill made his move, the rest of us promptly exited elsewhere so the 'gator would not get confused.

Moments later all four of us were standing safe and sound in shallow water near the ravine, idly chatting with two elderly ladies who had watched us submerge at the start of the dive. The alligator was nowhere to be seen.

"We were worried about you boys," one of the ladies called down the bank. "As soon as y'all went underwater, our alligator went in, too."

We quickly moved to even shallower water. One of the ladies was holding a bag of those strange ping–pong things that I had seen in the water earlier.

"What's that in your hand, ma'am?"

She laughed. "Oh, this is just some marshmellers. We always feed Ollie this time of day."

It did not take us long to get out of the water.

More than a year before our first dive in Knight's Sink, we had visited Tarpon Springs, a quaint settlement of Greeks that is the center of Florida's sponge diving industry. Less than two miles from Knight's Sink is a park in the middle of town containing Spring Bayou. Every year the Greek Orthodox Church uses the park for its Epiphany ceremony. An orthodox priest climaxes the ceremony by hurling a large solid gold cross into the waters of the bayou, whereupon hundreds of young boys splash into the water after it. The boy who finds the cross

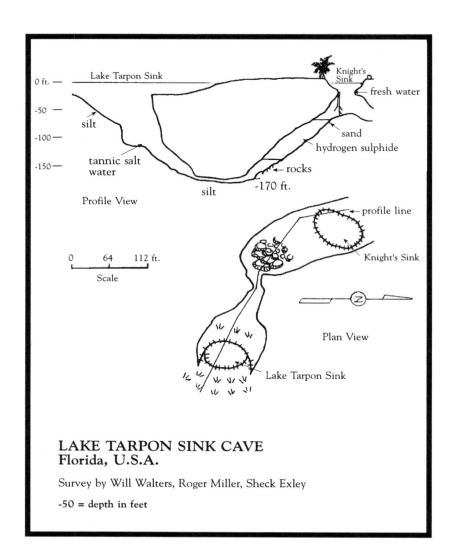

LAKE TARPON SINK CAVE
Florida, U.S.A.

Survey by Will Walters, Roger Miller, Sheck Exley

-50 = depth in feet

gets to be the next deep sea diver.

There is just one problem, however. Gold is very heavy, and a priest with a good arm could accidently toss the priceless object into the 125–too–deep throat of Tarpon Springs itself, far beyond the ability of any free diver in the world to retrieve. This is exactly what eventually happened, so nowadays a cheaper gold–plated version is used. The solid gold cross has never been found, so still lies under a dozen feet of muck in the bottom of the spring.

When we arrived in April, 1973, the cave in the spring had never been dived. The Anclote River, fed by several cypress swamps further inland, fills Spring Bayou with black, nasty–looking water. Since the source of the water that periodically gushed from the spring was believed to be the nearby, equally–black Lake Tarpon, there was no reason to believe that the cave was any clearer. In fact, every seven to 25 days, the flow in the spring would change direction, alternately filling the lake with dark salt water from Spring Bayou or vice–versa. During the reverse stages the sudden increase in salinity caused fish kills in the lake, covering the surface with their stinking, rotting carcasses.

Because of the fish kills, the U. S. Geological Survey purchased the sinkhole in Lake Tarpon to undertake the first engineering effort to alter the drainage characteristics of a first–magnitude spring. In the late 60's they put in an earthen dike to separate the lake from the sink, with a weir installed to prevent overfilling the lake from excessive rainfall. They were so successful that the mysterious seven to 25 day cycle—one that is still not fully understood—was permanently inter-rupted.

Leaning against a palm in the park, I stared hard at the inky water of the spring, trying to guess its secrets. I knew that the spring had flowed as much as a billion gallons a day when it had drained Lake Tarpon, more than any other spring in the western hemisphere, so it had to contain a significant cave. If some groundwater drainage had continued after the USGS built the dike, there was a chance that below the turbid surface of the bayou there would be water with diveable visibility. I needed to see only 10 feet to explore the cave.

With me were my favorite diving partners of the early seventies, Court and Lewis, and Dana Turner, a quiet young geology student from the University of Florida who, like Lewis, was a director and officer of NACD as well as a NSSCDS member. Court pointed at a raw sewage outfall near my foot, where disgusting unmentionables were oozing into the bayou. Lewis was sure that any cave opening that might have existed was now covered with bayou sand. Finally Dana consented to join me in a reconnaissance dive.

After a few minutes of groping around in the 10–foot–deep bayou we found the rock lip of the crater dropping into the spring. Our descent was quite slow because of the limited visibility, and more than once I asked myself what I was doing here. Gradually the visibility got better. I could see Dana's light, then was able to see Dana himself. We increased the speed of our descent.

By the time we reached the bottom of the crater, visibility had increased to 40 feet, and a large horizontal cave mouth yawned open before us. Inside, the floor of the cave gradually sloped down to 170 feet. We saw three small crevices in the floor, and dropped down the largest one. At 210 feet, it opened into a large horizontal passage, which extended out of sight to our left. Dana grinned and gave the OK sign. To avoid having to repeat our sluggish search in the bayou, I tied off the line and left the reel. Then we went up to get the others.

"It goes!"

Lewis was chagrined at having missed a chance at being the first to enter a significant cave, but joined us for a quick look before the inflow became too strong. We waited until low tide to make a push dive so we would not have to contend with the inflow and dark bayou water. On that dive, Court and I followed the 60–foot–wide and 10–foot–high passage at the bottom for 350 feet, the depth never varying from 210 feet. Our exit was assisted by a gentle outflow, confirmation of Tarpon Springs' blue hole characteristics.

On May 12, Court, Lewis and I returned with double 100–cubic–foot tanks to push past the 500–foot penetration reached on our third dive. This time we timed our dive for extreme low tide to take advantage of as much outflow as possible because it caused the best visibility. There was a pronounced slick on the surface from the upwelling water, and we found it unusually clear just beneath the surface. At the entrance to the cave at 130 feet, we startled a huge sting–ray out of the mud. It took off in a black cloud, wings flapping vigorously in protest at the intrusion.

At a penetration of 550 feet, we hit the end of our old guideline. I tied on a new line and led the way down the 210–foot-deep passage. I spotted a jumble of boulders extending the width of the passage, and swam over them toward what appeared to be a flat, completely black ceiling. When I stuck my arm into it I realized that it was a very dense layer of hydrogen sulfide. Progress in the chemical–laden water was very slow since it reduced our visibility to only three feet. We reached the crest of the boulder pile at 170 feet, then descended into a passage considerably different from the one by which we had entered. While the dimensions were roughly the same, 60 feet wide by 10 feet high, there was absolutely no flow. The ceiling was totally obscured by a coal–black hydrogen sulfide layer, but the lower five feet was crystal clear salt water. Court's powerful quartz lamp cut through it like a knife for 100 feet, illuminating walls and floor, which were covered by undulating ebony mung like a black velvet blanket. The depth of the tunnel was 210 feet, so we hit our preplanned air turnaround after progressing 400 feet.

In 1977, Will Walters, Roger Miller, and I made the first dive in Lake Tarpon Sink. As luck would have it, Ollie the

alligator had moved his residence to that location. Spurred on
by fears of decompressing with Ollie in black water, we pushed
a small passage at 170 feet until we connected to the southeast
side of Knight's Sink. Later, Paul DeLoach and I added
another 1,000 feet of line in the 60–foot–wide northwest
conduit of Knight's, discovering a huge fresh water–filled
room on the way. The northwest tunnel of Knight's is a mirror
image of the velvet passage Court and I found in Tarpon
Springs. Connecting them will be quite a chore, requiring a
three–hour swim in poison, plus 15 hours of decompression, as
well as stupendous amounts of air.

But it could be done. Who knows? Maybe they will find
a gold cross on the way.

There is no better place in the world for a cave diver to look
for gold than in the sacrificial sinkholes, or cenotes, of the
Yucatan Peninsula. Cortes and Pisarro took a fantastic treasure from the Aztec and Inca civilizations, but few riches have
been recovered from the Mayan Indians. The Mayans were
older than the other two civilizations and situated between
them geographically, so it seemed strange that nothing had
been found in Central America in the way of treasure. Then
divers entered the Sacred Well cenote at Chichen Itza in
Yucatan. In only 40 feet of open water they found hundreds of
priceless preColumbian artifacts as well as jade, emeralds, and
gold. Similar discoveries were made in another cenote at
nearby Dzibilchaltun. Did the Mayans have a fortune that
they threw into the many cenotes of Yucatan rather than have
it stolen by the Spanish?

In preColumbian days, most of the commerce in Yucatan
was along the rugged coast. Access to the sea was possible at
only a very few locales where short spring–fed rivers known as
caletas provided a safe harbor. One of these caletas, Xcaret,
is a short distance due east of Chichen Itza and on a direct line
between it and the sacred island of Cozumel, site of Mayan
pilgrimages.

Sheck Exley and Karan Pribble prepare to dive at Xcaret, Mexico. (*Photo by Ned DeLoach*)

Sheck Exley explores a shallow passage in Xcaret. (*Photo by Ned DeLoach*)

In 1979, Ned DeLoach, Karen Pribble, and I joined a group of open water divers on a boat at Cozumel to go to the Xcaret caleta. As we sped across the foam–speckled turquoise waves, I saw the caleta just as the Mayan pilgrims had 1,000 years earlier. A deep cleft in the jagged rocky coast, it poured clear blue water into the sparkling sea. After 300 feet, the caleta ended in a shallow pool at the bottom of a low limestone cliff. On top of the cliff were the ruins of a Mayan city, the squat stone buildings and walls covered with the profuse flowering plants and vines of the Central American jungle. As we unloaded the boat, the brisk sea breeze had a perfumed fragrance, and brightly colored parrots cawed at us.

The opening in the pool at the caleta was too small to be entered, so we hiked a 100 feet through the jungle to a wide, shadowy opening in the cliff. A few feet inside was a deep pool of limpid water 30 feet in diameter. The open water divers were to sightsee in the lake while we searched for a large passage that a French team had previously connected to a cenote 300 meters away.

I expected Xcaret to be like Tarpon Springs, a blue hole with reversing currents like those in the Bahamas. At high tide, however, the flowing brackish water, while slowed considerably, did not reverse. At the far end of the underground pool we found drooping in the current the yellow tape left by the French. We followed it into a large passage 25 feet wide and 15 feet high. The light gray walls were honeycombed with small holes and covered with a fine white silt. Our exhaust bubbles caused the silt to settle slowly from the ceiling behind us, ruining the otherwise superb visibility. At a depth of 15 feet, it momentarily settled on top of the halocline separating the cool brackish water from the warm sea water beneath it. The floor of the passage was at only 25 feet.

We reached the cenote after swimming 364 feet. Surfacing was difficult since a canopy of dense foliage grew down to the water's surface. The dangling vines looked like a fer–de–lance I encountered on a cave dive in northern Mexico, so we quickly resubmerged to check for a continuation of the passage. The way on was blocked by the collapse of the cenote, so we backtracked 100 feet to a low side passage I had noticed on the right. We followed this passage a couple of hundred feet until it lowered to less than three feet high, then turned back.

We had swum out less than a 100 feet when we saw the five open water divers following our guideline despite assuring us that they would not enter the submerged cave. Their fins were near the soft mud floor and churning up huge clouds of silt. The water behind them looked like an avalanche of liquid mud hurtling toward us. They did not know it, but they looked like five dead men to me.

Ned insists that he heard my barked order to our unwanted intruders clearly, despite being underwater and a considerable distance from me: "Get the hell outta here!" Fortunately, the five magically turned around and life-savingly placed their hands on our guideline so we could shepherd them out. On our trip back the leader of the five, a well-known scuba instructor from Texas, studiously avoided my gaze. It was just as well: I was busy getting seasick.

To avoid more episodes of seasickness, we moved our base to the Yucatan mainland, where we located the owner of Xcaret, Felipe Delgado. Felipe also owned the finest restaurant in the area, where we enjoyed seafood he had speared and other delicacies barbecued in tangy red achiote sauce. I like to think of myself as a gourmet, so I methodically tried them all. One of the delicacies tasted remarkably like pork, so I asked Felipe what it was.

"We call it *tepesquintle*," he said beaming.

I took another delicious bit. "What's that in English?"

He frowned, thinking. "How you say – rodent?"

I stopped chewing and pushed the half-finished plate away as unobtrusively as possible.

After hastily gulping down some Mexican beer, I changed the subject. "Any other cenotes around here?" I croaked, while Ned struggled to keep a straight face.

"Oh, there's one," he said.

Ned leaned forward. He had regularly made trips to Mexico ever since a teenager in Texas, taking photographs for various diving publications.

"Chakalal?"

"No, this is north of Chakalal. It is known as Nonec, but," he added with a grin, "I call it Paradise."

The next day Felipe took us by boat to the remote cave. There was no caleta, so we anchored just offshore, carefully ferrying our equipment to the rocks through the pounding surf. I was thankful that it was a relatively calm day. We hiked 300 feet down a sandy path covered with broad–leafed sea grape plants and many–spined prickly pear decorated here and there with fragrant yellow blossoms. Ahead of us appeared a huge L–shaped cenote of bright blue water, shimmering in the tropical sun.

We dived the upstream end of the cenote first. It was at the top of the L, where a sheer limestone wall dropped nearly 10 feet to the water's edge. Below the ledge brightly–colored angel fish frolicked in a gaping cave mouth nearly 40 feet wide. I tied off our guideline, then found it was unnecessary. We could clearly see daylight streaming in from another cenote in the distance. Since I had already started the line, I used it to measure the distance of the traverse: 380 feet – by far the furthest I had ever seen daylight in an underwater cave.

At the second cenote, we surfaced and climbed over a pile of rocks, glad that we were using single tanks. The continuation of the passage retained roughly the same dimensions: 30 feet wide by 10 feet high, with the floor at only 25 feet. At a distance of 1,060 feet from the second cenote we decided that we had seen enough for one day. While I tied off our line, a large white cave amphipod hovered nearby.

After returning to the L–shaped cenote, we used what little line remained to investigate the downstream end. The current in the brackish layer had increased, forming ripples on the surface of the halocline that caused our reflected light beams to flicker across the bottom. I thought the effect was fascinating, but I could hear Ned growling into his regulator as he struggled to get pictures undistorted by the halocline. Our underground path led us even closer to the sea through a chain of small cenotes separated by natural bridges 40 to 60 feet long. I ran out of line in a crevice–like cenote where evenly–spaced tree roots hung down to the water surface like bars in a jail. On the surface we paced off my survey notes and found that they led us to a tiny blow hole near the surf, where the crashing waves would periodically cause a 20–foot–high geyser of spray to shoot skyward.

We spent the rest of the expedition exploring and surveying the branching passages in Xcaret. At the end of the week we had nearly 3,500 feet of passage surveyed, making it Mexico's largest underwater cave. We never did find any gold.

Bermuda is a strange island for blue holes. Rather than having a limestone layer thousands of feet thick like Florida, Yucatan, and the Bahamas, on Bermuda you hit insoluble lava rock only 80 to 100 feet below the water surface. One would expect that there would not be much opportunity for cave development in so thin a layer. But Bermuda is loaded with caves. Dr. Tom Iliffe believes that it has more caves per acre than any other similarly–sized area on earth.

Because of Bermuda's proximity to the ocean, many of the caves are at least partly filled with water. Working from the Bermuda Biological Station, Tom started a systematic investigation of the caves that evolved into a major project of the NSS. A Bermuda Cave Divers Association was started by Tom, Rob Power, Paul Hobbs, Paul Meng, and Barry Warner. I was invited to join the BCDA in March, 1981.

Two hours after I stepped off the jet, Paul, Rob, and Barry took me into the sprawling Green Bay Cave System, which extends underground all the way across the island. With more than a mile of totally submerged, interconnecting passages, Green Bay was then the world's longest sea cave and would remain so until our expedition to Belize the following year.

A brilliant red sun plunged into Harrington Sound as we swam to the main entrance of the cave. It is a classic Bahamas–style blue hole, 40 feet wide and 10 feet deep, festooned with all sorts of colorful sponges and corals. It is also subject to Bahamas–type tidal fluctuations, and I noticed with alarm that we were diving on the *inflow* cycle, a sure way to commit suicide on Andros or Grand Bahama. I pointed at the rushing water, but Rob shook his head and smiled, continuing into the cave.

Two hundred feet in, Paul led me into a side passage while the others continued ahead with the current. A hundred feet

Stalagmites are highlighted by a diver's light in Green Bay Cave, Bermuda. (*Photo by Rob Power*)

further the passage opened into a room 60 feet wide and 100 feet long, where we had to choose from three large tunnels. Paul followed the permanent line into the center tunnel, and moments later we surfaced at Cliff Pool, the only other known entrance to the cave. Like many Bermuda cave entrances, Cliff Pool was in someone's garden. While we stood in shallow water chatting, bubbles announced the arrival of Rob and Barry, who had reached us by a different route.

Our exit from the Green Bay entrance was not as difficult as I had feared. The currents in Bermuda never approach the severity of Bahamian blue holes, so I was able to get out by pulling on rocks. One of the rocks I grabbed moved: a startled pink octopus that quickly jetted away from me.

On a later dive, Rob and Barry took me past Cliff Pool up the North Shore passage, a spacious hall 50 feet wide and 10–20 feet high and more than 1,000 feet in length. There was one nice difference from Bahamian caves: on Bermuda there are spectacular stalagmites on the floor of the cave as well as stalactites on the ceiling. One enormous pair of stalagmites was especially intriguing, and after the dive I was informed that they even had a name: The Mammaries.

Impressive as Green Bay is, my favorite caves in Bermuda are in the Walsingham area. In Deep Blue is a huge room where a stalactite–studded entrance silhouette is plainly visible more than 100 feet back. While we were there, Barry showed me a tiny hole where he and Tom had followed a strong inflowing current another hundred feet. Despite the fact that we were well inland, there was no fresh water lens like the one we had at Lucayan, and the water was quite cold. Apparently the reason for the cold and the absence of the lens is that the island is so porous that the Atlantic Ocean roars in one side and out the other with little or no opportunity for the temperature to be altered by the ground. If I had visited in the summertime, I could have enjoyed 80° F water instead of the 59° F water I was enduring.

The next day we dived Walsingham's Cave, a former show cave near the sea. From the concrete walkway we could see a deep cave lake surrounded by large stalactites. Underwater my companions showed me a 30–foot–wide by 15–foot–high passage leading to several dome–shaped rooms. The passage has a diversity of formations unrivalled by anything I have ever seen, even at Lucayan: hundreds of stalactites and stalagmites, cascades of flowstone, swirling ribbons of bacon rind, and even delicate, twisting spirals of helictites. Some of the rooms extended above the water surface. The mirror–like pool surfaces reflected our light beams downward, illuminating the formations from many different angles. The red clay floor, typical of Bermuda caves, gave some of the stalagmites a fiery glow.

A diver peers over drip formations in Walsingham's Cave in Bermuda. (*Photo by Rob Power*)

After conferring briefly in the last of the air domes, Barry and I looked for a lead in the far wall. We knew that several other caves were in this part of the island, but none of them had been linked together. We followed one fissure a couple of hundred feet, where it ended in clay–shrouded breakdown. Then I spotted a tiny slot at 60 feet where I could see ripples on the white sandy bottom. We squeezed through it and followed a slope upward into a vast room more than 100 feet across, easily the largest room in the cave. At the top of the room was another small air dome containing crystalline, china–like stalactites. We carefully skirted them and continued into a broad passage that ended after a couple of hundred feet.

On the next dive Barry and I tried two side leads in the left wall of the broad passage that we had stopped in previously. One of them was a picturesque canyon 14 feet high but only five feet wide, festooned with stalactites and draperies, but neither lead went for more than 200 feet. Still another passage leading from the top of the canyon led to a bedding plane more than 60 feet wide, but only two feet high, with a floor of fluffy red silt. A slot in the ceiling provided the only route high enough to swim through. Barry led the way while I carefully secured the line on projections to keep from slipping out of the slot into the low area.

After 100 feet the slot ended in a three–foot hole. Barry squeezed through into a high canyon, then spun and flashed his light at me. On the floor ahead of him was the end of the line that he and Tom had laid from Deep Blue.

A few days later Rob and Paul made the first entrance–to–entrance trip. The spiritual leader of the Bermuda cave diving effort, Tom Iliffe, missed both dives because he was overseas at a cave biology conference. This was sad, but Tom may get the biggest dive yet. Bermuda's most popular tourist attraction, Crystal Cave, is not too far away from Walsingham's/Deep Blue and has several promising leads. A connection between the two caves might result in their surpassing Green Bay as

Bermuda's longest.

If Bermuda is a strange place for blue holes, then the Canary Islands are bizarre. Located just off the African coast, these islands are almost totally volcanic, lacking any limestone at all. Yet we had been told that there were caves here also, giant tubes in the basalt that had been formed when lava continued to flow out from under a solidifying crust, leaving a cavity underground. One tube was rumored to extend all the way from the top of a volcano named Monte Corona to the sea, a distance of four miles.

Biologists Jacob Parzefal and Horst Wilkens of the University of Hamburg had contacted Tom Iliffe about some rare cave life they had found in a pool where the tube plunged under the ocean. So in early 1983, we traveled across three continents to find out what happened when the tube met the sea. Also with us were Rob Power, Mary Van Soeren, Dennis Williams, Ken Fulghum, and Clark Pitcairn. Mary is a lithe registered nurse from Canada whose favorite pastime is running marathons. Rob taught her how to cave dive while they were living in Bermuda. Ken and I had worked together in the 1978 exploration of Tennessee's Lost Sea, the world's largest underground lake; he had logged more than 500 cave dives. Clark is a strong young man from Pennsylvania with whom I had set several cave diving distance records.

The furthest anyone had been in a cave completely filled with salt water was 3,800 feet, a record set by Martyn Farr, a Welsh diver who showed me England's Wookey Hole in 1980. In 1982, Martyn had pushed to the end of Conch Sound Blue Hole on Andros, breaking a 1981 mark set by Spanish divers in Jameos del Aqua, the volcanic cave we were planning to visit. Since the Spanish had not found an end, we had high hopes of producing a new world record.

Access to the water in Jameos del Aqua is somewhat unusual. Since the cave is heavily commercialized, we had to tiptoe in full cave diving regalia past an underground restau-

Jameos del Agua expedition participants were (left to right) Clark Pitcairn, Dennis Williams, Ken Fulghum, Horst Wilkens, Rob Power, Sheck Exley, Mary Van Soeren and Tom Iliffe. (*Photo by Yolanda Iliffe*)

rant and bar and across a disco floor to go diving. Also in the cave were two more bars, swimming pools, dance floors, and even 1,000–seat modern auditorium.

Somber symphonic music poured from huge loudspeakers as we climbed down some boulders to get to the water. Brightly colored lights reflected from the boulders into the water, where permanent underwater lights further illuminated the deep blue pool. At 65° F, the temperature of the water was a little cooler than Florida, but the visibility approached 100 feet.

On the first dive, Clark and I followed a line installed by the original Italian explorers of the cave, while the others conducted a successful search for *Munidopsis*, a cave–adapted crab that was found nowhere else in the world. Since the cave is a blue hole of sorts with water flow reversing with the tides, we had timed our dive so the current would be heading out of the cave.

We followed a huge borehole 30 feet in diameter from the surface pool. Accustomed to the jagged, angular turns of limestone caves, I was fascinated by the flowing curves of the lava tube. There was absolutely no silt, no wall–encrusting growths in the cave, even on the floor, and the bare gray walls turned to a lovely azure in the distance due to the refraction of the water. Swimming around the swooping turns in the cylindrical tunnel was like swooping through a giant space-ship, a sensation which our underwater weightlessness did nothing to dispel. I missed the huge stalactites found in many other blue holes, but in some sections lava had dripped from the ceiling before cooling, leaving ebony icicles several inches in length.

As we swam, our depth gradually increased as the cave continued to follow the slope of Monte Corona into the Atlantic. At 1,710 feet from the surface pool we had reached a depth of 80 feet, and the yellow rope left by the Italians in 1981 changed to a thick white Spanish cord. In places part of the roof had collapsed, leaving a jumble of dark boulders on the floor beneath tall canyons more than 60 feet high.

At 2,300 feet, we rounded a bend to the left and were surprised to see a 20–foot–high mound of glistening white sand. Above the mound, Clark found a tiny slit leading up toward the ocean floor, but it was too small for a diver. We turned back at a penetration of 2,660 feet and a depth of 100 feet, without reaching the end of the Spanish line.

The next day Clark and I entered the cave with four tanks each. In addition to our back–mounted double 100's were two single 80–cubic–foot bottles, which we hung beneath us with snaps. By 1,550 feet into the cave, we had used one-third of the air in the two singles, so dropped both tanks on a pile of rocks to reserve two two-thirds air supply for the swim out.

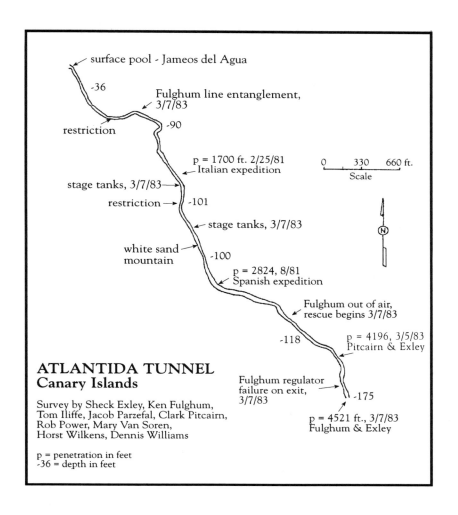

surface pool - Jameos del Agua

-36

Fulghum line entanglement,
3/7/83

restriction   -90

p = 1700 ft. 2/25/81
Italian expedition

stage tanks, 3/7/83

restriction → -101

stage tanks, 3/7/83

white sand
mountain   -100

p = 2824, 8/81
Spanish expedition

Fulghum out of air,
rescue begins 3/7/83

-118   p = 4196, 3/5/83
                       Pitcairn & Exley

ATLANTIDA TUNNEL
Canary Islands

Fulghum regulator
failure on exit,
3/7/83   -175

Survey by Sheck Exley, Ken Fulghum,
Tom Iliffe, Jacob Parzefal, Clark Pitcairn,
Rob Power, Mary Van Soren,
Horst Wilkens, Dennis Williams

p = 4521 ft., 3/7/83
Fulghum & Exley

p = penetration in feet
-36 = depth in feet

0   330   660 ft.
          Scale

N

Then we started breathing from our double tanks. Some 500 feet past the sand mound, we saw the end of the white Spanish cord tied to the left wall. A white slate commemorated their effort. Clark picked up the slate while I tied off on our guideline.

Beyond the end of the Spanish line, the lava tube assumed more impressive proportions, the ceiling rising 50 feet above the 120–foot–deep floor. After several hundred feet, we saw a bridge of dark basalt spanning the passage that looked like a double–barrelled shotgun lying on its side. A pile of boulders on the floor 300 feet further along heralded the collapse of the span, and the upper level again joined the lower in a high canyon. When we had used up one-third of our air, we tied off our line on the floor at a depth of 158 feet. We had explored another 1,372 feet past the Spanish line to a penetration of 4,193 feet.

That night, both groups swapped tales of their successes over huge mounds of paella. While Clark and I were setting a world record, the biology team had made an incredible find: Dennis had collected a new genus and possibly family of *Remipedia* over 3,000 miles from its only relative at Lucayan Caverns.

The next day, Clark had to return to the states, so Ken Fulghum was selected to join me in the next exploratory push. The sinewy Georgian intoned to me Elmer Fudd's solemn advice to Bugs Bunny: "Say your pwayers, wabbit!"

Our push dive was a team effort. Mary had prepared more measured guideline for us while the others had filled tanks and carried equipment to the water. Dennis and Rob entered the cave ahead of us carrying two full singles each which they deposited at 1,550 feet. Minutes later Ken and I submerged with double 100's, breathing from a single tank snapped beneath us. At 1,300 feet we passed Dennis and Rob on their way out and gave them a wave and grin. When we reached the tanks they had left us, we dropped the singles we had been using and picked up one fresh tank each. A third of the air in the fresh bottles lasted us until the bend before the white sand mound, where we left those tanks on a dark ledge.

An hour after we had left the surface, we reached the end of our old line. Ahead of us the tube became an irregular, distorted inclined fissure that slowly curved to the right. The gradient of the floor increased, so we swam near the ceiling to minimize our decompression requirements and to conserve air. The fissure bent back to the left. I tied off on the left wall near the ceiling at a depth of 160 feet. We had not used one-third of our air, and normally I would have added more than 325 feet, but I had a feeling that we had gone far enough. I spent a few extra moments at 4,518 feet, tying a Spanish–style slate with the names of the members of the group on it, while Ken started swimming out. He returned a minute later, I assumed to check on what was taking me so long.

We had swum out 400 feet when Ken showed me his pressure gauge. He had less than a minute of air left! At first I thought he was playing a trick on me by bleeding air out of his gauge to provide a false reading, but his eyes were deadly serious. I gave him my primary mouthpiece and insisted that he start using it while I switched to my secondary for the long swim out. Unable to converse with Ken except by hand signals, I could only assume that something had happened to increase his breathing rate enormously, since total scuba equipment failures during a dive are extremely rare.

This assumption meant that our position was especially precarious since my supply was theoretically enough to get two people with my breathing rate back to our single tanks, but not enough if a diver's air consumption was elevated by fatigue, anxiety, or physical trauma. I was also painfully aware that the longest successful buddy–breathing assist in the history of cave diving was less than 300 feet, while there were dozens of multiple fatalities from botched rescues. We were over 4,000 feet back.

After 20 minutes, there was still no sign of the white mound in sight. My head throbbed with pain from the carbon dioxide buildup in my body caused by my efforts to conserve air. I checked my pressure gauge, trying my best to look unconcerned to Ken. We had considerably less than 500 psig left, only a couple of minutes of air at that depth. We were going to die. I felt a profound sense of dismay, and tried to resign myself to our fate. I wondered if anyone would guess what happened when they found our bodies.

Our empty tanks became very light, forcing us to swim very hard to keep from being immobilized on the ceiling. It became very hard to breathe as my tank pressure fell below the minimal levels necessary to unseat the demand valves of my regulator. As my carbon dioxide content increased I became giddy. Like a half–imagined dream, the white mound swam into view with our single tanks just beyond. It was going to be close.

One last, labored breath, then my air was completely gone. I held my breath as I hurriedly turned on my single tank, my chest spasmodically contracting in my hunger for air. I did not know then that Ken had switched back to his own depleted supply as we approached the tanks, probably saving my life.

After we had caught our breath on the ledge, I grinned at Ken, and gave him a squeeze to signal that we had made it. Because of his elevated breathing rate, he again ran out of air just as we arrived at our other tanks at 1,550 feet. Instead of picking up both his tanks, he took only one, and started out leaving what I thought was his full tank behind. Accordingly, I picked up that tank and left my one–third–full bottle.

As we approached the 1,150 foot point, Ken abruptly paused and asked me to give him the other tank. Since I figured he needed it more than I did, I complied. At 900 feet, Ken's dangling scuba regulator snagged the guideline, but I quickly freed it and we continued through a constriction on some boulders at 820 feet – the only true narrow spot in the entire cave – without incident. At 230 feet, we were only 40 feet deep and again had to swim hard to counteract our increased positive buoyancy. I developed a bad cramp in the calf of my right leg, but was able to control it and continue swimming using a one–legged stroke called the shuffle kick.

Air was getting low again as the artificially lighted entrance came into view. Now we had a fresh predicament. We had originally intended to have one–third of our total starting air supply plus one–third of at least one other set of double tanks for our decompression stops. Now, however, we had consumed most of our one–third reserve air and left the rest of it at 1,540 feet in the partially filled tank. Dennis and Rob had left a set of used double tanks in the water for us, but it had only 500 psig – not nearly enough.

One or both of us would have to surface to ask for more air, a very risky procedure even if only seconds are spent topside. When I was younger and in better shape I might have chanced it with little risk. But those days were long past and on two recent dives I had developed minor symptoms known as skin bends – a burning rash of bubbles that goes away without treatment after a couple of days. Ken had developed more severe symptoms once—joint pain—so was probably as good a candidate for bends as I was.

Suddenly, Ken did a very brave thing and surfaced to yell for more air and inform the others of our predicament. Dennis and Tom quickly got our surface expedition members to drive for emergency air and oxygen. Thanks to their help and the assistance of the local Red Cross, we were able to get through our ordeal without further mishap or any symptoms of the bends.

After surfacing, I learned of the incredibly bad luck that had almost caused our deaths. While I tied off our guideline at 4,518 feet, Ken had started out, swimming to a point 100 feet from me. At that precise moment—the worst possible moment—the first stage valve in Ken's scuba regulator malfunctioned, causing a massive and rapid loss of air. Because the

Sheck Exley, Dennis Williams and Ken Fulghum look for lava tubes from camels on Lanzarote. (*Photo by Rob Power*)

air leak was unseen – behind him, on his back – Ken was aware only of the sound of the leak. Underwater sound travels much more rapidly than air, making it virtually impossible to tell where a sound is coming from. Because air leaks almost always occur at the mouthpiece rather than the first stage, Ken assumed I was the one with the air leak instead of him and started swimming back to me rather than checking his own regulator. By the time he saw I was okay and discovered the real problem, his air was almost gone.

To this day I do not know how we got out alive. The 500 psig of air I had left was probably not enough to get me out alone from the point where I checked the gauge, and not nearly enough for both of us. There was nothing wrong with the pressure gauge I had read; I continued diving with it for years afterward. I do not believe in magic or miracles, but I am unable to find a rational explanation for our survival. Sometimes I wonder if I really did drown in Atlantida. Perhaps everything that has happened to me since that day in 1982 has been a dream. At any rate, the incident certainly makes accepting the disappointments of life easier. After all, I could be floating lifeless in a volcanic blue hole on Lanzarote instead of dealing with the problems of life.

9

Hall of the Mountain King

I was slowly spinning on a thin wire cable in the middle of an icy waterfall. One hundred feet below me, myriad droplets splashed into the glistening surface of an emerald green subterranean lake. If I had not been so busy trying to stay warm and to keep from spinning faster, I might have risked a quick glance down, invoking my strong fear of heights. As it was, I barely had enough time to remember the warning of Bill Wallace far above me: "When you get near the lake, be sure to put your mouthpiece in your mouth."

I was a little mystified by this advice. The waterfall was bad, but it was not that bad. I had no trouble breathing in the torrent. Nevertheless, I followed Bill's advice and chomped down on the rubber bit of my regulator as the huge sunless sea loomed below me. It was just in time. In less than a heartbeat I was five feet beneath the surface of Missouri's Devil's Well, my numbed hands fumbling with the safety chain of my bosun's chair so that I could free my twin tanks. Someone had been a little late putting the brakes on the cable.

In another couple of minutes I was able to relax on the water's surface and enjoy the view of the largest underground lake in the Ozark Mountains. On the far side of the 400–foot–

Looking down at the bosun's chair at Devil's Well, Missouri. (*Photo by Sheck Exley*)

diameter lake, the floor of the huge jug–shaped chamber plunged to depths rumored to be in excess of 200 feet. From there an unknown corridor rambled the incredible distance of two miles before surfacing at Cave Spring, where four years earlier in 1969, Joe Prosser and I had found a horizontal tunnel at similar depths. Even before that dive, other divers had recovered ancient dugout canoes from the depths and had connected Cave Spring to a crawl cave only 150 feet away called Wallace Well.

Our main interest now was on the other side of Devil's Well, where the upstream source led out of the chamber and under a nearby ridge. Geologists had theorized that under that ridge would be still another huge natural air bell, which Jerry Vineyard thought served as surge chambers in times of heavy rainfall. Dana Turner, David Fisk, and I followed the undercut wall of the chamber to a 50–foot–wide passage at a depth of 40 feet. From the passage came a sluggish flow of clear green water. Visibility was about 40 feet, so we could enjoy the view of the ribbed, undulating roof. We had swum only 50 feet when we saw the tell–tale glisten of a surface above us. When we surfaced, however, we found that we were merely in an air bell that Don Rimbach had discovered previously. We continued another 400 feet up the submerged passage, which wound back and forth and gradually sloped to a depth of 70 feet. There was no sign of the conjectured air chamber.

The entrance to Cave Spring, Missouri is well hidden in the shadows. (Photo by Sheck Exley)

Ever since I spent several summers in the Appalachians as a child, I have loved the mountains, which contrasted so dramatically with the flat, featureless landscape of my native Florida. Therefore, when we visited the Current River section of the Ozarks in 1969, I thought I had found Nirvana—a combination of my beloved mountains and spectacular, Florida–like springs. We plunged into several of the alluring giant conduits including Welch Spring and the Gulf as well as Cave Spring and Devil's Well. My favorite was Blue Spring near Owl's Bend, where Lewis Holtzendorff, Court Smith, and I swam in air–clear water down a steep tunnel through the pure white Eminence dolomite to a depth of 280 feet. Later, Roger Miller and Frank Fogarty explored that fine cave on a helium dive to a depth of 325 feet. At that point the tunnel ended, with water seeping upward through the gravel floor.

But the real story of the Ozarks and other mountainous areas, as far as cave diving is concerned, is not the springs—it is the sumps. While cave diving in springs is an end in itself, in sump diving scuba equipment is merely a means to finding more air–filled cave. Nowhere is this better illustrated than in the Ozarks of Arkansas, where in the fall of 1970, Glen Thompson connected Blanchard Springs to the awesome air–filled show cave that bears the same name. In the same county in 1977, Don Monnot, Ed Arters, Paul Smith, Forrest Wilson,

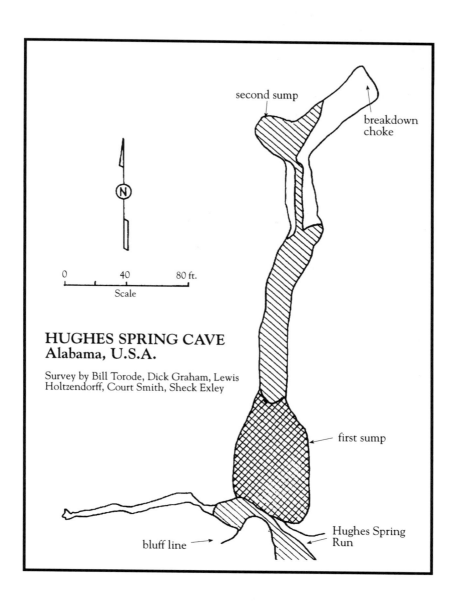

second sump

breakdown
choke

0   40   80 ft.
Scale

HUGHES SPRING CAVE
Alabama, U.S.A.

Survey by Bill Torode, Dick Graham, Lewis
Holtzendorff, Court Smith, Sheck Exley

first sump

bluff line

Hughes Spring
Run

Sheck Exley crawls out of a short sump that was free–dived. (*Photo by Glen Thompson*)

Carl Cowart, and I made similar discoveries in Cave River Cave and Nesbitt's Spring in expeditions organized by veteran dry caver Mike Warshauer. Despite all of this activity, the Ozarks remain an area with immense potential for cave divers.

In 1975, Bill Torode, an Alabama caver responsible for mapping most of Alabama's dry caves, gave me some fascinating underwater cave leads in his state. At the first spot, a large underground lake near Belgreen, Court, Lewis, and I discovered an air bell similar to the one that we had seen at Devil's

Well in 1973. The next day we drove to Hughes Spring, a small pool of ugly gray water nearby.

Under an overhanging ledge at Hughes, I found a water—filled tunnel only two feet high and six feet deep, but well over 30 feet wide. How much over 30 feet I do not know because I could barely see my hand in front of my face, much less a cave wall. The visibility was so bad I did not even try to avoid the soft red clay bottom. I worried that my guideline might drift into an area too low for me to follow it back out. That had happened to Court and me in 1973 in a remote section of Little River Spring which I named the "Rat Trap".

After nearly 200 feet, I glanced up to see stalactites hanging from the ceiling above an air surface. I arched up to check it out, and saw a large passage in air with a flowing river at the bottom. Its walls were covered with draperies and bell canopies of dripstone. Fifty feet away was a glistening bank of sand, unmarked by the footprint of any man since the dawn of time. There was a profound silence broken only by the occasional drip of water from an unseen stalactite somewhere in the labyrinth beyond the sand bank.

I had swum through more than a million feet of passage underwater, but the strangeness of my first virgin passage in air was a little frightening. Aware that air pockets in caves can contain dangerously high levels of carbon dioxide and other gases, I carefully removed the regulator from my mouth and risked a breath. The cave air had the musky smell of damp earth, but was okay. I swam across the surface of the river, then trudged up the sand bank, unwilling to take my doubles off for fear I would misplace them and become stranded. Overcome by an intense feeling of aloneness, I mumbled something just to hear a human voice. It did not work, so I shut up and left, but not before noticing that the 10—foot—diameter air passage continued beyond the sand bank.

The return route was straight and high enough to swim through easily, so I talked Court and Lewis into returning with me. We deposited our tanks on the sand bank, then walked down the passage. Beyond a sharp bend to the left we splashed back into knee–deep water to wade through an area whose high ceiling was covered with stalactites. After 100 feet the stream ended in a deep pool where the cave ceiling once more dipped beneath the water, We wiggled into a cobble–floored crawlway on the right in an effort to find a route around the new sump, but the low slot was blocked by boulders after 100 feet.

Two years later Paul Smith and I dived the second sump in Hughes Spring. After a short swim we surfaced in a small lake room at the base of a high wall of boulders that had collapsed from the ceiling. We climbed 20 feet up a crevice through the unstable boulders, but only succeeded in causing some rocks to splash into the lake. Disappointed, we retreated after survey-ing our discovery so that we could give Bill Torode a map.

Is there a way past the boulders in Hughes Spring? Bill says that the water rising in Hughes and nearby Skidmore Spring comes from the Newsome Sinks area many miles to the north. Between them lies a high limestone area which could contain Alabama's longest cave.

The biggest opportunity for discovery by sump divers in America may lie under a picturesque section of Virginia's Appalachians known as Burnsville Cove. Under the colorful wild flowers and split rail fences are both the longest and third longest caves in the state, sprawling Butler and Breathing Caves. Tests have shown that all the water from both caves, as well as from some less significant caves in Burnsville Cove, resurges at Refrigerator Spring several miles away. With potential for a huge cave rivaling the 300–mile length of Kentucky's Mammoth Cave, the world's longest, it is not surprising that NSS divers have long directed their attention there. In 1956, Bevin Hewett plunged a mere 30 feet into Refrigerator Cave and surfaced in an awesome virgin air cave with a ceiling 60 feet high. Later, dry cavers excavated an

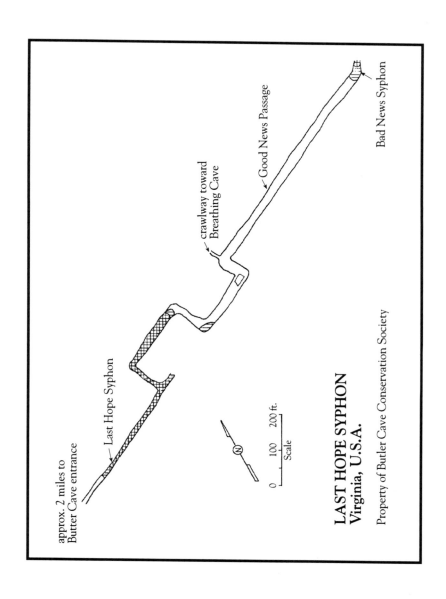

approx. 2 miles to
Butler Cave entrance

Last Hope Syphon

crawlway toward
Breathing Cave

Good News Passage

Bad News Syphon

0 100 200 ft.
Scale

N

LAST HOPE SYPHON
Virginia, U.S.A.

Property of Butler Cave Conservation Society

entrance in air and surveyed a half mile of cave passage before
it sumped again in an intriguing area known as French Lake.
Bevin's dive was the biggest American sump diving discovery
until the late 1960's.

By the time Court, Lewis, and I arrived at Burnsville Cove
in 1975, both Hank Hoover and Rick Rigg had pushed French
Lake and a tantalizing sump in the remote recesses of Butler
Cave without finding any new airspace. At the latter site,
which carried the ominous name of Last Hope Syphon, Rick
had pushed 300 feet into the icy 50° F water with no luck. This
should have told us something, since Rick is a very fine caver
as well as a cave diver and had discovered the world's longest
soda straw stalactites during a dive at Pennsylvania's Tytoona
Cave in 1965.

Nevertheless, we showed up at Burnsville expecting something similar to our previous experience at Alabama's Hughes
Spring, where a short walk from a parked car put us in the
water. We had along the heavy, bulky cave diving equipment
that we used in Florida that had served us well. The discoverer
of Butler Cave, Ike Nicholson, had told me on the phone that
Butler consisted of an easy two–mile walk to the water at Last
Hope Syphon. I should have known better, having done a
little dry caving in Georgia and Tennessee during my college
days.

Our first dive was in Refrigerator Spring's French Lake.
Because of the half–mile underground trek to the lake, we
decided that only two of us would dive. I volunteered to carry
equipment and help the other two get ready. At the lake I grew
restless waiting for the dive to start, so grabbed a snorkel and
started swimming around on the surface. I was able to swim
under the right wall by holding my snorkel in a narrow crack
that extended above the water surface. After nearly 100 feet
I entered a large room with a ceiling that shot up into air for
20 feet. A minute later Court and Lewis, wearing double
tanks, joined me, their 55–watt quartz lamps transforming the

Sheck Exley prepares to free dive a sump in Tennessee in 1973. (*Photo by Glenn Thompson*)

dark water into a blazing sapphire that clearly illuminated the recesses of the large room. Despite their lights, we never found Hank and Rick's passage leading from the lake. Maybe sump diving was not as easy as we thought.

Early the next morning, we assembled on a grassy knoll in the bright yellow sunlight. It was decided that I would make a solo dive in Butler Cave because of the difficulty of getting equipment to Last Hope Syphon. Nevin W. Davis, the red–bearded president of the Butler Cave Conservation Society, took one look at us and shook his head, skeptical of our chances. Instead of vibram–soled climbing boots we were wearing our slick–soled neoprene diver's booties, and the rest of our dry caving equipment was equally inappropriate.

With us were Tom Tompkins and a Marine from Virginia Beach whose experience, like ours, consisted mainly of diving in Florida's springs. The Marine did not like Nevin's attitude. "Look," he said, "I run two miles in the soft beach sand every day. Don't tell me I can't handle a two mile walk through a cave. Now, where is the entrance?"

Nevin sighed and stepped to the side. Behind him appeared an 18–inch–high opening in an outcrop of rock. In a

few minutes our efficient BCCS porters had passed my equipment and the five of us through the tiny opening. Just inside
was a sheer 30–foot drop that required climbing down a cable
ladder. So much for Ike Nicholson's easy two–mile walk. The
Marine muttered something like, "Neat, just like an obstacle
course," and started down.

"Wait," Nevin called. He carefully tied a loop of rope
around our gung–ho friend, then belayed him as he climbed
down. Halfway down the Marine slipped off the ladder and
had to be carefully lowered to the bottom. I looked at the
Marine's eyes, as big as saucers. The bravado was gone. "I've
had enough," he croaked. As Nevin hauled him back up I
realized that I didn't feel much better. Beyond me was a muddy
squeeze called the Glop Schlott, then a slippery climb over
slippery mud–covered boulders that bordered treacherous,
sheer–walled pits more than 100 feet deep.

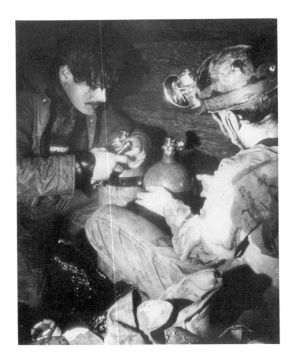

Climbing on all
fours (and some-
times fives when I
could bring my
fanny into play), I
managed to get past
the pits without
sliding into obli-
vion. Three hours
later we arrived at
Last Hope Syphon
having suffered
through all the
crawlways, chim-

Nevin Davis helps
Sheck Exley suit up at
Last Hope Syphon.
(*Photo by Lee Gilman*)

ney, and other nasties that any experienced dry caver would have expected on a two–mile cave trip involving a 590–foot change in elevation. Because of the frigid water—the coldest I have ever experienced in a cave except for a dive with Jochen Hasenmayer in Germany's Blautopf—I wore a fully sealed dry suit instead of the usual wet suit. With a thick woolen sweater on underneath, I was quite comfortable during the dive. After assembling my double tanks I followed a three–foot–high by five–foot–wide tunnel for 500 feet. While the maximum depth of the dive was only eight feet, there was no hint of any air above me.

I returned to tell the others what I had found, then asked Jack Igoe to open my drysuit zipper. But it had become jammed with clay and no amount of yanking by Jack and Fred Wefer would open it. Since I was not about to slice open a new $200 suit, I was a prisoner in my drysuit until we arrived back in our motel room 20 miles away, and became dangerously over-heated. Only repeated immersions in the cave stream averted heat prostration.

Our success in exploring 200 feet past Rick's furthest penetration encouraged Nevin, so he invited us back for another dive. That fall I returned with boots and other caving equipment, and pushed another 100 feet into air. Although the 600 feet of Last Hope Syphon was far shorter than our Florida cave dives and even sump dives in Europe, it was nevertheless the longest single sump ever successfully pushed in America at the time. Unfortunately, our search for the greater glory of a major cave discovery was foiled. When I returned to the start of the sump I told Nevin, "The good news is that we've found 950 feet of air–filled passage. The bad news is that there's another sump." Several years later David Whall and Karen Wark dived the Bad News Syphon and came back with the even worse news that it is clogged with mud. So the key to the vast Burnsville Cove Cave System remains undis-covered.

Sheck Exley submerges at Last Hope Syphon. (*Photo by Lee Gilman*)

In 1976, the largest cave in West Virginia was Organ Cave, a commercial cave that was also the sixth longest cave in the world. Organ is a favorite of tourists because of the musical tones that are emitted by struck stalactites as well as many saltpeter mining relics dating from the Civil War. That fall, Forrest Wilson, original Training Director of the NSS Cave Diving Section, invited me to help him dive a muddy sump at the end of Bowen Canyon. He had already made two unsuccessful attempts to pass Bowen Sump that had been stymied by the atrocious visibility.

Thanks to the help of a strong group of cavers from the D. C. Grotto, the oldest chapter of the NSS, most of the two–mile–long trip from the cave entrance to the sump was fairly easy. Halfway there we paused while Mike Dyas, Dennis Seekins, and Carl Cowart put ropes down a 130–foot–deep pit.

Sheck Exley on a winter trip to Organ Cave. (*Photo by Karan Pribble*)

Forrest Wilson prepares for a sump dive in West Virginia. (*Photo by Carl Cowart*)

I rappelled down the pit by threading the rope through the aluminum bars of a steel rack snapped to a seat harness I was wearing. In the dark it was easy to pretend that the pit was only 30 feet deep, so I had no trouble with my fear of heights. At the bottom of the pit was Bowen Canyon, the passage in the cave, averaging 15 feet wide and more than 20 feet high. As we waded down the stream–covered floor of the canyon, the dramatic opening strains of Strauss' *Thus Spake Zarathustra* crept into my head. I felt that we were on the verge of a big discovery.

After a mile the canyon ended at a 20–foot–wide pool of red, clay–laden water. Our heavily–laden porters eased their packs off and watched while Forrest and I quietly suited up. Since it is safest to dive solo in caves with poor visibility, we decided to take turns diving the sump. Nicknamed The

Wizard because of his bushy blond beard and long, thinning hair, Forrest graciously suggested that I go first.

"That way you can see the passage before we silt it up," he said.

"What makes you think that I'm going to see anything anyway?" By this time the clay disturbed by our trip down the canyon had been carried by the stream into the sump, making it look like red paint. I carefully felt my way under a ledge at five feet to a wide passage only two feet high. I eased into it, pushing off slowly from the ceiling with my cave boots. I was diving without fins since they serve no purpose in short low visibility sumps and add to the weight and bulk of gear that has to be carried through the cave.

After 100 feet, I dropped to a depth of eight feet, and visibility increased to five feet over the fluffy red clay floor. Now that I could see, I swam faster, and a couple of minutes later came to the end of my 200 foot line. I tied it off on the left wall. Ahead of me the ceiling seemed to be rising. I returned to tell Forrest the exciting news.

Forrest was gone a long time. I was just on the verge of going back in to check on him when he popped up from the scarlet depths. His grin said everything. Fifty feet from the end of my line he had popped into a small airspace, then crawled through a low area into a huge hallway every bit as impressive as Bowen Canyon!

We swam back through the sump and dumped our single tanks on a mud bank next to a startled reddish–brown sala-mander. We trudged up the bank into a booming borehole 15 feet wide and 20 feet high. It seemed to go on forever as we followed it past glistening stalactites, strange red flowstone, rare white gypsum flowers, high waterfalls, and great austere hallways fading away into the unknown. We turned back after an hour to keep our porters from worrying, but not before surveying 3,800 feet of virgin passage. It was easily the biggest sump discovery ever made in the eastern United States.

In February, David Morrow and I returned to explore more of Wilson's Wonderland. It continued undiminished in size, but the gradient increased, causing the stream in the floor to cascade noisily down a series of low rapids. After another 1,000 feet the passage curved to the right to head west, then continued the curve to the north. The passage finally ended 6,200 feet from Bowen Sump in a large room 100 feet in diameter, where the stream tumbled through white foam to sink through tiny cracks between huge boulders. I climbed to an upper level passage to check for a continuation or a connection to the Lipps Syphon in another part of Organ Cave, but after several hundred feet it dropped back into Wilson's Wonderland near a bright red flowstone area that we had previously named the Scarlet Pimpernel. Oddly, all the formations beyond Bowen Sump including the Pimpernel were in the right hand wall of the passage.

We returned to Bowen Sump six hours after starting up Wilson's Wonderland. Rather than have our porters worrying and waiting for us in the cold cave air, we had sent them out of the cave as soon as our gear was deposited. They were to return the next day to retrieve our equipment, but we elected to carry out everything except the tanks since we still felt fresh. It was a little tricky climbing back up the 130–foot pit with my jumars, but I was able to keep my balance by pushing off on one wall with my feet. At the top I coiled the rope and threw it over my shoulder also.

We had been underground for more than 15 hours. Fatigue had begun to set in, making us wish that we had left our burdens in the cave for our porters. I had lost track of the time, so was surprised to exit from the cave at night in a raging blizzard. A low, picturesque waterfall that tourists love in the summer had turned into an icy glacier blocking our path. Even with a hand line to help us it was too slippery to get across without great danger of a nasty fall. Finally we got across on our hands and knees, pushing the coiled rope and packed equipment ahead of us.

We might as well not have bothered. Our brightest cave lights penetrated the falling snow for only a few feet. My damp coveralls and wetsuit froze solid, so that I felt as though I was wearing stovepipes on my legs. The bone–piercing cold had to be approaching 0° F. My right hand felt frostbitten from crawling over the glacier, and after we had wandered blindly through the snowstorm for several hundred yards, we decided we would be much better off in the cave. Even though it was damp and muddy and our bed would be on sharp rocks, at 50° F it would be much warmer than the blizzard or even the unheated D. C. Grotto fieldhouse. Unfortunately, now the snow was falling with such ferocity that our tracks were covered as soon as we made them. We were lost, the cold rapidly sapping our dwindling reserves of strength as we searched for shelter.

I was nearly asleep on my feet when we finally stumbled up the steps to the fieldhouse, and only vaguely remember climbing into my dry down bag for dreamless sleep.

Later dives elsewhere have resulted in the discovery of passages of similar lengths, but none have been larger or more grand than Organ's Wilson's Wonderland. Only at Iowa's Cold Water Cave, where in 1967 Dave Jagnow and Steve Barnett pushed through a series of long swimways separated by short sumps, has cave diving resulted in a significantly larger find in the U. S. Even there, most of the eight miles of cave thus far mapped has been explored through a man–made air–filled entrance.

Dedicated American sump divers like Stephen Maegerlein, Tom Cook, and Jim Pisarowicz will tell you that some day, somewhere they are going to make a dive to discover a new Mammoth Cave. Already, in Mexico, Bill Stone has led a dive to connect two sections of the third deepest cave in the world, and by the time you read this it may be *the* deepest.

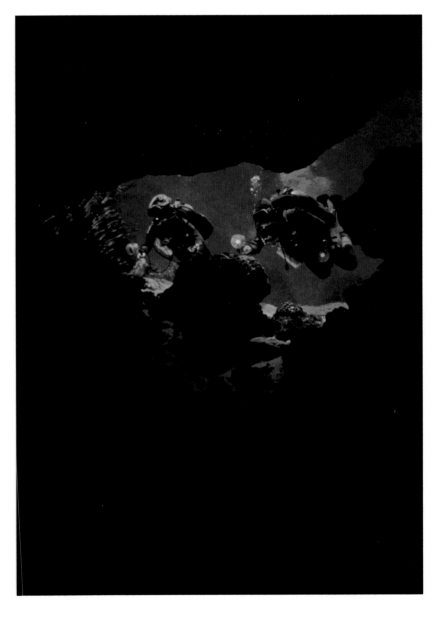

Sheck Exley and Mary Ellen Eckhoff prepare to enter Ginnie Spring in Florida. (*Photo by Ned DeLoach*)

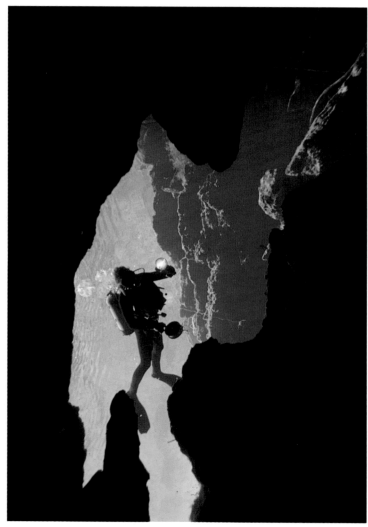

A diver is silhouetted in one of the entrances to Running Springs Cave System. *(Photo by Ned DeLoach)*

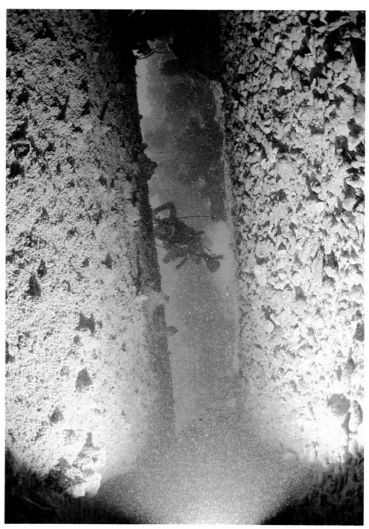

A diver pauses in the entrance of a Bahamian blue hole. (*Photo by Sheck Exley*)

The water is amazingly clear in this cave pool near Walsingham's Cave, Bermuda. (*Photo by Rob Power*)

A diver submerges in a crystalline pool near Walsingham's Cave, Bermuda. (*Photo by Rob Power*)

A diver "staging" through a stalactite forest near Walsingham' Cave in Bermuda. (*Photo by Rob Power*)

The Xcaret caleta (spring-fed river) on the Yucatan peninsula in Mexico. (*Photo by Ned DeLoach*)

Mary Ellen Eckhoff suits up for a 400–foot dive in Nacimiento del Río Mante. (*Photo by Sheck Exley*)

Sheck Exley starting down on a record 780–foot deep dive in 1988. (*Photo by Ned DeLoach*)

Sheck Exley before his record 867-foot dive in Nacimiento del Río Mante. (*Photo by Ned DeLoach*)

Sheck Exley decompresses on nitrox at 80 feet after his record 867-foot dive in Nacimiento del Río Mante. (*Photo by Ned DeLoach*)

Sheck Exley uses a compass to survey underwater passageways. (*Photo by Ned DeLoach*)

10

Manatee Springs Cave

I could not breathe.

I coughed violently as I inhaled some water, and spat the defective regulator out of my mouth. Since my double 100's were empty, I was trying to breathe from a single tank that we had placed in the cave for decompression. I knew that only 30 feet above me was the surface of Friedman Sink, but to swim to it now, with nearly three hours of decompression stops left, would have meant a serious case of the bends and possible paralysis or death. My lungs aching for air, I flashed my light at Bill Main, who was hovering nearby in the cave. While I swam to Bill, I reached behind my head to the valves of my empty double 100's, trying to free one of my regulators to replace the defective one on the single tank. Full of the nervous energy that make him an exceptionally alert diving companion, Bill saw my signal and handed me his spare mouthpiece. I signalled thanks for the air, then finished getting the regulator off my doubles and putting it on my stage tank. Switching from Bill's mouthpiece to my chest–mounted single tank, I used a hand signal on the troublesome regulator that is not found in any of the diver communication lists.

I pulled my slate and pencil out of a pocket in my B. C. vest and wrote a note explaining our predicament to Bill. While we were decompressing at 40 feet, our rising exhaust bubbles dislodged a dense rain of red clay from the ceiling of Friedman Sink's entrance room. The fine–grained sediment turned the water above us into red paint, totally obscuring a niche where I had put two more decompression tanks at 20 foot depth. Without those tanks we would run out of air in 40 minutes.

I tied a short length of guideline to a ceiling pendant and wandered into the scarlet liquid, one hand extended to keep from bumping my head on a rock projection. I had an image in my mind of how the area of the niche looked, and tried to translate it into how the shape of the walls and ceiling felt to my outstretched hand. After a few minutes of searching I felt the smooth, cold metal of our tanks and carefully tied off my guideline so we could retrieve them.

When we checked out those tanks, however, I discovered that the valve on mine had bent when I had dropped it down the entrance shaft, making it impossible for me to open it. Fortunately Mary Ellen and Bill's girlfriend, Jane Grey, came down to check on us and brought us more air, so the bad regulator and tank valve were merely inconveniences on the world's first 5,914–foot cave penetration.

Every field of human endeavor from tiddly winks to space exploration has its champions and its marks for human endur- ance and achievement. Without them there would be little or no human progress, for we would have nothing to measure our efforts by or to encourage us to try harder. It is difficult to imagine any aspect of our lives that is not enhanced by competition, the drive to excel, and the recognition of excel- lence.

In the open water diving community, one scuba record has gotten a bad reputation: open water depth on compressed air. Lives have been lost in the pursuit of that record. Also, it now serves little purpose since techniques developed by Dale Sweet and Jochen Hasenmayer have demonstrated that scuba divers can go much deeper on helium/oxygen mixtures. Otherwise, diving records are generally applauded as long as they are accomplished without unnecessary risk. This is especially true in cave diving, where the people who set the records have been almost exclusively responsible for all the improvements in cave diving safety equipment and procedures. Those safety advances would probably have never been made except for the interest those divers had in making record dives. The entire scuba diving community has benefitted from forearm knives, octopus regulators, buoyancy compensators, dual valves, third rule dive planning, and other cave diving innovations.

There are all sorts of world records in cave diving, from depth, distance, and duration to safety records like my 3,000 cave dives. But the best known cave diving record is for penetration, or distance from the nearest air surface in a cave. This is probably because it is the best measure of a cave diving team's ability, challenging its physical and psychological endurance as well as its equipment and procedures. Since cave diving has always been a technology–dependent activity, anything goes: there is no distinction between swimming dives and scooter dives, for example. Getting there (and back) is the thing.

Records have played an important part in the exploration of the Manatee Springs Cave System. In January, 1961, NSS divers connected the Manatee Springs entrance to a 120–foot–diameter sink called Catfish Hotel because of the large numbers of catfish found there ("there's one in every room"). This 467–foot dive was the world's first cave diving traverse, or through trip from one cave entrance to another.

Bob and Sue Friedman explored upstream from Catfish in 1969, finding the largest tunnel in the cave, a conduit 50 feet wide and 15 feet high that they followed 915 feet to the third entrance to the cave, Sue's Spring. Their progress was hindered by the tremendous velocity of the water, which has caused divers to compare a dive in Manatee to swimming up Niagara Falls. They quit 510 feet upstream from Sue's Spring.

1973 was the 100–year flood for the Suwannee River. As the river rose it exceeded the hydrostatic pressure of most of the tributary springs, causing them to reverse their flow to send blackwater into the caves. Only Jugg Hole and Manatee stayed clear. Jugg Hole is a relatively small cave (Court Smith and I walled it out at a penetration of 600 feet), so we concentrated on Manatee.

On February 25, Court and Lewis Holtzendorff explored 360 feet past where Bob and Sue had stopped. Returning the next weekend with Dana Turner, Dutch Vande Noord, and me, Lewis added another 160 feet. The visibility in this area was only 10 feet instead of the 30 feet typical in the rest of the cave, so we named it The Sewer. We stopped at a high dome whose floor was covered with small fossil bones. Since the dome had no opening to the surface, how did the bones get there? They were possibly a couple of million years old, but the limestone of the cave was approximately 50 million years old, so the bones had not been dissolved from the rock. Since the cave does not contain any stalactites, there is no evidence that it was once dry. The most likely explanation is that an enormous ancient flood of the Suwannee had washed the bones back into the cave, but we were awed by the thought of a reverse current strong enough to send heavy bones more than 1,000 feet over high sand dunes and boulders and down an irregular, winding corridor with several minor restrictions. An archaeologist, convinced that excavation by scientists was impossible upstream from Sue's Spring, asked me to retrieve samples of the bones and any human artifacts we found, after carefully noting their depth and position in the cave.

While struggling upstream against Manatee's ferocious torrent is an ordeal, exiting from the cave is quite pleasant. I was drifting out with the current, enjoying the physical sensation of flight when I noticed that the water became clearer. I

Silvery bubbles glisten as a diver exits through the Catfish Hotel entrance to the Manatee Springs Cave System. (*Photo by Henry Nicholson*)

Divers exit Manatee Springs via the Catfish Hotel entrance. (*Photo by Henry Nicholson*)

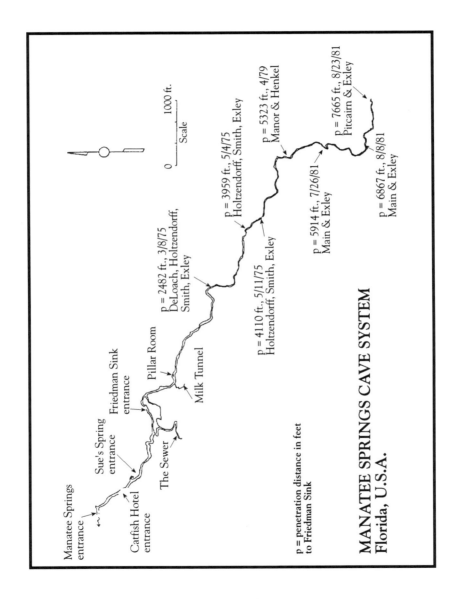

Manatee Springs entrance

Sue's Spring entrance

Friedman Sink entrance

Catfish Hotel entrance

Pillar Room

Milk Tunnel

The Sewer

p = 2482 ft., 3/8/75
DeLoach, Holtzendorff,
Smith, Exley

p = 4110 ft., 5/11/75
Holtzendorff, Smith, Exley

p = 3959 ft., 5/4/75
Holtzendorff, Smith, Exley

p = 5323 ft., 4/79
Manor & Henkel

p = 5914 ft., 7/26/81
Main & Exley

p = 7665 ft., 8/23/81
Pitcairn & Exley

p = 6867 ft., 8/8/81
Main & Exley

0   1000 ft.
          Scale

p = penetration distance in feet
to Friedman Sink

MANATEE SPRINGS CAVE SYSTEM
Florida, U.S.A.

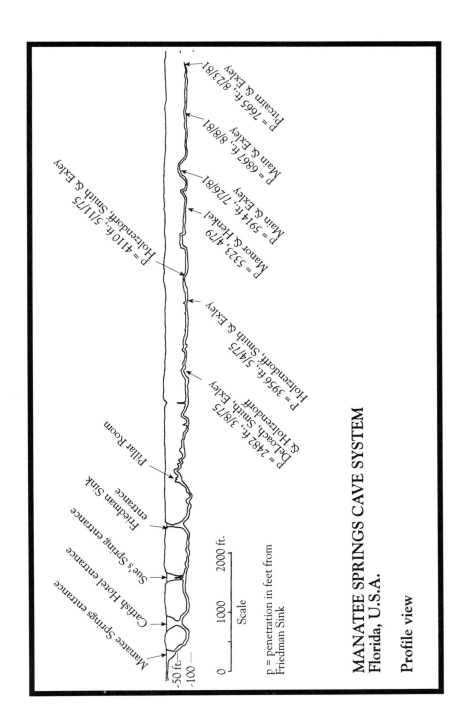

MANATEE SPRINGS CAVE SYSTEM
Florida, U.S.A.

Profile view

p = penetration in feet from
Friedman Sink

Scale

0   1000   2000 ft.

~50 ft.
-100

Manatee Springs entrance
Catfish Hotel entrance
Sue's Spring entrance
Friedman Sink entrance
Pillar Room

p = 2482 ft; 3/8/75
DeLoach, Smith, Exley
& Holtzendorff

p = 3956 ft; 5/4/75
Holtzendorff, Smith & Exley

p = 4110 ft; 5/11/75
Holtzendorff, Smith & Exley

p = 5323; 4/79
Manor & Henkel

p = 5914 ft; 7/26/81
Main & Exley

p = 6867 ft; 8/8/81
Main & Exley

p = 7665 ft; 8/23/81
Pitcairn & Exley

swam up a high sand dune on the right that seemed to extend to the wall. Beyond its crest, however, I saw a hidden 10–foot–diameter conduit that appeared to be carrying the main flow of water. We had learned that following the main flow in underwater caves usually led us to the most extensive areas, so I tied off a small spool of line and beckoned to the others to follow. After 170 feet, I ran out of line, but the cave was still going strong. It averaged 20 feet wide and 10 feet high. The nearly black walls made following the undulating sand floor much like flying over a white glacier on a starless night.

The next weekend Court, Lewis, and I installed another 600 feet of line in the new passage. The river was receding, so the current in the cave was even stronger than on our previous dives. On the way out, I found what appeared to be a clay vase on top of a sand dune. I turned my lamp off and strained my eyes upward. There was no daylight coming down to reveal another entrance.

At the surface Lewis turned to us and spat out his mouth-piece. "Whew," he sighed. "That current is really something. We aren't going to be able to go much further without the help of another entrance."

"Well, I didn't find another entrance, but I did find this." I pulled out my heavy flower pot and passed it to Court. He was unimpressed. "K–Mart sells these for a quarter each," he explained.

But I thought Lewis' eyes would bulge out of their sockets. "Vase my ass," he explained. "Don't you know a Spanish water jar when you see one?"

"A what?"

"Yeah. See here?" He pointed to the irregular rim of the pot. "This is where the top broke off."

"I didn't see any top, but I didn't look very hard." I frowned, thinking. "Hey. Do you know who crossed the river near here?"

Lewis' eyes widened. "DeSoto."

"Sure. They probably stopped to get water and accidentally dropped it, then a reverse current carried it all the way from Sue's Spring."

Court hefted the heavy jug. "Ain't no current carried this thing nowhere."

Five days later we were joined by Dana for another dive upstream from Sue's Spring. Our main objective was to explore more cave, but my archaeologist friend wanted me to look for the rest of the water jar. Mindful of Court's comment, I also wanted to give the ceiling above the sand dune where I found the bottom of the jug another careful examination. Perhaps I had missed something.

We were only 300 feet into the dive when Lewis flashed his light at me and gave me the thumb up signal to abort the dive. Since anyone on a cave diving team can call any dive at any time for any reason, the four of us immediately turned back. Back at Sue's Spring it turned out that Lewis had broken the waist strap on his tank harness, a minor problem that he probably could have contended with. It would have reduced his ability to handle emergencies because of his unstable body position, however, and possibly jeopardized the safety of the other members of the team.

Since we had used a substantial amount of air on the aborted dive, the three remaining divers spent a few minutes planning a new air turn–around point. Half an hour after resubmerging, we reached the dune where I found the bottom of the jar. I decided to check the ceiling on the way in since our rising exhaust bubble might knock silt loose from the ceiling and hide any surface openings. The ceiling was very irregular, with lots of pockets, pendants and arches, and surprisingly large, 30 feet wide by 50 feet long. Precariously balanced on one of the arches was the missing top of my clay jar! There had to be an opening somewhere above me. After several minutes of searching I had found nothing but dead ends. Maybe the opening had collapsed and closed up in the

past 300–400 years. While my companions below me flashed
their lights at me impatiently, I decided to check one last area
before continuing on. This spot was only 16 feet deep. I swam
up to it and peered upward. Through a mess of logs and rocks
I was certain that I saw daylight coming through a tiny hole an
inch in diameter! Then my exhaust bubbles hit the silt around
the hole and obliterated the visibility.

We continued upstream against the vicious current, pushing off the ceiling with our fins and pulling on rocks since the
flow was too strong for swimming. We explored another 400
feet, discovering another side passage discharging murky water
similar to that of The Sewer. Beyond that point, the water
became very clear in the main passage, with visibility approaching 60 feet. We rode out with the current, swooping up
and down over the undulating floor. It was like being on a
roller coaster, with the added fun of having to stay alert to
avoid running into rock projections.

Back at the surface, I excitedly told the others about the
opening to the surface. Lewis was skeptical. "You sure you
didn't just see your dive light reflected from air bubbles on the
ceiling?"

"No, I'm certain it was daylight."

"But it was only an inch in diameter. How are we going to
get through?"

"Dig."

"Dig?" Lewis frowned. "Underwater?"

"Why not?" I replied. "Dry cavers have done it for years.
How do you think they got Floyd Collins out of Sand Cave?"

"Dead," said Court.

"Besides," Lewis added, "We don't have any ideas where
this sinkhole of yours is."

He was right. The primitive cave surveying methods we
had in 1973 were impossible to use in the severe current of
Manatee. My tentative compass readings in the cave suggested that the cave was headed toward a remote area of the

park, so the four of us spread out in the forest and started to search. All we had to find was a small pond in the dense woods. Unfortunately, the ground was packed with dozens of small, water–filled depressions, all of which looked alike. Most were covered with duckweed, a dense floating plant that made the surface look like a bright green carpet. Below the duckweed was only the dark brown of surface water rather than the azure tint of the cave, however.

We had just about given up hope when I heard a shout from Lewis. Hurrying through the palmettos and scrub oaks, I saw him standing on the edge of yet another duckweed–covered pond, holding a stick in the water. "Look at this," he said, swirling the stick to clear a spot through the dense floating plants. The water was blue!

Two days later, Dana, Court, and I dived Sue's Spring again with the idea of trying to dig out the opening from inside the cave. Two hundred feet before reaching the new sink, the exhaust port of Dana's regulator began to leak water, so we had to abort the dive. Then, on the morning of March 24, I spent a miserable two hours free diving from the surface without equipment to clear the opening. Since the opening was very narrow – only 3 feet wide after all my work – I was the only one in the water. Court, Lewis, and Dana sat on the bank and laughed while I wrestled dozens of logs, sticks, and rocks to the surface in the cool 73° F water. Every time I surfaced to hand my helpers another chunk of wood, I was attacked by clouds of voracious mosquitos, most of which seemed to instinctively head for that one spot between my shoulder blades that I could not reach.

"I thought that last mosquito was big enough to cart you off," Court observed as he doused himself liberally with more insect repellent.

"He would have, but I was drained of all blood an hour ago." I sat on the bank to wait for the silt that I had stirred up excavating to settle so I could check to see if my suffering had been worthwhile. I was coated with the slimy duckweed.

Lewis puffed thoughtfully on his pipe. "We took a vote while you were down wallowing in the mud. If you didn't come back we were going to name this place Exley Sink in your memory."

I grinned, and took another look at the mud and slime. "Naw. Even a place this awful deserves a better name than that. Let's name it Friedman Sink since Bob did a lot of the original exploration here. Now let me borrow your light."

I took a big breath and pulled my way down the narrow shaft. At 16 feet the beam of my light revealed a large room below me. I bounced back to the surface.

"It goes."

Over the next two years we gradually pushed exploration of the main passage 2,482 feet past Friedman Sink. Joining us for some of the dives were Paul DeLoach, Tex Chalkley, Bob Goodman, and Kirby Sullivan. We discovered two 60–foot–diameter rooms, one with a large solution pillar five feet in diameter. Just past the Pillar Room, the tunnel ascended to a floor depth of only 34 feet, then gradually sloped back to the 90–foot level down two long gravel slides that we named the Slippery Dips. The severe current made further exploration extremely difficult and tiring. We decided to wait until a severe flood of the nearby Suwannee River backed up over the spring, dimishing its flow.

Meanwhile we explored nearby Devils Eye, pushing its main passage to a penetration of 3,305 feet on April 20, 1975. The depth and size of Devil's Eye was nearly identical to Manatee, but the reduced current enabled us to stage extra tanks, a technique I had devised during our 1970 explorations at Blue Springs near Madison, Florida. Stage tanks are single tanks with regulators that we breathe a third out of before dropping them; then we switch to the double 100's on our backs, breathing a third of them before turning back. On the way out we would pick up the stage tanks so that we always had

Court Smith and Sheck Exley surface with the shard that led to the discovery of Friedman Sink. (*Photo by Henry Nicholson*)

a two–thirds reserve for the trip out. Originally we had carried the tanks, but Court devised a system of hooking the stage tanks to a diver's chest and waist freeing his arms for other tasks and further streamlining his body.

Floods severe enough to slow Manatee's current occur only a few times in a decade. The relatively slack period lasts only two or three weeks at the most. One such period occurred in the spring of 1975. On May 3, Court, Lewis, and I made a dive in Friedman to check conditions and found that the current was greatly reduced and visibility had improved. We left one full stage tank for each of us on a pile of rocks between the Slippery Dips about 1,100 feet from Friedman Sink.

The next day we entered Friedman Sink with one stage tank each in addition to the double 100's on our backs. We breathed from the stage tanks until we reached the full tanks we had left the previous day, then dropped them. We clipped all the tanks to the permanent guideline so that we could find them even in a silt–out. After checking the other tanks to make sure that they were still full, we continued into the cave, breathing from our doubles.

I enjoyed being able to swim leisurely through passages where we had to push, pull and fight to make any progress at normal flow. Visibility was in excess of 60 feet, imparting an attractive blue hue to objects viewed in the distance. Two thousand feet from Friedman, I passed under the Big Crevice, a 30–foot–high dead end rift in the ceiling, and signalled to Court and Lewis that we were almost to the end of the line. Six minutes later I spotted the end of the line next to the left wall and looped around it the end of my 600–foot spool. We checked air and exchanged okay signals, then I led the way onward.

The passage averaged about 20 feet wide and half as high, ascending to a depth of 60 feet over a series of sand mounds and low rubble piles, then returned to 70 feet to enter a flat sand plain. We were surprised to see a four–foot–high step of bedrock extending the width of the cave. At the step the cave made a dramatic 90 degree turn to the left. The floor of the cave started to change character as the bedrock began to appear regularly through the clay layers, sand piles and fallen rock.

One hundred feet further along, my line spool ran out and I started to tie off the line. Someone flashed a light at me, so I stopped and turned, catching an unmistakable gleam in Lewis' eyes. He held up his 600 foot spool. We had never added more than 600 feet of line on a single line on a single dive. I checked my air pressure gauge. There was still a long way to go before I reached my two–thirds reserve, so I signalled okay and held out the looped end of my line to Lewis. He threaded the end of his spool through it, wrapped the line once against a nearby projection, and took off. Cave divers generally adhere to the concept of penetration in increments in exploring caves. That way they gradually familiarize themselves with the landmarks and features of the new area, which helps navigation on the way out, and minimizes the stress of confrontation with the unknown. Tom Mount, who helped explore Devil's Eye and Blue Springs near Madison, often cited 200 feet as the ideal amount of additional cave to explore per dive. Our team frequently exceeded that figure, but now we had more than tripled it. Soon added to that stress as we passed the 3,305 foot mark was the stress of knowing that we had been farther from air in any cave than anyone. To combat the anxiety I reassured myself with frequent air checks and by mentally humming a relaxing tune, appropriately named "Fool on the Hill."

Two hundred feet further, Lewis pulled his way into a three–foot–high restriction. Red clay silt streamed out behind him, reducing the visibility to a few feet. Court glanced back at me, shrugged and followed. The current was still strong in the restriction, so to make progress I had to use my fins to push off the ceiling. As I struggled through the tight spot, I reflected that negotiating the restriction at normal flow would be impossible. Beyond that point the passage opened up again and the water cleared. While Court prudently waited for me, Lewis progressed 50 feet further, full of the excitement of virgin cave and record setting. He led us through 300 feet of passage 30 feet wide and 10 feet high, then paused beneath a 20–foot high dome, out of line.

Not to be left out, Court quickly produced his spool of line and charged off into the unknown, Lewis hot on his heels. We had already added 1,200 feet! Logically my mind said that we were quite safe since we still had more than two thirds of our air left, but emotionally, anxiety still fought for control, as my body tried to elevate my heart rate and respiration. I tried not to think about the distance and the unknown, concentrating instead on the fascinating cave features, beautiful blue vistas, and inner rendition of "Fool on the Hill."

The passage made two 90–degree turns, first left, then right; then Lewis flashed Court down, pointing at his air pressure gauge. He had reached his two–thirds reserve so it was time to turn around. Court quickly tied off under a 10–foot–wide span of rock I named the Arc de Triomphe, then we drifted out. My anxiety decreased each minute as we drew nearer to our stage tanks and our reserve air grew percentage–wise from twice as much as we needed to get out to three times as much, then four times as much. Nearly two hours after entering the cave we picked up our stage tanks and continued to Friedman Sink. During a very cramped hour and a half of decompression in the entrance shaft at Friedman I totalled up our accomplishments. We had explored an additional 1474 feet of tunnel to a record distance of 3,956 feet from Friedman Sink. It had been exhilarating dive, but it somehow was not enough.

It never is.

The next weekend we installed fresh stage bottles at 1,900 feet, then on May 11 the three of us returned to the Arc de Triomphe to explore more cave. We hoped to make the first 5,000–foot cave dive, but Court inexplicably flashed his light at me after I had installed less than 200 feet. Usually he was the least conservative of my diving partners, but he called the dive only because he had a bad feeling. Since Court is not especially superstitious, he was undoubtedly affected by the same distance–record anxiety that I had felt the previous weekend. Since excessive anxiety can reduce a diver's ability to handle emergencies, we quickly headed out without any discussion, inwardly appreciating Court's good judgement.

You can always dive another day.

Almost always. By the next weekend the river had dropped and the current in the Manatee Springs Cave System was nearly back to normal. Over the next several years further exploration was precluded by change in park policy restricting access to Friedman Sink and the lack of floods severe enough to slow the spring substantially. Meanwhile, Paul DeLoach, Dale Sweet, John Zumrick, Mary Ellen Eckhoff, and I made long dives in Hole in the Wall and Blue Springs near Marianna, Florida. Using two stage tanks per diver in addition to back–mounted double 100's, we progressed from double–stage dives to triple– and even quadruple–stage dives requiring several set–up and retrieval dives in addition to the long push dive.

In early 1979, Dave Manor and Lewis Henkel quietly secured permission to enter Friedman and extended explora-

Dana Turner, Court Smith and Sheck Exley clown around with add–on spools of guideline. (*Photo by Lewis Holtzendorff*)

tion to 5,323 feet. Their ordeal was such that they did not return to retrieve their expensive stage tanks for several months, risking having them ruined or stolen. A borrowed guideline reel was left at 5,323 feet for posterity. "No one will ever reach that reel," Henkel told the reel's owner.

News of their dive and Friedman's reopening soon leaked out. In 1981, Paul DeLoach, Clark Pitcairn, Mary Ellen Eckhoff, John Zumrick, and I pushed exploration of a huge section of Big Dismal Sink near Tallahassee to a penetration of 5,847 feet using motorized scooters. The torpedo–like devices enabled us to save time and effort while hauling four–stage tanks and to overcome the greater depth of the dive (135 feet). Unfortunately, the scooters were not powerful enough to make any headway against the severe current of the Mana-tee Springs Cave System. On the other hand, we could not wait for a flood of the Suwannee that was substantial enough to slow the water flow. Sometimes it was more than three years between floods, and the two weekends of slack–water diving caused by the flood were not nearly enough for the many set up and retrieval dives needed for a multiple–stage push. We needed some way of handling the current at normal water levels.

During our 1979 dives at Blue Springs near Marianna, I experimented with a new technique which John Zumrick promptly christened groveling. Far from the graceful swim-ming and pulling techniques which take advantage of our weightlessness underwater, groveling consists primarily of crawling on the bottom. The only difference from crawling is that the groveling diver has to balance on fin tips instead of knees so that stage tanks hooked below him do not drag along the bottom. A big disadvantage of the technique is that it stirs up so much silt that visibility can be very limited for divers downstream. We solved this problem by proceeding into the cave alongside one another instead of in the single file ar-rangement customary for cave diving teams. The optimum size for a groveling cave diving team is two divers since larger groups would run the risk of losing contact with the guideline even if the passage was wide enough.

On July 26, 1981, Bill Main and I made our first long push in Friedman. Aside from the difficulties we had diving and decompressing described at the start of this chapter, the dive went very well. We followed Manor and Henkel's guideline through three tight restrictions at 4,300, 4,350, and 4,500 feet, dropped down a 12–foot pit at 4800 feet and found the missing reel at 5,323 feet. Then we went another 588 feet, discovering another pit and some bizarre rock formations, including a huge hollow boulder that vaguely resembled an elephant. Perhaps equally important, we surveyed all of our discovery as well as Manor and Henkel's and added it to the rapidly–expanding map I was making for the park staff.

The dive took five stage tanks, so two set–up dives were required to get all the equipment in place. As our expedition continued, it became obvious that getting the last stage bottles in place (those to be used farthest in) was a major problem. To avoid long stage dives to install stage tanks, we began the practice of leaving our farthest full stage tanks in the cave unless they were needed on the way out to handle an emergency. This practice and the severe current of Manatee made frequent maintenance of our equipment a necessity. Fortunately, Bill is one of those rare individuals who can fix almost anything, and has the energy to do so.

The next weekend we tried another long push, but Bill felt unusually fatigued at 2,000 feet and called the dive. On August 8, we tried again, with six stage tanks in addition to our back–mounted double 100's. This time we managed to explore an additional 953 feet to a distance of 6,867 feet. Strangely, this entire section headed due south instead of the ESE trend dominant throughout the rest of the main passage. We tied off at an apparent fork in the cave. Would this cave never end? Our dives were becoming exceptionally tedious, lasting more than seven hours including four hours of decompression. The exceptional exposure tables that we were using to calculate our decompression requirements were poorly tested and not as reliable as the shorter schedules. Then there was the cold. The 10–foot decompression stop in Friedman's three–foot–diameter entrance shaft did not permit any moving around. While Bill and I cracked jokes about decompressing in each other's arms, the reality was that after seven hours immersion in 73° F water, our bodies and minds were numb. We read cheap paperback books underwater to take our minds off what we were doing and to keep from going crazy from the boredom of decompression.

Then there was the financial drain—and logistics problems. Our dives required more than a dozen tanks and regulators per diver, more than most dive shops stock. Both of us had invested thousands of dollars in equipment and had to borrow or rent more to make the dives. There was also the expense of frequent overhauls to stage regulators as a result of being dragged in the silt and banged on rock. Also, the rubber parts were ruined by algae and bacteria in the water.

Late one night I got a phone call from Bill. "Sheck," he began, "Jane and I have talked it over and I really don't want to go on this next dive."

I was surprised, because on our 6,867–footer, Bill had installed the last section of the line and I was the one who had called the dive. I normally do not believe in talking people into making dives, but this was different. Bill is one of our best divers, and lad a lot invested in our Manatee project. "Are you sure? If you need some help finding more tanks and regulators, maybe I can scrounge some."

"Thanks but no thanks," he laughed. My regulators were famous for their rundown appearance, whereas Bill was a perfectionist about all of his equipment being shiny and clean at all times. "Why don't you make the dive with Clark? I'll help you any way I can."

Clark Pitcairn is one of the best cave divers I have ever seen, very strong and determined as well as calm and knowledgeable. He has the added advantage of youth, being more than 10 years younger than Bill and me. If he lived in Florida instead of Pennsylvania he would break all of the distance and depth records. Clark had already contributed to our project by lending me regulators and tanks and giving me free air at his dive shop in Jacksonville.

We spent the weekend of August 16 installing stage bottles, then made a 3,850 foot dive on August 22 to replace some of our more distant stage tanks. These set–up dives served the additional purpose of familiarizing Clark with the cave and our groveling technique. Fortunately, Bill and I had taken full tanks to 4,700 feet, our most remote stage point, and left them in full on our last dive, so it was not necessary to replace them. We spent the evening of the twenty-second with the map, carefully going over our plans and all the what–ifs: what if the cave silts out? what if we miss locating of our stage tanks? what if some of the regulators malfunction?, etc. Manatee Springs is a wonderful cave, but not wonderful enough to die in. A foolproof plan to contend with every emergency situation, no matter how unlikely, had to be evolved and committed to memory.

We entered the water early the next morning so we could avoid the blistering midday heat of Florida summer and be out of the park by the sundown closing time. Beneath our thick neoprene dry suits were three layers of wool. Perspiration trapped in the wool during the walk to the water would eventually cool, causing us to lose valuable body heat during the dive, so it had to be minimized. Likewise, the wet–suit–clad diver's privilege of urinating in his suit could not be permitted. Clark utilized Paul DeLoach's external catheter, the collection bag strapped to the inside of his thigh. I relied on a large bladder and will power.

There is a certain amount of pre–dive stress before any

major dive. Some divers have trouble sleeping, others try to relieve the stress by talking, telling jokes, etc. I never have trouble sleeping, but have been known to talk. This dive was different. Our preparations were quiet, without any pre–dive banter; our thoughts consumed by the many details of our dive. Once or twice I paused to use my unusually aware senses, sharpened by the stress of the forthcoming dive, to listen to the call of a bird in a tree or to smell the musky aroma of the wood. If being alive is a relative condition, then I attain my highest degree of aliveness just before a big dive.

Underwater, my mood changed. Now I was a beast of burden, whose sole purpose was to get a certain amount of equipment to the end of the line at 6,867 feet. My mind shifted into neutral and my hands and legs automatically sought the best purchase to propel my heavily–laden body along the bottom. From our many previous dives, I instinctively knew what part of the passage provided the easiest route. Another part of my mind provided a subconscious awareness of Clark's location, condition, and mood. It was as if I had the lateral lines of a fish and could sense minute vibrations from him in the water.

At each staging area, we mechanically discarded spent bottles and picked up fresh ones. Our air was planned so that at no point would we have less than twice as much air to come out on as we had used going in. If a stage tank had somehow developed a leak and lost some air, then the dive would be automatically cancelled.

At 5,323 feet, we passed the end of the Manor/Henkel line, and Clark and I got ready to drop our last stage tanks. We deposited them on the lip of a 15 foot pit that Bill and I had discovered, then switched to the doubles on our backs. We were making excellent time now, unencumbered by stage bottles. Two hours after the dive started, we reached the end of Bill's line at 6,867 feet. Now my mind snapped into focus and I was fully alert. I tied off my new line and led the way into the right–hand passage at the fork, which was carrying most of the water. A hundred feet further I spotted another opening in the left wall, confirmation that the left–hand fork was merely a bypass that paralleled the main passage like many similar passages throughout the system. Our route was now due east instead of along the southward trend Bill and I had recorded on our previous dive.

To avoid poor visibility on our way out, we stopped groveling as soon as we reached the end of the old line, switching to less efficient techniques that were more tiring but stirred up less silt behind us. I was relieved when, at 7,200 feet, we entered a larger area with greatly reduced flow. Unfortunately, this nice subway–sized tunnel, almost perfectly straight for 400 feet, had a ceiling covered with flaky, light–colored material that fell like snow behind us, dislodged by our rising exhaust bubbles.

I ran out of line at 7,300 feet and Clark tied on his line. He swam so quickly that I had trouble keeping up with him. At 7,600 feet, the Snow Tunnel ended in a high jumble of boulders. Clark squeezed into a narrow, silty slot, his bubbles instantly silting it out. We spent the next several minutes checking the fissures in the boulders; most were emitting a substantial flow of water, but none were big enough to squeeze into. Clark tied off our line in the first slot at 7,665 feet, and I began surveying out. Since we had planned for enough air for an 8,000 foot dive, we were able to check all of the side passages in the Snow Tunnel on the way out. None went more than a few feet. Slowly it was dawning on us that we had walled out Manatee. The unconquerable was conquered.

We coasted with the current from the Snow Tunnel to Friedman Sink in an hour and a half. Our four–hour trip had taken nine tanks per diver. We consumed five more tanks each during our five–hour decompression schedule, then surfaced. We were happy with our achievement, but we felt a sense of loss. Now there would be no future expeditions in the

Manatee Springs Cave System, no renewal there of that strange yet somehow intimate companionship of divers and impossibly remote, virgin cave.

11

The Eternal Challenge

The sudden noise was deafening.

EARTHQUAKE! my mind screamed. In the thunderous roar, greatly magnified by the 140 feet of water which enveloped us, it seemed as if the entire cave was shaking to pieces and would come crashing down. Tensing my neck in expectation of the deluge of hundreds of tons of limestone, I instinctively steered my torpedo-like scooter away from the center of the tunnel and the greatest exposure. Then I realized that there was no safety to be found, and settled down in despair to wait. At the very least I expected a cloud of liquid mud at any moment, the result of a cataclysmic cave-in elsewhere, sealing us in our watery tomb forever. For an instant my eyes met Paul DeLoach's. His eyes were cool as ever, but he frowned, puzzled by the noise.

After minutes that seemed like hours, the din drained away. Paul tied off our guideline at a penetration of 2,480 feet from the entrance to the cave at Florida's Suwanacoochee Spring, our enthusiasm for the beckoning new passage greatly diminished. We gratefully started out of the cave, never encountering the wall of mud or the dreaded cave-in. Not until we were back to our 20-foot decompression stop and traditional underwater checkers game did the truth suddenly occur to me and I scribbled on my slate: Train?

After surfacing we asked at the nearby state agricultural inspection station, "Yep, the 8:05 was right on time." When we plotted our survey data, we learned that we had been directly under the tracks of the Seaboard Coast Line Railroad, separated from it by only 170 feet of rock. Unfortunately, we also learned that the tunnel was headed northwest, almost directly away from the gigantic Cathedral-Falmouth Cave System, to which we had hoped it connected. Since Clark Pitcairn and I had just connected the only other tunnel in Suwanacoochee to nearby Edward's Spring, where the water was much warmer than that of Cathedral, our hopes for a connection to that magnificent cave now seemed frustrated. What we had instead was a tightly coiled system of corridors that crossed under *two* major rivers (the Suwannee and the Withlacoochee), *three* of Florida's rural counties, and the Seaboard Coast Line Railroad.

ᘉ

I spent New Year's Eve of 1970 the same way that I have celebrated 20 of the last 21 New Year's: in an underwater cave at the stroke of midnight. Over a late breakfast in Live Oak, Florida, the next morning, Carl Fowler and I discussed the prospects for the day's diving. "Why not Devil's Eye?" I asked.

Carl glanced at his watch. "I dunno," he said. "The Eye is over an hour away, and by the time we made a long dive in there we'd be late getting to bed again."

"Well, we dived Madison Blue last night so that's out. How about Little River?"

"Squirrelsville. I'm tired of that place."

I slid a pair of coffee-stained topographic maps from a tube and spread them on the table. "Ever head of Falmouth Springs?"

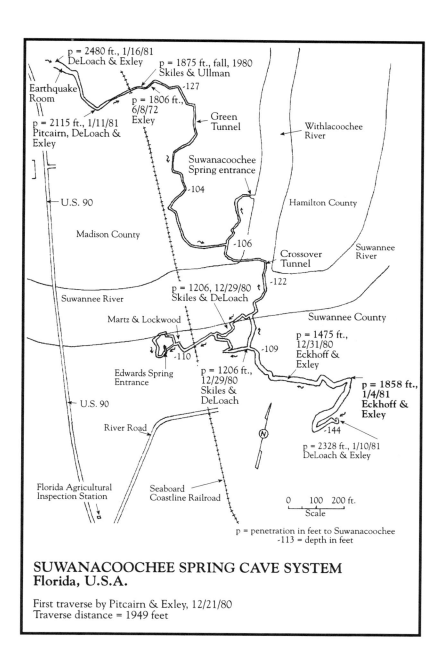

p = 2480 ft., 1/16/81
DeLoach & Exley

p = 1875 ft., fall, 1980
Skiles & Ullman

Earthquake
Room

-127

p = 1806 ft.,
6/8/72
Exley

Green
Tunnel

Withlacoochee
River

p = 2115 ft., 1/11/81
Pitcairn, DeLoach &
Exley

Suwanacoochee
Spring entrance

-104

U.S. 90

Hamilton County

Madison County

-106

Crossover
Tunnel

Suwannee
River

-122

p = 1206, 12/29/80
Skiles & DeLoach

Suwannee River

Suwannee County

Martz & Lockwood

-109

p = 1475 ft.,
12/31/80
Eckhoff &
Exley

-110

Edwards Spring
Entrance

p = 1206 ft.,
12/29/80
Skiles &
DeLoach

p = 1858 ft.,
1/4/81
Eckhoff &
Exley

U.S. 90

-144

River Road

N

p = 2328 ft., 1/10/81
DeLoach & Exley

Florida Agricultural
Inspection Station

Seaboard
Coastline Railroad

0   100   200 ft.
Scale

p = penetration in feet to Suwanacoochee
-113 = depth in feet

SUWANACOOCHEE SPRING CAVE SYSTEM
Florida, U.S.A.

First traverse by Pitcairn & Exley, 12/21/80
Traverse distance = 1949 feet

Carl took a bite out of a slice of jam-covered toast. "Sure. It's listed on my road map as a tourist attraction along with Silver Springs and Wakulla."

"Right. It's located three miles from the Suwannee just west of here."

"Three miles from the river?" Carl frowned. "Can't be much to it if it's that far from a discharge point. Caves around here usually wall out less than half a mile from the river."

I smiled. "That's the intriguing part. Falmouth flows along the surface for a hundred yards before returning underground, and the geological survey says the flow is more than any other spring in north Florida. Heck, *Ripley's Believe-It-Or-Not* calls it the "World's Shortest River.""

Carl dropped his toast and leaned forward. "There must be an enormous cave there. What are we waiting for?"

"Dogs and a barbed wire fence. Falmouth has been closed since two teenagers drowned there in 1962. But look at this." I traced a line from Falmouth to the closest part of the Suwannee River with my fork. About halfway there it crossed a small blue oval next to some railroad tracks. "Think we ought to check it out?"

"Shootahreckon."

After a short ride, we struggled across the tracks in our gear, then crossed the remnants of a barbed wire fence. The rusty wires were down at one point, and technically we were not trespassing since there were no posted signs. Nevertheless, we kept carefully out of sight from traffic on nearby US 90. Adverse publicity from cave diving accidents and lawsuits made it highly likely that the landowner would tell us to leave if he saw us.

"That's one big sinkhole," Carl ventured, admiring the 150-foot-long oval pool before us.

"Why don't we name it Fowler Sink," I suggested.

Carl grinned. "Sounds good to me."

Despite the pretty blue-green hue of the water, the visibility was only five feet. After tying our guideline to a submerged log near the surface, I dropped slowly feet first to avoid impaling myself on any branches from the many trees that had fallen in. The sink appeared to be two 70-foot-diameter vertical pits in the limestone that had joined in one wall. The water was unusually cold, which made a direct connection to the 70° F water of Falmouth unlikely. After a half hour of searching the base of the shaft walls and dodging javelins of waterlogged saplings loosened from their resting places above us by our rising exhaust bubbles, I paused near the northwest end at the deepest point. The only way on was a tiny, log-and mud-choked slot at a depth of 90 feet. I shivered, not just because of the cold water. No way anyone was ever going through that nasty opening. So much for a back door into the Falmouth System.

Later that year, John Harper and Randy Hylton tried a more direct approach. Randy's philosophy toward dogs and barbed wire was simple: "A good man never lets a fence stand in his way." They used Randy's Land Rover to make a trail through the forest behind Falmouth Springs, then slipped through a gap in the fence and hiked half a mile in the night to dive the upstream entrance to the spring. Beyond the 50-foot maw of the spring where the teenagers had drowned a decade earlier, they found an enormous passage 60-80 feet wide and 10-15 feet high. From the entrance at a depth of 50 feet, the deep sand and mud floor sloped to a depth of 120 feet, then leveled off. Two hundred feet back they passed the end of previous explorations by NSS divers in the 1959-1962 era. Then 737 feet further on, the roof of the vast cave opened above them to reveal a silvery moonbeam plummeting through a hundred feet of water. John named this perfectly round, 50-foot-wide opening Aquarius Sink.

Continuing upstream from Aquarius on their secret mid-night dives, John and Randy found that the tunnel narrowed to about 40-50 feet wide and ascended a huge sand dune before plunging back to the 120-foot base level. Not only was it the widest underwater cave passage ever discovered in the Suwannee River Valley, but also John and Randy were amazed that there were no side passages. Virtually all Florida's caves form patterns like the shape of a tree – a short trunk near the spring followed by an extensive system of smaller branches containing most of the cave's total length. Yet here they were, nearly four miles from the nearest possible spring, and they were still only in the trunk section! Their excitement increased on every dive, but finally they had to stop their explorations 1,200 feet upstream from Aquarius for fear that they would not have enough air in their double 90's to return to the surface.

They feverishly searched the woods beyond Aquarius for another entrance. Finally Randy found an oval duckweed-covered pool about 60 feet long and half as wide on some old church property. Located at the base of a 50-foot-deep depression and shielded from the sky by immense hickory and gum trees as well as a near-record live oak that hung completely over the pool, the pond had completely escaped the notice of surveyors, so was not shown on any topographic maps. Aware that several of Florida's best cave dives lay below similar weed-covered ponds, Randy dived in holding his breath. Beneath the duckweed he saw a couple of logs spanning a circular opening 16 feet in diameter. Farther down, the shaft opened into an immense canyon where everything dropped into a blue-green void.

Returning with tanks, Randy and John swam down the canyon, gawking at the parallel rock walls 40 feet apart and nearly 300 feet long. The canyon was as high as a 13-story building, making it easily the largest single room ever discovered in the Suwannee River Valley. It was capped by a flat roof of purest white limestone. A broad beam of sunlight illuminated the canyon through the 16-foot diameter opening. The water was so clear that after their exhaust bubbles had made

John Harper and Randy Hylton, discoverers of Cathedral Canyon. (*Photo by John Harper*)

an opening in the duckweed they could look up from a depth of 130 feet and see clouds in the sky above the limbs of the overhanging oak. Because of the sink's unsurpassed combination of size and beauty, it was named Cathedral Canyon.

The base of the far end of the canyon opened into a 50-foot-wide tunnel with a strong flow headed away from the Cathedral entrance. Five hundred feet further on, they spotted the end of the line they had laid from Aquarius, and continued to that sink. The 1,711 foot traverse from Cathedral Canyon to Aquarius was the second–longest dive ever made from one cave entrance to another at the time.

On October 15, 1971, I made our first dive in Cathedral. Because of its enormous distance from the Suwannee River, it is very unusual for the dark brown river water to backflood into

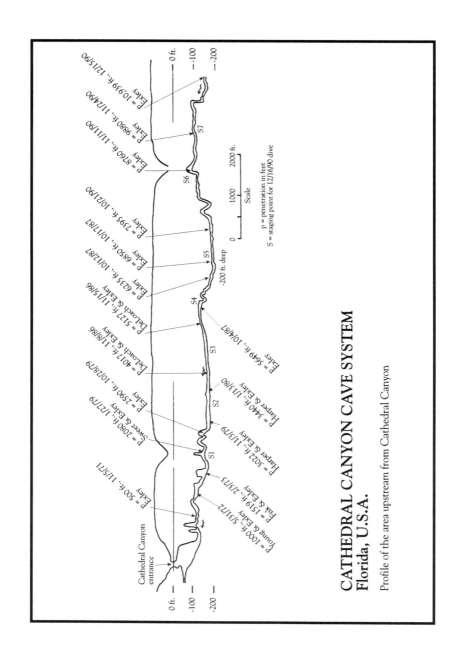

CATHEDRAL CANYON CAVE SYSTEM
Florida, U.S.A.

Profile of the area upstream from Cathedral Canyon

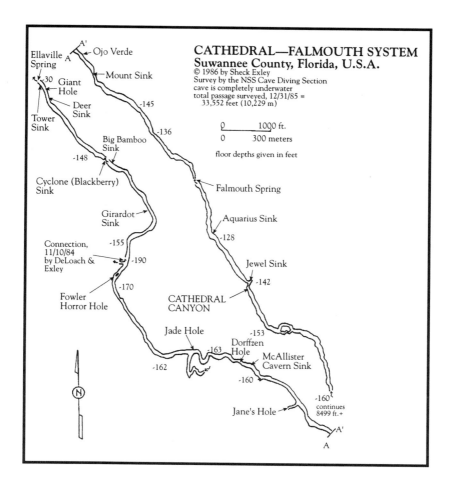

CATHEDRAL—FALMOUTH SYSTEM
Suwannee County, Florida, U.S.A.
© 1986 by Sheck Exley
Survey by the NSS Cave Diving Section
cave is completely underwater
total passage surveyed, 12/31/85 =
33,552 feet (10,229 m)

0   1000 ft.
0   300 meters

floor depths given in feet

Ojo Verde
Ellaville
Spring
A' A
30 Giant
Hole
Mount Sink
Deer
Sink
-145
Tower
Sink
Big Bamboo
Sink
-136
-148
Cyclone (Blackberry)
Sink
Girardot
Sink
Falmouth Spring
Aquarius Sink
-128
Connection,
11/10/84
by DeLoach &
Exley
-155
-190
-170
Jewel Sink
-142
Fowler
Horror Hole
CATHEDRAL
CANYON
Jade Hole
-153
Dorffzen
-163 Hole
-162
McAllister
Cavern Sink
-160
-160
continues
8499 ft.+
Jane's Hole
A'
A
N

the cave at Cathedral. Unfortunately, this was one of those times, so instead of the usual clear blue-green water with visibility that has been known to exceed 100 feet, I could only see only about 15 feet. Since I could see only a small portion of one of the immense canyon walls during our descent, the entrance room seemed even larger to me than it really is.

I landed on a clean sand and rock bottom at a depth of 130 feet. Falmouth Springs was near its peak discharge of 500 cubic feet per second, all of which passes through the bottom of Cathedral, so it was all I could do to hang on to a car-sized boulder. Downstream was the route John and Randy had pioneered to Aquarius, a traverse I was anxious to duplicate. My objective, however, lay in the other direction: the unexplored passage leading upstream from Cathedral Canyon. While I caught my breath in an eddy behind the rock, I saw large black objects sticking out of the white sand. Swimming closer to investigate, I found that they were huge fossil bones, the remains of large animals that had fallen into the entrance room over the centuries. The bottom was literally covered with them.

I emerged from behind the boulder and grabbed rocks on the floor, pulling my way into the torrent. After 30 feet I saw the flat ceiling of a tunnel a dozen feet above me. I was in the virgin upstream passage of Cathedral. I curved over to the right wall, then swung back to the left. The mammoth conduit was nearly 60 feet wide, easily the largest underwater cave passage I had ever seen.

Two weeks later the visibility had improved to nearly 100 feet, allowing me to appreciate the great size of my discovery. The passage was 50 to 150 feet wide, quite large enough for a small submarine. There were stratospheric domes in the ceiling that shot straight up out of sight for more than 50 feet. Beneath the second of these domes I saw a huge sand dune so rippled by the current that it looked as though it were straight ·⊦ of the Sahara Desert. Near the top I found an ancient wooden washtub like those used by the pioneers, deeply imbedded in the sand. Swimming up the dome above it, I encountered a perfectly flat ceiling at a depth of 50 feet, with no hint of an opening to the surface. I concluded that the heavy washtub had fallen into Cathedral and had somehow been swept through 200 feet of passage by a reverse current during a severe flood of the Suwannee River. Since the tub had to be moved over the sizeable dune beneath the first dome, this was a considerable accomplishment and I could only shake my head in awe at the power of the current that must have raged through the cave.

On May 31, 1972, Billy Young and I pushed another 500 feet to a point 1,000 feet from Cathedral. The cave got even larger as we went back, the domes and depths even more spectacular. At one point we paused at the foot of a gigantic mountain of white sand, its ribbed side sloping steeply upward out of sight. Swimming upward, we found its crest 50 feet higher and named it Mount Everest.

A week later, we explored onward 450 feet into the awesome Grand Canyon, with perfectly straight, parallel, vertical walls 50 feet high and 300 feet long. At this point, the passage constricted to 30 feet wide and the floor was a roller coaster-like series of 15-foot-high waves of sand. Midway down the Grand Canyon, we discovered a low, 20-foot-wide side passage that we dubbed the China Route. Had the cave finally started to branch out?

We dived again two days later, and followed the winding China Route 300 feet. At that point our path was blocked by a vertical wall of peat mud. I ascended in a corkscrew pattern while shining my light on the mud and rock walls nearby. After swimming upward 40 feet, I found the way onward over the top of the huge pile of peat, which we named the Great Wall of China. We checked the ceiling for an opening above the peat, but once more found instead the flat roof character-istic of the domes in the Cathedral-Falmouth Cave System.

On the other side of the Great Wall, we followed the mud slope steeply downward to the base level of 130 feet, where it spilled outward into a gargantuan passage extending left and right out of sight. Had we discovered a completely new tunnel, or rejoined an unknown major passage leading out of the Grand Canyon? Unfortunately, we were now 1,928 feet from Cathedral, so the dives were very long and cold and required very large amounts of air. We had to go back.

Looking for something easier to explore, on October 26, 1972, Charlie Sturdevant and I moved some logs out of the virgin downstream opening to Falmouth Springs. Since the opening was only five feet in diameter, the rushing water sucked us into the ground like soapsuds down a bathtub drain. After a few feet we tumbled into a 40-foot-wide passage at a depth of 30 feet. I looked back at the narrow opening and scratched my head, vaguely wondering how hard it would be to get back out. I caught Charlie doing the same thing, and he shrugged at me and laughed a hoarse, inhaling laugh that was remarkably similar to my own. We followed the downward sloping passage for 500 feet first, then returned to try the opening. It was not easy, but we got out.

On a later dive, we added another 500 feet in the 40-foot-wide downstream passage, most of which was at a depth of 120 feet. Our success reminded me that earlier that year, Tom Mount had told me after I had taken him on a dive in Cathedral that he had been down to a similar depth in a nearby sinkhole. Since the sink was quite large and the passage leading downstream from Falmouth seemed headed straight toward it, we decided to check it out.

Two weeks later Lewis Holtzendorff, Court Smith, Dave Fisk, Dutch Vande Noord, and I dived Mount Sink. Normally the idea of five cave divers attempting to explore a virgin cave would be ridiculous, but we were confident that we would find another entrance to the Cathedral-Falmouth System, and by now we knew that Falmouth was typically large enough for a team of a dozen or more divers.

At Mount, we again struck paydirt, discovering a huge outflowing tunnel at 145 feet that headed off toward Falmouth. In a series of dives over the next two months Court, Lewis, Charlie, and I pushed this new passage nearly 2,000 feet. One strange discovery was that of still another giant mound of sand, this time with a Styrofoam cup of recent vintage sitting on top. Looking directly above this mound, dubbed Vendo Hill, we saw a three-foot-diameter hole in the ceiling. Peering into it with a light, I saw a large silty room with an unstable pile of logs and boulders perched directly above the tunnel we were traveling in. I started to ascend, then hesitated. There was no opening to the surface above me, and I certainly did not want to make one accidentally. We wisely continued on, leaving the room above Vendo Hill unexplored.

Sheck Exley hovers over huge boulders. (*Photo by Ned DeLoach*)

Meanwhile, Lewis found still another sinkhole between Fowler and Mount that Paul DeLoach, Billy Young, and I entered on November 25, 1972. We named this one, a virtual mirror image of Mount Sink, Jade Hole after the telltale blue-green hue of the Falmouth water. Then it was back to Cathedral, where on February 3, Dave Fisk and I found the main tunnel leading out of the far end of the Grand Canyon. We were making so many discoveries so fast in the cave that it was getting hard to keep track of them.

Then the 100–year flood intervened. Early 1973 was marred by the worst flooding of the Suwannee in recorded history, even worse than after the hurricanes of the mid-1960's. The river rose so high that it threatened to wash away the wooden trestles of the bridge for the Seaboard Coast Line Railroad, a disaster averted only by placing heavily loaded railroad cars on the bridge to hold it down. Every spring in the Suwannee River drainage basin except Jugg Hole and Mana-tee was reversed; millions of gallons of muddy river water poured into the ground. Even Falmouth was affected.

By summer, the water had receded, and Dave Cameron and Rory Dickens rediscovered McAllister Cavern Sink, a sink in the area that had been reported in *Skin Diver* magazine in 1962. A long-time cave diving instructor who has seen more than his share of caves, Rory's interest in the area had been whetted by a dive he and I had made in Cathedral the previous year. Surfacing in the night, he had pronounced to me in a hushed, reverential tone used by most Cathedral explorers, "That's the best cave dive I've ever made."

Located midway between Mount Sink and Jade Hole, McAllister Cavern Sink gave us renewed hope of somehow linking Jade with Mount. Court, Lewis, and I soon pushed nearly 1,500 feet from McAllister during a series of dives, discovering more large passage and high domes. Under one of the domes we found the remains of an old moonshine still, and I ran 100 feet of line up into the dome, to a depth of 60 feet, without seeing any daylight indicating a new entrance. Fearing another unstable situation similar to Vendo Hill upstream from Mount, we reluctantly retreated.

At McAllister, like so many of the sinks in the area, the only access to the water is down a steep game trail used by various wild animals. After the last dive, I was trudging back up the trail with all of my equipment on except my fins, which I was carrying in one hand. Near the top, I paused in the gathering darkness to rest, bending over to take the weight of the heavy twin 100-cubic-foot tanks off my shoulders. Suddenly there was a movement directly in front of me and I heard a loud thump followed by an ominous rattle. I straightened up and turned on my dive light to see the angry coil of a six-foot diamondback rattlesnake right next to me.

I carefully backed up and called down to the others to come on up while I had the snake spotted with my light. While Lewis went to my van to get my machete, I could

High domes are common in Cathedral, but are usually much bigger. (*Photo by Ned DeLoach*)

not help wondering about the thumping noise. Obviously the snake had been lying across the game trail waiting for food and my next step would have landed right on him if I had not stopped to rest. Was the thump simply caused by the weight of the heavy snake settling into its coil? Or had it actually struck at me with the lightning speed for which rattlers are famous before I could turn on my light, striking something like my fins to cause the noise?

My speculations were interrupted by the return of Lewis, who chopped at the snake and missed. It struck angrily at him twice before retreating down the steep bank of the sink. Lewis chased after him like a madman while I carefully followed, trying to keep the huge reptile in the beam of my light. Finally the snake was cornered against an oak tree and Lewis raised the machete high above his head to deliver the coup de grace. At this moment my gaze wandered to the steep slope between Lewis and me, where an abandoned gopher hole was directly above and behind him. My heart skipped a beat when I saw what lay there: another huge, coiled rattlesnake, its ugly head no more that 3 feet from the back of Lewis' neck!

"Lewis," I said very quietly but firmly, "don't move. There's another snake directly behind you."

Lewis carefully turned to confront the second snake, which for some reason was not rattling. With a sudden, violent downstroke he dispatched that reptile, then quickly spun to hack the other one to pieces.

Our progress through the bushes back to the cars was unusually slow and cautious.

The rattlesnake incident robbed us of our enthusiasm, and it was not until more than two years later that any more exploration was done in the area's caves. We were further dismayed by having put a lot of line in five different, obviously related caves and not making a single connection. Finally, in the fall of 1975, Court and Lewis put 500 feet of line in the hitherto unentered downstream side of Jade Hole, and our interest returned. The three of us put 350 feet more line in the upstream side of Jade, then returned with Ed Hall to explore another 500 on the downstream side.

A bombshell hit the cave diving community four days later when Lewis Holtzendorff died in a freak accident on an experimental mixed gas dive in a deep spring near Tallahassee. Lewis was not only a charter NSSCDS member and vice president and director of NACD, he was also one of our very best divers at the time. He had completed a dive to 260 feet and was proceeding though what should have been a routine decompression schedule on pure oxygen when suddenly at 50 feet he went into a convulsion and died. Pure oxygen can become toxic and cause convulsions to swimming divers as shallow as 30 feet, but incidents involving resting divers during decompression are extremely rare. It was ironic that he perished on a dive on which he was trying to find a way to prevent a repeat of the mysterious death of another friend and expert cave diver, Dana Turner.

Court and I connected to a new sink a month later and named it after Lewis. Entering the downstream side of McAllister, we added only a few feet onto the previous 400 I had installed when a huge pile of logs made our arrival at another opening quite obvious. We surfaced briefly in the cool night air at Dorffzen Hole then continued downstream another 400 feet into a huge room more than 200 feet across that Court named Gargantua.

A week later we were the first divers to enter Ojo Verde, still another sink we had discovered just northwest of Mount Sink in 1973. Swimming only 50 feet back under the lip of the sink, we discovered a line that Court and Lewis had laid from the downstream side of Mount some time earlier. Rather than swimming back 600 feet to Mount to complete the first traverse, we headed further downstream into virgin territory. We managed to add only 400 feet before hitting our air turnaround point.

John Harper, one of the discoverers of Cathedral. (*Photo by John Harper*)

Then, on December 26, Court and I made still another dive into the Gargantua section below Dorffzen Hole and managed to connect to the elusive upstream Jade Hole line by adding 275 feet and dropping down a large crevasse to a lower level.

There followed a lull of more than three years in the Falmouth exploration. When we renewed our efforts, we discovered that this magnificent cave eats line. Normally our 1/16 inch nylon guidelines last indefinitely (lines installed by John Harper in Hornsby have lasted more than 20 years without any noticeable deterioration). After only four years, the lines in Cathedral Canyon, Mount Sink, and elsewhere in Falmouth had broken at numerous points, sometimes disappearing for hundreds of feet.

We still do not know what causes this, but there are several theories. One is that there is an inordinate amount of acid in the water, but we have nothing to suggest that that is true or that the acid is in sufficient quantities to react with the highly-resistant nylon. Still another theory is that the many large cave crayfish, known to attack cotton line, cut the line with their claws in their never ending search for food. Surely they do not eat nylon?

Perhaps the missing sections provide us with a clue. When we reentered Cathedral in December, 1978, we found that much of the cut line was buried in the sandy floor. Obviously the sand moves around quite a bit, probably during the rare but violent periods of reverse flow when the Suwannee backfloods into the cave. Grains of sand act like tiny saws on nylon fibers. Cavers sometimes discard a climbing rope that someone has carelessly stepped on with a muddy boot. Maybe moving sand eats the lines in Falmouth. At any rate, we had to replace virtually all the lines in the caves.

On one of our first dives, John Zumrick and I reinvestigated Fowler Sink. Again the visibility was poor down to about 80 feet, then it started clearing up near a tiny crevice at the bottom that was choked with sticks and mud. I noticed what appeared to be a slight inflow at this point, so started digging out the crevice, gradually enlarging it until it was wide enough for a human body. Unfortunately, the digging procedure had totally wiped out visibility, so I asked John to wait while I backed into the crevice feet first.

I knew I had loads of air, so I continued down the crevice laying line, periodically pausing to wiggle forward or backward to find an area large enough to pass through. It seemed to be gradually getting larger and was definitely getting deeper, which spurred my hopes. Finally I dropped out of the crevice into a large horizontal tunnel filled with clear, blue-green water that was obviously Falmouth. I returned to get John. The extraordinarily nasty entrance via the crevice led to our re-christening the place Fowler Horror Hole. To this day it remains by far the least popular of all the Falmouth entrances.

By the fall of 1980, we were in the age of the torpedo-like underwater scooters. Encouraged by our successes in the Wakulla Springs area, we turned our interest back to the elusive connections of the Falmouth area. First, Clark Pitcairn, Jamie Stone, and I connected Ojo Verde to McAllister on October 19; then a week later, Clark, Paul DeLoach, and I

"Uncle" Paul DeLoach just before a dive. (*Photo by Mary Ellen Eckhoff*)

penetrated 3513 feet upstream from Mount until we could see light coming in from the downstream side of Falmouth Springs. Finally, on November 18, Clark and I re-entered Fowler Horror Hole to discover a line that we had laid 3,090 feet downstream from Jade Hole two days earlier. We now had a fully explored and mapped cave extending all the way from just below Fowler to the dim recesses above Cathedral Canyon, more than three miles in a straight line, an unprecedented distance for cave diving. It was time to think about connecting downstream Cathedral/Falmouth to the Suwannee River.

As mentioned at the beginning of this chapter, the Suwanacoochee Cave System, which discharges into the Suwannee River at the closest point to Falmouth, had proved to be a disappointment as far as a possible connection goes.

The next most likely candidate for a connection was a chain of murky sinks and intermittent springs in the Suwannee River State Park a little farther north. The key to this chain was a giant swirling syphon 200 feet across that was first entered by Court and Lewis in the early 70's. The immense whirlpool and tannic water there is so frightening that specially trained divers of the Florida Highway Patrol, almost certain that mass killer Ted Bundy had thrown a murder weapon into it, refused even to step into the water. Another possible link was a large sink whose water was so chilly that Paul DeLoach wanted it called M. F. Cold Sink. Paul relented only when I suggested that if we did not name it Girardeau Sink after the owner, he would never let us dive there again. And, of course, there was also Fowler Horror Hole.

For this kind of cave diving – bad visibility, narrow restrictions, dangerous inflowing current, cold water, and unstable, silty entrances – I needed really hard–core partners. John Zumrick, a former chairman of the NSSCDS and medical officer with the U. S. Navy Experimental Diving Unit, was one. Mary Ellen Eckhoff, the only woman ever to log 1000 cave dives or set a world record for cave diving penetration, was another. But the real sparkplug of the project to connect Falmouth to the river was Paul DeLoach. Known as Uncle Paul to the diving community, Paul is a big, strapping ex-Navy Seal who has frequently put his training as a psychologist and public relations director for the Miller Brewing Company to good use in diving. Acting as the Farmer Charmer, he has been responsible for getting more hostile and suspicious landowners to open their springs to diving than any other person. Free cases of Miller's beer may have something to do with it. More important to our project is his unsurpassed experience. He was the second diver in the world to log more than 2,000 cave dives, and has participated on many record dives. I called him on the phone late one night in 1984.

"Uncle Paul," I started, "I've found just your kind of dive."

"What's that, Ex?" Paul calls everyone by a nickname, the shorter the better. Occasionally he even refers to initials: Billy Young is B. Y., Mary Ellen is M. E., and John Zumrick the shortest of all: Z.

"Oh, the usual. Zero vis, major restriction, excessive depth, cold as a well digger."

Paul laughed. "Hey, that sounds great."

"I'm serious."

"Well, does it have a cave?"

"Of course."

"And do you still have that case of Miller Lite?"

"Well, most of it."

"Then see you in the morning."

Paul, John, and I started by squeezing through Fowler to add more than 1,000 feet of line downstream. We were encouraged when I plotted our survey notes and discovered that the cave had turned north to head toward Girardeau Sink. On the last dive in Fowler Sink, Paul and John had wrestled scooters through the squeeze, triggering a landslide of silt and debris that still had not cleared when they returned to exit nearly an hour later. For a while, Uncle Paul thought he would have to abandon his scooter below the squeeze because of the difficulty in finding a way out after the line was accidentally loosened.

Then Mary Ellen and I added 1000 feet of line onto the 400 feet she and Paul had installed in upstream Girardeau. This 40-foot-wide passage was very similar to downstream Fowler and headed directly toward it. We were discouraged by the terrifying entrance at Fowler and the cold water at Girardeau, however, so decided to work on the shorter links next.

Even the most experienced cave divers require at least 10 feet of visibility in Falmouth-size passages for any kind of significant exploration, and even more if scooters are used. This is because of the large amount of time required for route-finding in water having poor visibility, given the limited amount of time that a diver can stay in a cave. The chain of sinks in Suwannee River State Park northwest of Girardeau have visibility in excess of 10 feet for about a month once every three years or so. This unique situation arises only after a severe prolonged flood of the Suwannee, when recharge to the local aquifer is sufficient to cause the water to flow through the sinks for a considerable length of time. But if the ground water table drops so rapidly that the flow ceases before it has had time to remove the flood waters of the Suwannee, then the water ponds, is very cold from rain water, and has zero visibility because of the suspension of silt.

In the fall of 1984, however, conditions were good. Paul and I began by diving Cyclone Sink. Paul paused at the water's edge and scowled at the violently swirling water that had scared off the FHP divers. "Anything with this big a whirlpool over a cave entrance 100 feet deep has got to have a heck of an inflow, Ex."

"Don't worry. Court and Lewis went in here a dozen years ago."

"Yeah, but they might have been diving in bad vis at no flow."

"Well, if it was easy, someone would have already done it."

Paul looked pointedly at an immense spool of exploration line I had hanging on my belt. He had heard stories about Charlie Sturdevant and me getting sucked into downstream Falmouth, and had experienced worse himself at Spring Creek, a violent syphon south of Tallahassee. "Why don't you listen to your Uncle Paul and put that line up? Let's just see if we can get out of this place."

The current was not as bad as we feared, so we returned for more dives. On August 19, 1984, we finally connected the 140-foot-deep conduit to an immense sink 2,000 feet farther west called Giant Hole. Then we quickly connected Giant Hole to Ellaville Spring in the park, a connection that Howard Tower had reportedly made in the 70's. Ellaville Spring was where the water entered the Suwannee, so now we had to work upstream from Cyclone. Mary Ellen and Bill Stone had connected Cyclone to Big Bamboo, a large sink only 200 feet away, but the access to Big Bamboo was so bad that we decided to enter at upstream Cyclone instead. Upstream Cyclone was a 100-foot-long vertical slot that was easy for us to get our scooters down. On August 26, we penetrated 1,130 feet, connecting a 400-foot line that Paul and Mary Ellen had laid from downstream Girardeau.

One missing link remained: Girardeau to Fowler. On September 2 and 3, Paul and I made two dives at a depth of 175 feet with scooters, ultimately pushing to a point 2,551 feet from Girardeau on a single stage dive. We decompressed for three hours in the chilly water on the last dive, and surfaced shaking severely despite our thick dry suits. Paul said what was

"Uncle" Paul DeLoach attired in full cave-diving gear. (*Photo by Dan Lenihan*)

on both our minds: "Maybe the Horror Hole ain't so bad after all."

At home I plotted our survey notes from the last dive and gave Paul a call.

"How close are we?" Paul wanted to know.

"We are past it."

"What?"

"Yep. What wall did we lay line on coming south from Girardeau?"

"Left." Paul cursed. "You mean we have been paralleling ourselves on the other wall?"

"Exactly." In the poor visibility we could not see across the 40-foot-wide passage.

Our first attempt from the Fowler side was disappointing. Flow in the right fork toward Girardeau and Ellaville Spring had ceased, so visibility had decreased to only five to eight feet. Paul and John's old line had come loose, so I had to pull it out of the mud. I swam with it to the right side of the tunnel, but did not see any sign of the Girardeau line. At that point we ran low on air and had to exit.

A week later, on November 10, we tried again. We did not say it, but both of us knew that this would be the last attempt at a connection for a while, possibly for three years. The rapidly dropping visibility and temperature in Fowler were making diving very cold and difficult. I led the way down the tight crevice. The butterflies that I always feel when deprived of sight in an irregular constriction underwater were in my stomach. Finally, at 160 feet, I swam out into the clear Cathedral/Falmouth water, and paused to wait for Paul. Seconds later a yellow glow emanated from the dense cloud of silt raining down the crevice, then the powerful white beam of his light broke out of the mud and bounced off the cream-colored walls to vanish in the emerald-hued distance.

Paul flashed me an "okay" signal, then I led the way down the broad passage. A few hundred feet further we passed the deepest point in the cave, 190 feet, then the junction with a large passage on the left that Paul and John initially thought was the main route. Briefly I wondered where it went. It apparently took all the low flow Falmouth water. Did it go to Suwanacoochee after all, or did it come out in some unknown spring in the river bed, permanently hidden by the deep, dark water of the Suwannee?

Visibility in the right fork seemed even worse than the previous week. On the floor was deep fluffy silt, so we swam near the ceiling to avoid kicking it up. Above us our exhaust bubbles loosened silt that had accumulated on the ceiling in the stagnant water. The passage was nearly 100 feet wide and was very irregular. I tried to lay line along the right wall, straying into two dead–end pockets on the way. I had to reel up the line and start over each time I exited one of the pockets, wasting precious time and air, neither of which lasted very long at 175 feet. After adding 180 feet of line, Paul flashed me with his light. Low air, time to go. I felt immense disappointment at having failed to make the connection again, but Paul had made the only acceptable decision. When you are down to two-thirds of your starting air supply, you call the dive, no matter what.

I could not find a tie-off along the right wall, so swam over to the left to try to find something. With Paul shooting me exasperated glances, I finally spotted a small ridge in the ceiling near the left wall. I started to tie off, then noticed a thin brown-stained thread a few feet further left: our Girardeau line! Excitedly flashing Paul, I rapidly followed the old line 15 feet to its end and tied the new line to it. The old line was in a tunnel parallel to the passage we were following from Fowler, separated from it by a thin rock wall whose only gap was near the ceiling ridge I had tried to tie off on. We had been incredibly lucky.

At home I totalled up the surveyed length of the Cathedral-Falmouth Cave System now that it was connected to

Ellaville Spring and the Suwannee River, while Paul and sipped our beers. I looked at the number and gave a start.

"What's the matter?" Paul asked.

"Oh nothing much," I said, trying to hide my excitement. "Nothing except that Cathedral is now the world's longest underwater cave."

"What?" Paul jumped out of his chair to take a look. 34,000 feet. That made it more than 1,000 feet longer than Lucayan Caverns. And still going. At both ends.

The most exciting end, of course, is the upstream end of the cave beyond Cathedral Canyon. Protected by a thick layer of the impermeable Hawthorne formation, there are no more entrances past that point, making it an ideal location for an attempt to break the penetration record we set at Manatee Springs. Best of all, the awesome cave seems to represent in every respect the endless labyrinth that every cave explorer dreams of: the farther you go, the bigger it gets.

The fact that, for once, this dream appeared to be reality became increasingly apparent during a series of dives in 1979. On January 27, Dale Sweet and I single-staged upstream from Cathedral, repaired a break in the old line at the Great Wall of China, and added 198 feet of line to the 1,928-foot end installed in 1972. We were able to confirm that the gargantuan passage previously found just beyond the Great Wall was in fact merely a continuation of a major passage leading out of the Grand Canyon. This latter passage, explored by David Fisk and me in early 1973, turned out to be the main passage, since its cross-sectional area was about three times that of the China Route. Happily for exploration (but sadly for record penetrations), the main passage is also shorter, so the end of the new 198 feet of line Dale and I installed wound up being "only" 2,080 feet from Cathedral.

On October 28, 1979, I returned with my new Farallon scooter and added 510 feet of line, discovering the large Double Rooms, where immense breakdown piles are almost

Dave Fisk helps survey a passage. (*Photo by Ned DeLoach*)

completely covered with sand and mud.

Seven years earlier, John Harper, the best cave diver of the 1960's, had quit cave diving when his favorite partner, Randy Hylton, suffered an apparent heart attack and drowned at Eagle's Nest. Recently John had become interested in diving again, and, working with Jamie Stone, pioneered the modifications necessary to make scooters sufficiently safe for cave diving. I couldn't resist making a phone call a day before Halloween to the man who had been my number one diving inspiration when I started cave diving 15 years earlier.

"Hi John, this is your protegé."

"Sheck?"

"Yup. I've been adding line in one of your caves again," I teased.

"So what's new about that?" John had always been modest

about his amazing accomplishments, and very open about sharing information with other divers. His generous, unselfish help had saved me considerable time and effort in numerous exploration projects. I hope I will be capable of the same attitude when I quit diving.

"Well, we're a half mile upstream from Cathedral and it's still getting bigger."

"Sounds like scooter country."

"None better," I agreed, then hesitated, carefully phrasing my next words to give my friend the respect he deserved. "How about taking me on a dive in there?"

"I can't think of any better way to spend Halloween than to go 'Ghoul-ing' with you." (He was referring to "Ghoul Sink", the original name he had given Cathedral.)

We both laughed and hung up, but were not able to dive until November 3. John led us 432 feet further into the cave, discovering the remarkably uniform and straight Subway at an average depth of 165 feet. Then, on January 13, 1980, John and I added more line in the Subway to a penetration point 3,440 feet from the Cathedral entrance. At the time, this was the longest penetration ever made below 150 foot depth.

Unfortunately, this good news was tempered by some bad news. One of the Falmouth Springs property caretakers (who had actually been known to shoot at divers), drove up to our parking lot and informed us that Cathedral was part of the Falmouth tract and we weren't welcome there. Worse, John got bent on the dive despite his liberal use of pure oxygen (a concession to the increased susceptibility to bends of divers more than 40 years of age). He quietly endured the pain and dizziness and decided not to go to a chamber. He did decide, however, not to make such advanced dives anymore, a sad loss to cave exploration.

Over the years I had developed considerable respect for property owners' rights in general (not to mention the Falmouth caretaker's rifle in particular), so sneaking back into Cathedral for more exploration without John's help was not an option. Discreet inquiries at a nearby real estate office revealed that I could buy Cathedral (as well as the rest of the Falmouth Springs property) from the St. Joe Paper Company (also owners of Wakulla Springs) for "only" half a million dollars (later increased to $750,000). No, they weren't interested in dividing the property so I could buy only Cathedral, by far the most significant of the entrances.

Meanwhile, we made the record dives at Big Dismal Sink and the Friedman entrance of Manatee Springs described in the previous chapter of this book. With further progress at Manatee hopelessly blocked by hundreds of tons of unstable rubble, Cathedral was by far the most promising location in the Western Hemisphere for a new penetration record. I felt like a baby who had his favorite candy taken away.

Imagine my surprise when, on a routine wistful drive past the property in 1983, I spotted a new home less than 100 yards from Cathedral! Knocking on the door, I learned from the new owner that, despite the information given me by the caretaker and the real estate office, Cathedral was on a separate four-acre tract surrounded by St. Joe Paper Company land. He had just bought the acreage at an incredible bargain from an absentee owner who had no idea what was on his property.

Now I felt like a complete idiot for having missed such an opportunity. But there was worse to come:

"Can we have permission to dive on your property?"

"Nope."

"Well, would you consider leasing diving privileges to us?"

"Nope."

"How about selling your property?"

"Nope."

I was desperate. "I'd be willing to pay you six times what you paid for it two years ago." It was all I could conceivably scrimp and borrow.

"Nope."

I was so depressed after my negative conversation with Cathedral's new owner that I turned around and drove 100 miles home without even making the nearby dive I had planned. During the long ride back, I tried different techniques to cheer myself up. I reminded myself of the bright side of things: heck I'm still alive. But then, is any cave explorer who is denied access to his favorite cave really alive? Now in a real funk, I threw my favorite music into the cassette player: the exalted final movement of Beethoven's Ninth Symphony. Then I remembered that I had requested in my will that the same piece be played at my funeral. Somehow, it seemed fitting for my morbid mood.

More years passed, and Switzerland's Olivier Isler broke our Friedman Sink record with an incredible 10,168-foot penetration at Doux de Coly, France. It looked as if Americans were out of the cave diving record business for good, especially with Hasenmayer's astounding deep dives at Vaucluse, France (see the next chapter).   Then, late one night I got a phone call: "Mr. Exley, are you still interested in buying my Cathedral property?"

Soon we had the first completely legal access in more than 20 years to any of the 19 entrances to the world's longest and largest underwater cave. Best of all, the entrance we owned—Cathedral—is arguably the most scenic and certainly the most significant, being further upstream, closest to the major unexplored area of the cave, and the most likely area for a penetration record. By fall of 1986, we had run power to the water's edge and installed America's first hot water warming system for decompression. Wes Skiles, Tom Morris, and Paul Smith had even placed the first "Habitrough" at 20 feet—an inverted cattle trough filled with air so that divers could drink hot liquids and stay warmer during decompression. We also invested in expensive German Aqua Zepp scooters and a variety of other equipment. In three dives, Paul DeLoach and I pushed to 5,127 feet.

Then the winter rains came, causing the Suwannee to rise and reverse into the cave, reducing visibility to zero. By October, 1987, the water had cleared again, enabling me to solo in three dives to 6,850 feet, the second longest penetration in America. But the Wakulla Project intervened, demanding our full effort for the rest of the year. Then it rained again.

The next two years were frustrating. Visibility in Cathedral was worse than ever, too poor for high speed exploration with a scooter, despite some of the driest weather since 1981. Evidence points to huge agricultural concerns that have moved into Suwannee County (where Cathedral, Peacock, Little River, and many other springs are located), pumping many millions of gallons a day out of the aquifer. This unrestricted mining of the aquifer has had predictable results: many springs have stopped flowing, including the largest in the county, the great subterranean river that courses through Cathedral and Falmouth. Beginning in May, 1989, the run at Falmouth, considered a first magnitude spring averaging more than 100 cfs, dried up completely for the first time in the memory of the local residents or the stories of their parents, a period going back well over 100 years. The spring only outflowed for five of the next 28 months, but readily drained billions of gallons of black, polluted river water into the aquifer used for drinking water by local residents, poisoning their wells. The uncontrolled mining of ground water also means that the surface water component of the springs, carrying nitrates from dairies into the aquifer, is a much higher percentage, drastically reducing the visibility in springs and polluting their water. For example, when the flow ceased in Cathedral and Falmouth, the pristine, almost-white walls of the cave became heavily coated with dark algae and tannin, and oxygen levels plummeted, resulting in a massive kill of what cave biologist Tom Morris believes was the largest colony of *Procambarus pallidus*, the rare and endangered blind crayfish. The great cave, once teeming with thousands of cave crayfish, large schools of catfish, and the like is now nearly devoid of any animal life.

Over the years, cave diving has survived the lack of good equipment in the 1950's, the ostracism of the open water diving community in the 1960's, the many fatal accidents of the 1970's, and the continuing efforts of junior state legislators, ever eager to get publicity, to interfere with the sport by passing senseless regulations. Can it be that the activity we love will succumb to the destruction of the springs by Florida's population pressure and the selfish interests of big agricultural concerns and phosphate mining?

By fall, 1990, our efforts at Mante, Mexico, and Chips Hole, Florida, had brought the cave diving depth and distance records back to Florida, and surveying efforts had established Cathedral as the world's longest (and by far largest in volume) underwater cave, but my dream of a penetration record at Cathedral remained. And I was not getting any younger. I had vivid memories of John Harper and Jochen Hasenmayer getting the bends at my age on easier dives. Growing weary of waiting for the only possible cure for the poor visibility, prolonged and substantial rainfall, I finally resolved to attempt more exploration in Cathedral regardless of conditions.

Visibility in the entrance room of Cathedral Canyon itself is usually pretty good because of seep springs in the canyon walls. But visibility in the tunnel at the bottom was only 15 feet, the walls dark brown from the water pollution, and the bottom covered with deep deposits of easily-riled gray-tan silt from the lack of flow in the system. The bad visibility was made even worse when my rising air bubbles knocked silt loose from the ceiling, obscuring my return path. The worst, however, occurred 1,500 feet back, where the main tunnel leaves the Grand Canyon to enter an area 150 to 160 feet deep. This section (the Black Lagoon) had completely filled with frigid river water because of the lack of flow, limiting visibility to as little as two feet for a distance of more than 200 feet. Another section of similar conditions and length (the Brown Lagoon) was encountered just 200 feet past the end of the Black Lagoon. Fortunately, my memory of the line position in relation to the walls and rock projections in these areas was good. Because of this, I was able to cruise at high speed on my scooter through these sections, carefully keeping my head down and my attention riveted to the line. If I veered from it for just an instant at that speed in a cave that large, I might never find the line again. Of course, diving with a partner in such conditions was out of the question, but then, buddy–diving on very long or deep cave dives even in clear water is seldom practical or safe.

On October 21, 1990, I pushed to a distance of 7,395 feet, noting with dismay that the deep section, Thirty Fathom Freeway, discovered three years earlier, was continuing. Even with the hot water and habitrough, the decompression was already an ordeal. Much more of the 180-foot-depths would mean that I would have to switch from the 160-foot decompression schedule designed by Dr. John Zumrick to avoid the bends, to the much longer 170-foot or even 180-foot schedule. The number of stage bottles required would become logistically excessive, since substantially more air is breathed at those depths. Already I was taking more tanks on one dive than most dive shops stocked. Most sinister was the possibility of oxygen toxicity from the prolonged exposure to depth, especially if I had to swim out due to scooter failure. An oxygen convulsion in the water would result in certain death. Reducing the amount of oxygen breathed to prevent toxicity would result only in impossibly long decompression schedules on high-risk tables and dangerously high levels of narcosis. And speaking of narcosis, some diving physiologists predicted that the narcosis would become more severe with time, so that the amount of narcosis normally felt at 200 feet on a short dive, would be much more on Cathedral's long bottom times. I didn't need to be driving drunk through an underwater cave at two feet a second in visibility of 15 feet or less.

Fortunately, the next dive was like a prayer answered. After adding 300 feet, I started up a long slope that took me to a depth of only 120 feet. The cave would get no deeper for the next 2,500 feet. Exhilarated by the shallower depths, I didn't stop until reaching a point 8,760 feet from Cathedral, surpassing Friedman and making it once more the second longest penetration in America. This dive was also significant in that it represented the first time that Americans had staged scooters (Isler had done it at Coly in France).

The next push, to 9,880 feet, was much the same. The huge 60–foot–plus–wide trunk was continuing as big as ever, more than seven miles from its terminus at Ellaville Spring in Suwannee River State Park. No other trunk in the world, even in Kentucky's fabulous Mammoth Cave (by far the world's longest cave in air), can compare to it for uninterrupted length. And it looked as if the penetration record was only one push away.   But to make each push dive, several extra dives were needed to stage extra bottles and scooters in the cave. To ensure my survival, I insisted on providing enough air to complete a worst–case scenario: having to swim out from maximum penetration. I had learned that swimming took about three times as much air as scootering. Also, the extra bottom time incurred from a catastrophic breakdown of one or both scooters at the worst possible moment would be substantial, requiring much more nitrox and pure oxygen for decompression.

As luck would have it, I was "road-tripped" by my scooter on my longest setup dive, more than a mile from Cathedral. I was able to limp out on the much slower 12 volt power, but was unable to place the bottles at 6,850 feet as planned. Subsequent examination revealed a broken terminal wire on one of the two battery packs, rendering it inoperative. Rather than re-solder it myself, I hired a professional to do it at the local TV repair shop.

So guess what happens on the next dive? Right! The same wire breaks again, leaving me stranded at 3,000 feet. Fed up, I replaced the wire and completely redesigned the terminal connection. But now the record that seemed so easily in reach was beginning to appear unattainable. If the winter rains came early, the zero visibility would make further progress this year —and maybe ever, with the increasing pollution in the cave and my advancing age—impossible.

Finally, on December 12, I got the 6,850-foot setup dive completed, and three days later staged a scooter at 3,200 feet. Now everything is ready. The biggest question mark is hypothermia. While Cathedral ground water temperature is 65 to 69 degrees F, and the Black and Brown Lagoons some 5 to 10 degrees cooler, the nearly four hours of bottom time on a scooter is a real ordeal. At Chips Hole, I had endured five hours of swimming time in 69 degree F water, but the convection of heat at the much faster scooter speeds makes an enormous difference. Too bad that a dry suit cannot be used. To do so would mean freezing during the long decompression, where I could not avail myself of the hot water heating system.

Of course, the other question is, what will the cave do? While it is very unlikely that the trunk will end anytime soon, it could plunge to depths in excess of 200 feet, making further progress at that distance impossible. I am well aware that Mary Ellen Eckhoff and I had explored two caves nearly 300 feet deep less than ten miles away, and parts of the Thirty Fathom Freeway in Cathedral itself were 200 feet deep.

I had tried to carry all of the equipment needed for the dive to the water's edge the night before so I could get an early start. Nevertheless, on the morning of December 16, 1990, I fell victim to several of the many last minute tasks that invariably crop up at the start of such a dive if one is committed to doing everything he possibly can to survive: reboiling a couple of chemical heaters that served as a backup to the hot water decompression system, repairing a last minute tear in a slate pocket, replacing a regulator that looked as though it could cause problems during the dive. Finally, I submerged at 11:11 AM.

On the long dives at Friedman and Chips Hole, it was possible to slip into a comfortable sort of trance for the hours of travel through passage all too familiar from the tedium of recent setup dives. But at Cathedral, I could afford no such luxury. In addition to the regular, continuous scanning of instruments and equipment checks to maintain maximum safety and efficiency, I had to stay sharply alert to my surroundings because of my high rate of travel through restricted visibility. More than once, I wished for the days of the 1970's, when the vast cave was filled with perfectly-clear, 100-foot visibility water.

Ten minutes into the dive, I veered off the main line into the China Route. Though it forced me to travel 83 feet further than the main route, a distance that could not be added to my penetration record (since it had to be the shortest known distance to the closest entrance or air space, whichever is closer), its slightly shallower depths meant that I could avoid the dreaded near-zero visibility of the Black Lagoon. The Brown Lagoon could not be avoided, however, and I grimaced in pain as my wetsuit-clad body ripped into its chilly brown layer. I tried not to think about what it would feel like coming back out nearly three hours later, infinitely more cold and tired than I was now.

Another detour was made 3,500 feet from the Cathedral entrance, where I chose the 118-feet-longer West Loop instead of the shorter but much smaller East Loop, whose narrow, twisting walls would have slowed me down. As I proceeded into the cave, I had to watch out for more than just the cave walls. My lifesaving guideline was in some ways more dangerous than crashing into a wall or dangling ceiling projection would be. It could easily snag me or my equipment if I strayed too close, or even catch my prop and hopelessly jam it.

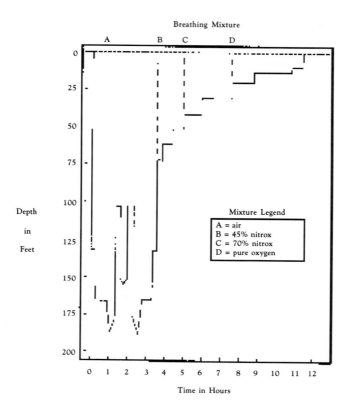

Profile for 12/16/90 dive by Sheck Exley to a penetration of 10,939 feet at Cathedral Canyon, Florida.

Yet I dared not stray far from the menacing strands for fear of the even worse fate of losing my way in the visibility, no better than 15 feet and frequently worse. Several times I had to steer carefully over or under the line to avoid contact with ceiling and wall obstacles. I also had seven stage stops scheduled at intervals of 1,000–2,000 feet (depending on the depth and conditions of the intervening passage), where I had to stop briefly to exchange and test stage bottles. A redesign of my air requirements and contingency plans enabled me to skip a couple of the stops, but each stop still required quick, alert action to avoid delays that could have wreck the dive.

An hour and a half into the dive, I dropped my 13th and 14th stage bottles at the end of the line at 9,880 feet, parked my scooter, hooked on my line and started swimming. On earlier dives I had discovered that adding line while swimming is more practical in the limited visibility (somewhat better in the back of the cave, but still less than 30 feet). It also enabled my body to warm up and the scooter to rest, cooling the motor and recharging the batteries slightly.

The cave maintained its impressive 60-foot-plus width and 15 to 20 feet height, and its depth was thankfully only 100 to 110 feet. Then I rounded a bend after 500 feet and frowned in dismay as a long pit opened in the floor along the left wall. I swam its full length to the far wall in hope of a shallower continuation, but found nothing. Luckily, the pit quickly opened into a huge tubular borehole 40 feet wide and 20 feet high at a depth of 150 to 165 feet. After swimming several hundred feet more, I noticed that my air was down to two-thirds, so I tied off. The new record penetration distance was 10,939 feet, the world's first four-mile (round trip) cave dive. (I actually had to travel a one-way distance of 11,140 feet because of detours into the China Route and the West Loop to avoid bad visibility.) But before turning around to survey out, I couldn't resist spending a few seconds squinting on into the vast unexplored distance, trying to fathom the grandeur of this most measureless of caverns.

Maybe it just goes on forever.

12

Mante

I need to buy some panty hose."
I glanced around nervously to make sure that no one was watching. The department store clerk waiting on me was a no-nonsense type, built like a female drill sergeant. She fixed me with a baleful glare, then put on her best professional smile. She had just helped me select a sweater for my mother's Christmas present, so maybe she would think the panty hose were for my mother. A little weird, maybe, but not likely to have me burned by the Baptists in Lake City, Florida.

"What size, sir?"

It just wasn't going to be my day.

I glanced down at my legs and mumbled, "What size do you think would fit me?"

On some of my longer dives the skin behind my knees was cut by the rubbing of the wrinkles in my neoprene rubber diving suits. The abrasions were painful and distracted me during the dive. Occasionally the pain was so bad that it affected my swimming kick. The cuts usually became infected and were slow to heal causing me to postpone future dives. The wrinkles couldn't be helped: they were the normal result of the stretching and compressing of the rubber as I kicked while swimming. Mary Ellen finally came up with the solution to the problem: broad strips of moleskin held in place by panty hose. Unfortunately, after I ran through all her old nylon hose, she didn't volunteer to buy any more for me.

A cut behind the knees may seem insignificant, but on deep dives the smallest details can make the difference between life and death. On these dives it's not just matters of endurance, propulsion, and logistics, which were enough for the record long dives in Friedman Sink and Cathedral Canyon. On deep dives you move into the physiological and psychological unknown, where all the components of the air you are now breathing become poisonous, where the normal problems associated with scuba diving in caves are magnified a hundredfold, where bizarre disorders arise that medical scientists have never even dreamed of.

At the time we made the deep dives below 200 feet described in Chapters 4 and 6, we were on the cutting edge of cave diving technology. Even today such dives are possible only for the most experienced and careful deep cave divers. But they are child's play compared to the record deep dives of the 1980's.

The first of these dives was made by Dale Sweet at Florida's Die Polder Sink No. 2 on June 8, 1980. Dale was attempting to break my three-year-old record of 340 feet, set at Boiling Hole in the Bahamas (see Chapter 6). Although "Deep Dale" has one of the best tolerances for narcosis of any diver in the world, he decided that the safest way to descend below 340 feet in a cave was by using helium in his mix. By substituting helium for nitrogen, a diver can eliminate most if not all of the numbing effects of narcosis.

This required a remarkable amount of perception and courage on Dale's part. He was well aware of the two previous attempts to make helium dives in Florida: Hal Watts' open water descent to 355 feet at Mystery Sink, Florida, in 1970, on

Dale Sweet before his record 360 foot dive at Die Polder Sink #2. (*Photo by Dale Sweet*)

which he got a severe case of the bends and a support diver drowned; and Lewis Holtzendorff's death during decompression following a 260 foot dive in 1975. He was not aware of the only "successful" helium dive prior to 1980, by Frank Fogarty and Roger Miller at Missouri's Blue Spring in 1978. While Frank and Roger did survive a descent to 325 feet, they became dangerously chilled due to the high conductivity of the helium in their mixture.

Dale faced enormous obstacles. First, how would he mix his breathing gas and make sure of its contents? How would he stay warm, since helium conducts heat away from the body, rapidly cooling a diver with each breath? Most importantly, how would he decompress to avoid the bends? Only U. S. Navy decompression tables were available, and they were unreliable even when used as intended in a dry decompression chamber under the careful supervision of a physician. Dale would have to do all of his decompression in the water. An attempt to do this by Court Smith and Lewis Holtzendorff ended tragically, even though it was a shallower dive and therefore required less decompression. Not only was Dale's dive going to be at least 80 feet deeper than theirs, but also it involved a horizontal penetration of about 1,000 feet through two silty restrictions.

When Dale invited me to accompany him into Die Polder Sink No. 2, it didn't take me very long to turn him down. I was tempted to try the dive on compressed air, since I had been to 465 feet that way in the sea in 1971. I hadn't made any extremely deep dives lately, however, and was well aware that some unknown psychological trigger made the intoxicating effects of nitrogen much more pronounced in a cave.

Despite the odds, Dale succeeded in setting a new record of 360 feet. The age of mixed gas cave diving had begun.

Six months after Dale's dive, I tied his record on a compressed air dive. But I had the advantage of following the guideline he had left. Route-finding, especially through the silty restriction at 340 feet, may have been impossible except with helium. If I had any reservations left about the superiority of helium over nitrogen for deep cave diving, they were dispelled by the German Jochen Hasenmayer's record descents in Vaucluse, France. He reached an astounding 476 feet on helium in 1981, followed by an even more amazing 656 feet in 1983. The decompression tables he used were based on some that I had sent him. Now I felt that I could start a cautious program of helium diving with acceptable safety.

An obvious immediate goal was Dale's American mark of 360 feet. But where could I do the dive? On my compressed air dive in Die Polder No. 2, I had discovered that the cave ended at 360 feet. The only other site in Florida with depth potential in excess of 360 feet was Mystery Sink, but that location had been strictly closed to diving since the accidents in 1970. Nevada's Devil's Hole would be ideal, but diving there was forbidden because some biologists felt that it would interfere with the survival of the rare and endangered Devil's Hole pupfish. Nothing in the Bahamas or Caribbean was likely to be deeper than the 340 feet I had descended in Boiling

Hole. In all the Western Hemisphere there was only one cave where Dale's record might be broken: the giant spring at the city of Mante in northern Mexico.

In 1979, before Dale's record dive in Die Polder Sink No. 2, I had led a team of nine NSS divers on an expedition to the mountainous area of northeastern Mexico, where John Fish, Bill Russell, Bill Stone, and other members of the Association for Mexican Cave Studies (AMCS) had found many large, clear karst springs. Most of the springs had never been dived before. They typically arose at the eastern base of the Sierra Madre Oriental and dropped nearly vertically to 100 to 200 feet before ending. The Nacimiento del Río Mante appeared to fit this pattern precisely, except on a more grand scale. An average flow of approximately a quarter of a billion gallons per day— as much as any single outlet spring in the eastern United States—gushed out of a river cave at the base of a 2,000-foot-high ridge of mountains.

During the expedition I rotated the divers so everyone could make the first dive at at least one location. That way each diver had a chance to enjoy a first exploration of virgin cave. The first dive at Mante was by Terry More and Frank Fogarty. After a hard swim upstream, they found that the river in the cave sumped 100 feet inside. The ceiling sloped down to enter a large underwater horizontal passage 20 feet in diameter. The violent outflow was reminiscent of the torrent at Manatee Springs and Friedman Sink. They dived into the sump and followed the sloping floor another 100 feet to a depth of 40 feet. There they saw a 100-foot-long crack in the floor, out of which the entire flow was gushing straight up.

Meanwhile, Paul DeLoach and I, the next to dive, were anxiously awaiting the news of Terry and Frank's discoveries. We knew that the longer their dive, the better the cave. I was very excited when they finally surfaced after nearly three hours.

"How'd it go?" I asked, helping Terry lift his equipment

Aerial view of Nacimiento del Río Mante, Mexico. The spring is at the start of the river. (*Photo by Sergio Zambrano*)

from the water.

His grin told it all. "We followed a crevice straight down to 270 feet," he replied. "Then it dropped out of sight!"

"All right!"

It was too late for another dive that day, so Paul and I entered the water early the following morning. Because of the severity of the current, I decided to pull my way into the cave by grasping the jagged wall projections with my bare hands instead of attempting to swim. Suddenly I yanked my right hand away from the wall as pain shot up my arm. In the dim light from the entrance I could see a green cloud streaming from a dark gash in my palm. When I shined my light on the cloud, it turned a bright red, confirming a steady loss of blood. Ordinarily I would have been tempted to call the dive, but I couldn't bear the thought of waiting any longer to follow up on Terry and Frank's exciting discovery. Besides, it could have been worse: large fer-de-lance snakes were frequent visitors to the cave entrance. At least the cave's "bite" wasn't poisonous.

Paul and I continued to pick our way gingerly along the walls, then down the crack below 40 feet. The 100-foot-long vertical fissure was only five feet wide at a maximum. It narrowed to three feet below a depth of 80 feet. At several points it was necessary to move back and forth along the length of the pit to find an area wide enough to get through with our twin 100-cubic-foot tanks on our backs.

At a depth of 180 feet, the fissure narrowed even more, and I signalled a halt to Paul. Instead of continuing down Terry and Frank's line, I tied off a new line and started pulling my

View looking out of the entrance to Mante, Mexico. (*Photo by Dan Lenihan*)

way horizontally along the fissure in search of easier going. After 100 feet I saw that the fissure expanded to a width of eight feet, so I turned and gave Paul the thumb down signal to renew our descent.

In contrast to the slow going we had encountered earlier, now everything happened very quickly. The velocity of the current decreased in the wider passage. It seemed that only seconds later we were at a depth of 290 feet and out of line. Below us beckoned a dark void, out of which the humming current sang an alluring, siren-like song.

Our group held council around the campfire that night while Jamie Stone serenaded us with his guitar. Virtually all of America's top deep cave divers at the time were present. Besides the five already mentioned were Dan Lenihan, Ken Fulghum, Steve Forman, and Carol Vilece. Carol had recently set a new women's cave depth record of 280 feet, breaking the 260-foot-mark shared by India Hendley, Karan Pribble, and Zidi Goldstein Mount. Of course, "Deep Dale" was also present.

"How deep do you think it goes?" he asked.

"China," Uncle Paul replied.

"Seriously," I added, "it could be very deep. The temperature of the water here is 78° F, a full 12 degrees warmer than the closest springs at Frio and Sabinas. It's reasonable to assume that the water has been heated up by the earth's interior at great depth."

Dan Lenihan pushed his tattered black hat back and stroked his blond beard, his eyes gleaming in the firelight. "Yeah, 'Dr.' Exley, but that doesn't mean that the cave goes there. At Warm Mineral the hydrologists told us the water was coming from 1,000 feet, but the cave only went to 230."

"Besides," added Frank, "the deepest underwater cave that's ever been found is the 340 feet you got on our trip to Boiling Hole, and at that point the cave ended."

"But what about the 600-foot-deep echo soundings at Red

Snapper Sink in the Atlantic off Florida?"

"Well, we all know how inaccurate sonar readings can be, especially when they are surrounded by rock walls. Besides, that's a vertical sinkhole open to the surface, not a real cave like here at Mante."

"Then look at it this way," I responded, leaning back to point with my bandaged hand at a dark silhouette looming high above us and blotting out the stars. "These mountains are classic fault block. The coastal plain we are sitting on was uplifted to form the central Mexican plateau. So the fault at the front of the mountains is at least 2,000 feet deep, probably deeper."

"Which makes Sheck's compass readings of the position of the pit in the cave very interesting," Paul added.

"Oh? Why's that?"

"The pit goes straight down the fault."

Despite repeated assaults by all of our team members at Mante in 1979, the deepest dive was 330 feet, by Paul and me. While 10 feet shy of breaking my record, the dive was particularly noteworthy because we could see rock ledges 30 feet below us. Attempting to reach them while breathing air, particularly while working against the strong current, would have been suicidal. In 1987, eight years later and after Dale and Jochen's helium diving efforts, attaining those ledges—and what might lie beneath them—was an exciting and very real possibility.

In American cave diving, small teams have often accomplished more than the few large-scale expeditions attempted, but I usually like to have more support than would be present for my renewed assault at Mante: one diver. That one diver was Mary Ellen, however, which was more reassuring than nearly any group of support divers I could envision. The fourth diver in the world (and only woman) to log 1,000 cave dives, she had also broken Carol's women's cave depth record with a 300-footer, and had been to 345 feet in the sea, also a record.

I considered asking Mary Ellen, Paul, or one of the other 1979 participants to dive with me, but it was obvious that it would be far safer to solo. To minimize the possibility of decompression sickness or hypothermia, it was absolutely essential to descend as quickly as possible. A minute's delay could be translated into another two hours of decompression and require the use of a riskier decompression schedule. I believe partners should stay together at all times to watch each other and give help quickly and efficiently if either should need it. In Mante, the lead diver would be slowed by having to pause periodically to glance up to check on his partner, and of course the pace of the team would be the pace of the slowest diver at all points. Delays for gear checks, negotiating difficult sections of the cave, and changing tanks, etc., would all be multiplied by two if there were two divers instead of one. Worse, the higher diver would be blinded by silt and the rising bubbles of the first diver for much of the dive due to the vertical path of the team. Finally, the need for deeper stops to prevent decompression sickness when using helium meant that many stops would occur between 80 and 180 feet, where there simply was not room for two divers and all the accompanying decompression tanks and related paraphernalia.

In the months before the dive, I was uncharacteristically apprehensive. Despite detailed planning and practice dives on helium mixtures to 130 feet at Cathedral Canyon and 260 feet at Holton Spring, I knew that the bottom line was that I was venturing into completely unknown territory, at least as far as my side of the Atlantic was concerned. Advice from my friend Jochen Hasenmayer had to be tempered by the difference between Vaucluse, where he dived, and Mante. Vaucluse was far colder than Mante, a real disadvantage for decompression, but Mante's current introduced a severe exertion factor throughout the dive, which increased chances of narcosis, carbon dioxide toxicity, oxygen toxicity, overbreathing regulators, and helium high pressure nervous syndrome as well as decompression sickness. In addition to all of these and other poorly-understood hazards of helium diving, both Jochen and Gene Melton described instances of mysterious "vestibular hits" causing sudden death when divers switched from helium back to nitrogen on ascent, as was necessary to avoid decompression sickness. And speaking of decompression sickness, the only decompression tables with any reasonable degree of safety were some top secret commercial diving tables that Gene had sent me. Unfortunately, they were designed for use with a dry decompression chamber like the one we would have in later projects at Cathedral Canyon and Wakulla Spring. But this was impossible at Mante with its irregular, unstable ceiling and lack of a firm floor. So the tables had to be modified by a certain car dealer, recently turned math teacher. At least if I got the bends, I would have no one to blame but myself. All factors considered, the dive would easily be twice as difficult as any dive I had ever made.

The morning of April 22, 1987 was cloudy and wet at Mante, a welcome change since it prevented my overheating while I struggled into my thick insulating underwear and dry suit. Now that the time for action had arrived, I felt confident. My attitude was not unlike Robert Falcon Scott's before departing for the South Pole: "I can think of nothing undone to ensure our success." Of course, Scott in fact left many things undone, which caused him to fail to beat Amundsen to the Pole and cost him his life (and the lives of his companions). I hoped that our expedition would be more like Amundsen's: small, meticulously planned, based on practice sessions, and, in the end, safe and successful.

When we entered the water, I had on most of my usual cave diving equipment, including twin 100-cubic-foot tanks filled with compressed air. Added to this was a spare depth gauge, special tables, a special light designed by Lamar English to handle the extreme pressure, and two 80-cubic-foot bottles filled with 50 per cent helium and topped off with air. Mary

Ellen and I had placed extra tanks containing special mixtures for decompression in the cave two days earlier.

Mary Ellen accompanied me on the long swim up the river and into the cave, which I took as slowly as possible to reduce overheating and carbon dioxide buildup. One hundred feet back in the cave, I rested at the surface on a ledge for 10 minutes, using the time to clear my mind and to increase my body awareness through meditation exercises I had learned two decades earlier in karate training. I would have to make life-or-death decisions quickly, and stay alert for any faint symptoms of decompression sickness, oxygen toxicity, etc., which would require immediate action. After meditating I felt calm and in control, which dispelled the last of the counter-productive apprehension I had been feeling.

At the end of 10 minutes, I reset my watch, then did something that had never before been necessary on a dive by an American: I turned on all five of my backup lights, since they might be impossible to turn on below 360 feet. I said goodbye to Mary Ellen and started down. It was precisely 12:00 noon.

The key to the descent was speed. To set a new American record, I would have to reach 361 feet no more than 20 minutes after leaving the surface. I was able to progress against the current by emptying my buoyancy compensators to make myself as heavy as possible. I pulled myself down the walls (this time I wore gloves), taking advantage of the rare downward eddy currents caused by the undulating walls of the vertical fissure. Whenever the cave permitted, I would brace my fins against a projection to push my way downward. Meanwhile, the part of my attention not devoted to route-finding, propulsion, and continuous gear checks was absorbed in monitoring my pulse and respiration to make sure that my carbon dioxide levels remained safe.

At 240 feet I switched from air to the helium mixture. I would use decompression tables based on having made this changeover at 180 feet. I could make the changeover 60 feet deeper because of my experience at depth with compressed air, and this was a big safety factor in my favor since it meant that I would have more gas available for the bottom part of the dive. Decompression would also be safer, since some of the deeper stops required by breathing helium would not be necessary and many of the other stops would be shorter. A third of several reasons to breathe compressed air to as great a depth as possible instead of the helium mix is that it would reduce the possibility of my getting dangerously chilled by helium heat loss.

At 330 feet, I hooked the new pre-measured guideline to the end of the old line, happily free of the narcosis I had felt the previous day. A minute and a half later I had a new record with time to spare, but the pit wasn't finished yet. It had also expanded to a width of 25 feet and was really looking interesting. I had tables for 400 feet and extrapolations for even greater depths, so continued on down.

At 400 feet the pit narrowed to about 10 feet again. I intended to switch to my second helium tank for the ascent when the gauge pressure in the first tank dropped to 1,500 pounds per square inch (psig). The gauge of my first helium tank still read 1,700 psig, so I kept on going down. The pit opened again, then narrowed again. I felt that I had gone far enough, so I started to tie off, surprising a cave crayfish. But my depth gauges showed 470 feet – too close to a nice round number to stop since I still had 1,600 psig in my first tank. So I picked out a rock projection below me and quickly dropped to it, just as I ran out of gas in my first tank. After switching to the other tank, I checked the gauge of the first and discovered that it was still reading 1,600 psig instead of zero. Apparently the extreme pressure had bent the gauge lens inward, pinning the needle that gave the reading.

After tying off, I quickly checked my depth gauges to verify the depth. Both read 500 feet, and since they are calibrated for heavier salt water, that meant that the actual depth was 515 feet in Mante's fresh water. My feet were five feet deeper. The easiest part of the dive was over.

Ahead of me were 26 decompression stops—more than twice as many as had been required for any other dive by an American. At 290 I paused to check the time, and discovered that my watch was gone! I had checked it a moment earlier, at 340 feet, so it had to have been dropped in the vicinity. This was critical, since now I had no way of timing the 26 decompression stops, each of which varied in length and had to be precise in order to avoid the bends. Understaying a stop could cause life-threatening bubbles to start forming in my body, and lingering too long altered the entire desaturation profile, making it necessary to extend some of the shallower stops. But which ones? And how long? Even a scientist with a mainframe computer would be hard-pressed to answer that. I had lost a watch only once in more than 3,000 cave dives; why did the second time have to be now?

Feeling more like the careless, impetuous (and dead) Scott by the minute, I frantically spent a couple of minutes searching for the watch, hoping a ledge had prevented its falling all the way down the pit. The bare rock grinned back at me. I could almost hear it speak: "So you think diving at Mante is easy, fella?"

I couldn't afford to look any longer without having to change to an even longer and more dangerous decompression schedule, so I resignedly started back up. At 260 feet and 250 feet I counted sixty-second stops with my fingers, then addressed a new source of concern: Jochen and Gene's mysterious vestibular hit. At 240 feet I had to switch from breathing 50 percent helium and 40 percent nitrogen to air, which contains 79 percent nitrogen. According to their information, the abrupt increase in nitrogen could result in instant death. And all authorities predicted a sudden onset of severe narcosis.

To make the switch as gradual as possible, I took only a

single breath of air from the tank we had earlier left at 240 feet, then switched back to the helium mix for two breaths. Then came two air breaths, then back to the deep mix for one inhalation. Finally I switched over to air completely, bracing myself for the severe narcosis and dreaded vestibular hit, all the while doing my best to count off the seconds required for the stop. Nothing happened, no narcosis, no sudden lapse into unconsciousness. The only thing I felt was warmer, thanks to not having to breathe helium any more. Apparently my strategy of keeping a maximum amount of nitrogen in the deep mix worked.

As I worked my way up and the stops grew longer, I thanked my lucky stars that I had taught cardiopulmonary resuscitation (CPR) for years. The 60-beats-per-minute pace of chest compressions for adults in the old method of two-person CPR was firmly imbedded in my mind. as I counted off each sixty beats, I made a tally mark on my slate to keep track of the minutes. During the three-minute stop at 170 feet I was alarmed to feel a hot pins and needles sensation in my right leg, which continued to persist for most of the rest of my ascent. While this is a classic early symptom of spinal decompression sickness (which can result in paralysis and death), it is also a symptom I often experience as a result of a back injury sustained during our 1982 Caye Cawlker Expedition to Giant Cave (Chapter 1). Another symptom of decompression sickness appeared during the five minute stop at 150 feet: pain in my right shoulder. Again, this might not have been the bends, since I was recovering from a three-month-old kayak injury characterized by the same sort of pain. The pain subsided by the time I arrived at the 140 foot stop, then returned at 110 feet.

At 130 feet my throat felt dry. My refreshments were in a net bag at 30 feet, high above me and hours away. Dehydration is a major cause of decompression sickness. Mexican water is a major cause of Montezuma's Revenge. People seldom die from the runs, so I helped myself to some of the bright blue Mante water, absently wondering what the tiny particles in the water were, and hoping that the vast school of minnows that had gathered around me, attracted to my light, hadn't had to go the bathroom recently.

During my 15-minute stop at 80 feet (ever try counting off 9,000 seconds?), Mary Ellen came down to check on me and offer a kiss of congratulations. For the only time ever, I was more interested in her watch than her kiss. She gave me her watch, and ascended to get my spare watch at 60 feet, where it was attached to one of my decompression tanks. (I had not worn both watches to the bottom because they were guaranteed to only 328 feet. Of course, if Amundsen were a cave diver, he would have thought to leave the backup watch at the first planned decompression stop, right?)

At 50 feet I started breathing a mixture of 50 percent nitrogen and 50 percent oxygen. The more oxygen one breathes, the faster and safer the decompression. But breathe too much—and the amount varies according to depth, time, and individual differences—and one can suddenly either lose the ability to breathe or launch into a violent convulsion, losing one's mouthpiece and drowning. Victims of oxygen toxicity who have survived because they convulsed while in a dry decompression chamber often report that they had no warning symptoms. Just such an occurrence had killed Lewis Holtzendorff and more recently Xavier Goyet, one of France's top cave divers. Normally during a 40-minute stop like this one, I would catnap, but sleeping now was out of the question since I had to keep a close watch for any of the few faint symptoms that have been associated with oxygen toxicity.

Sure enough, after five minutes I felt a little lightheaded, so switched back to air (21 percent oxygen instead of 50 percent). The feeling quickly disappeared. After three minutes on air, I tried the 50 percent nitrox again. Five minutes later I was lightheaded again. The pattern continued, my taking air

breaks whenever the giddy feeling returned. Once or twice I
felt muscular twitching in my left calf, a more serious symptom
of oxygen problems, but also a symptom of my chronic back
disorder. For safety, I went back on air for a long break.

About halfway into the 90-minute 40-foot stop I began
having spells of severe intestinal cramps accompanied by
chills. Surely the revenge of Montezuma couldn't strike that
quickly? I had carefully watched my diet before the dive,
avoiding any contact with Mexican water, milk products, and
even fruit and vegetables. The most likely alternative expla-
nations were not pleasant: decompression sickness and possibly oxygen toxicity, either of which could be fatal. Regardless
of the cause, I was confronted by a real dilemma, locked in a
dry suit that could not be removed underwater and 210
minutes from the surface. As the attacks became more severe,
I knew that there was no way that I could last. After 40 or 50
minutes of fighting it, I muttered into my regulator, "Heck,
astronauts do it," and gave up. Another first in the diving
career of Sheck Exley. Ech!

At 30 feet, I was scheduled to switch to pure oxygen for 85
minutes. Soon muscle twitches started in my face, the most
certain sign of an impending convulsion. I quickly went back
on air and started hyperventilating, a preventive measure
recommended by NOAA (the National Oceanic and Atmospheric Administration), for whom I had worked briefly as a
professional saturation diver in 1973 (Chapter 7). The twitching went away, and after a few minutes I tried the oxygen again
for a brief period. During the rest of this stop and the brief
stops I added at 20 feet and 10 feet, I used the same pattern of
alternating periods of pure oxygen and air.

Finally, seven and a half hours after I had submerged, I
surfaced just in time to enjoy a splendid Mexican sunset over
the Sierra Madre high above us. The view, however, was
partially obscured by a regulator in my mouth. I continued to
breathe pure oxygen for additional insurance against the

bends. It may have been very fortunate that I did. When I removed my foul dry suit and undergarments, I discovered a mottled red rash on my arms, chest, and stomach, similar to a disorder known as "skin bends", which can progress to more serious types of decompression sickness. On the other hand, I have a mild allergy to wool, so could easily have reacted to the long contact with my skin. At any rate, I had to assume the worst for safety's sake. I was back on pure oxygen, drinking lots of bottled water and taking aspirin to thin the blood and reduce any possible platelet involvement in any gas bubbles that might be moving around in my bloodstream. The rash disappeared an hour later, after a good cold bath. The next day there was no noticeable fluid replacement of the rash, so the problem was probably not decompression-related.

I had made mistakes, and most of the dive could at best be described only as an ordeal, but I had learned a lot about the cave and about deep diving. I also had a new American record for depth in an underwater cave, as well as depth while scuba diving from the surface under any conditions. An obvious question had to be answered. Mary Ellen said it first, as we shopped the following day in the local mercado.

"Are you going to come back?"

I was so tired from my dive that I could barely walk down the street. All I could think of was getting home to my bed and a Burger King Whopper with double lettuce, tomato, and onion.

"You've got to be kidding!" I said.

I squinted against the glare of approaching headlights. I couldn't believe that there were any other fools on this lonely Texas road at this time of night, especially since we were still an hour from Brownsville. I looked at the cheap Casio watch that had served me so well at Mantel Yes, we had gone back only two months later. And Mary Ellen had found the darn thing on a rock at 320 feet, right where I had dropped it. She had been on the way up from 400 feet, only the second

American to go that deep in a cave and of course the first woman anywhere. The following day I had tried to lose it again on a dive to 660 feet, but it refused to leave. Maybe it was like me, obsessed with finding the bottom of that darn pit and wanting to stick around until we did. Not satisfied with the 660–footer, especially since the paltry four feet was not enough for me in good conscience to claim to have broken Jochen's world record of 656 feet, my watch and I had returned the following Easter for a 780–footer. Once more I had benefitted from an outstanding support team (Mexico's two top divers, Sergio Zambrano and Angel Soto, and longtime friend Ned DeLoach).

It was hard to believe that this tiny $29.95 timepiece, which wasn't even waterproof (merely "water-resistant", and that only to 328 feet), was still ticking, or computing or whatever it is that these Japanese digital marvels do. And didn't the batteries ever run out? Yet there it was, telling me it was 11:30 p.m. on March 25, 1989.

Ned DeLoach leaned over from the seat beside me and interrupted my reverie. "Since it's quiet now, why don't we get back to work on the background for that article I'm writing?"

I was dog tired, and at that point could not have cared less about Ned's article, but he had been a great friend for many years and an unbelievable help with these marathon 3,000–mile round trip drives to Mante. "Go ahead," I murmured resignedly.

"Well, let's see. You set your first world records for distance and depth in 1970. Two decades later you are still setting records and making more dives than anyone else. How do you do it?"

"That's easy," I grinned. "Controlled paranoia."

"What?" He turned to stare at me.

"Controlled paranoia," I repeated. "It's sort of a mind game I play with myself. I pretend that the cave is out to get me, any way it can."

Angel Soto, Sheck Exley, and Sergio Zambrano getting ready for the 780–foot dive into Mante, Mexico. (*Photo by Sergio Zambrano*)

"Aw, c'mon."

"No, seriously. You see, this forces me to take the time to examine all of the potential hazards of each dive, and devise ways to surmount them. And conjure up backup procedures in case those ways don't work."

"Sort of like 'plan your dive, and dive your plan'."

"Well, it's more than that," I continued. "Lots of divers have the self-discipline to go through that process, and have the ability to perceive the hazards and weigh the risks so they can decide whether or not they can dive with an acceptable degree of safety. But to survive a long-term career of hairy dives, you can't afford to stop at that. You have to convince yourself that the cave is a fickle friend, harboring malevolent thoughts. If you leave any danger unaddressed, no matter how remote, the cave will definitely and gleefully kill you."

"So you see underwater caves as enemies to be conquered?"

"Not at all. The cave is my friend as much as it is an enemy. It has given me some of the greatest pleasures in my life, as well as some of the greatest heartaches. But the reality of course, is that the cave doesn't care one way or the other. Even if caves were sentient beings, their life–spans are so great that the instant of my exploration is no more noticeable than a blink of your eye. My claiming ownership of Cathedral Canyon, for example, makes no more sense than a flea claiming to own a dog. But before and during the dive," I summed up, "I use the pretense of the cave's enmity to ensure my survival, and the pretense of its friendship to reduce my anxiety."

"Hey, here's Brownsville."

In many ways this trip was more relaxed for me than the earlier Mante expeditions. Those dives had been for the numbers. Depth records had to be set and broken. Now the records were all comfortably mine. This trip would be for the cave, and to satisfy my curiosity. How deep could an underwater cave go? Could our campfire speculations from a decade earlier possibly be true?

There was also psychological strength in our numbers. This would be the biggest Mante expedition yet. Besides those three unsurpassed support divers who had helped me the previous year— Sergio, Angel, and Ned—several other highly regarded cave divers were coming along to help: Paul Heinerth, Tom Bussell, Randy Bohrer, Dave Hodgetts, Paul Smith, and newlyweds Tom and Nancy Morris, whose honeymoon would be diving at Mante. In addition, John Harper, Paul DeLoach, Mary Ellen Eckhoff, Bill Stone, Clark Pitcairn, Wes Skiles, John Troutner, Dale Sweet, Jochen Hasenmayer, John Zumrick, Rob Anderson, and Kelly Brady had all provided equipment and assistance for the dive. I also had six commercial sponsors: Air Products, Batso Products, Dive Rite Manufacturing, English Engineering, Scuba West, and Spring Systems Dive Resort. My decompression tables were based primarily on some that Bill Hamilton had designed for the 780–foot dive, with modifications from my extrapolations of the tables that Gene Melton had sent me as well as the calculations of Angel Soto and Randy Bohrer.

All this support and assistance was essential since all phases of this dive would be considerably more complex than that of the 520–foot dive. For example, as the dives became deeper, the amount of helium in the mixture increased from 200 cubic feet to over 1,200 cubic feet. On the 660–foot and 780–foot dives I had solved the need for increased gas by staging additional single 80 cubic foot tanks at 270 feet and 330 feet on set-up dives, plus putting a helium mixture in the twin 100's on my back. Since this mixture could not be breathed near the surface due to insufficient oxygen, this meant that I had to rely on an additional stage bottle containing air to get me from the surface to the depth at which I switched to the helium, now increased to 270 feet. (On the 660-foot dive, a regulator malfunction had made it necessary to stay on air until a depth of 330 feet).

Another added hazard was that my primary tanks—the twins on my back—would no longer contain a mixture that I could use to "bail out" to the surface in an emergency ascent. But these problems were nothing compared to what I faced on this latest dive. To go deeper and still have a third of my gas reserved for emergencies, I would need considerably more than the 500 cubic feet of gas carried down on the 780–foot dive, where I had cut it uncomfortably close. Gas would also be needed for decompression, since I would have 20 stops below 330 feet, the deepest point at which we could leave extra tanks on set-up dives. The only solution was to redesign my scuba rig completely.

After months of careful study, I decided to use a wrap-around set of five tanks on my back which, when filled to 4,000 psig, contained 600 cubic feet of gas. Adding two stage bottles to be snapped on my chest and four more bottles staged on earlier dives at 270 feet and 330 feet would give me the 1,200 cubic feet of gas that I needed.

I made several test dives with the five tank rig, the "quint set". By itself the monstrosity weighed more than 200 pounds out of the water. The center of gravity and center of buoyancy was adjusted for a perfect head-down descent by adding and shifting lead weights and the buoyancy compensator donated by Dive Rite Manufacturing. Incredibly, the outstanding lift and other characteristics of their stock, sold-across-the-counter buoyancy compensator was perfect for my needs.

Meanwhile, Lamar at English Engineering was hard at work designing a primary light to work at the unheard–of–depths of 800 feet and below. I had carried his lights on all my Mante dives and had experienced absolutely no problems with the light heads, generally considered to be the most delicate part of a lighting system. To place this remarkable achieve-ment in proper perspective, one must realize that the finest primary light heads available in dive shops generally implode from pressure somewhere between 230 feet and 300 feet. The few problems that we had encountered were occasional battery pack flooding, which resulted in a minor loss of buoyancy. But the light always kept burning! His latest design had survived without even flooding problems to 780 feet, but then the pack had imploded and flooded. Since flooding did not harm the batteries, and the concussion from a violent implosion could stun me, I suggested that we just flood the pack with distilled water to start with. I had already been preflooding my tank pressure gauges to prevent the needle sticking problems I had experienced on the 520 foot dive.

Various kinds of regulators had proven inadequate during the previous dives until I was left with only one type of regulator that I could hope would deliver the vast volumes of gas required at 800 feet: the Poseidon Odin. Likewise, only one backup light had resisted implosion below 400 feet – the Pelican light. The nearly 400 pounds per square inch of pressure that I would experience on the dive would literally crush the fancy, expensive diver's watches that the jet set liked to show off at plush dive resorts. My three $29.95 Casio watches would be OK.

One concern on previous dives had been the purity of the helium I was using. Even small impurities can cause major problems at depth. One tragic example of this was the fatal accident involving the secretary and director of NACD (the National Association for Cave Diving), Dana Turner, in 1974. While diving at 300 feet, he became confused and impaired, then experienced breathing difficulties and drowned with over two-thirds of his air left in his tanks. After we made the recovery, Lewis Holtzendorff had Dana's air analyzed and it was found to contain a significant percentage of deadly carbon monoxide. The amount would not have become life-threatening on the surface for several hours, but at 300 feet the effect is magnified ten times. A 25–minute exposure, combined with the toxic effects of oxygen, carbon dioxide, and nitrogen, were enough to kill one of America's top cave divers of the early 1970's. At the depth that I would be diving, the effect of any impurities would be magnified nearly 28 times.

Fortunately, Bruce Watson of Air Products, a major sponsor of our recent project at Wakulla Springs, agreed to donate the helium needed. Our experience at Wakulla had proved that they could be counted on to furnish the highest possible quality of gas. Likewise, the danger from impurities meant that not just any dive shop could be relied on to pump the gas and furnish the compressed air. Paul Heinerth at Scuba West pumped the gas with his ultra-clean system, and Arwyn Carr at Spring Systems added the nitrogen and oxygen needed with his carefully maintained compressed air equipment.

The business of installing the 23 tanks that had to be placed in the cave before the dive could be made was quite a complicated task in itself. Each tank, carefully numbered and with its contents tagged twice, had to be installed at a specific location in the cave. In many instances, loops of line that Sergio, Angel, and others had tied on the walls for the tanks had to be replaced, or new loops added in a cave where there was a lack of projections strong enough to support the weight of a tank. Most of the projections that were strong enough were also sharp enough to cut the line, so quite a bit of ingenuity was required to rig new loops. As Tom Morris once observed, staring pensively down the fissure, "This is not a place where you want to drop your dive gear."

Because of his experience and outstanding help with my 780–foot dive, I asked Sergio to head the complicated support effort. My two dozen tanks would be difficult for many of the divers to carry because the carry snaps and straps were adjusted for me and not for them. None of the new members of the team had ever dived Mante before, or even a cave containing Mante's unique combination of strong current, depth, silt, and sharp ledges. In such a situation one expects a lot of confusion. Tanks could be installed at the wrong depth, regulators with their hoses and delicate internal parts could easily be damaged, and worst of all, the tanks could be be dropped down the shaft "to China", as Paul DeLoach had said a decade earlier. It was largely due to Sergio's excellent leadership and the great help of the others that the tanks were installed with no problems. Paul Heinerth and Tom Bussell, our two most experienced deep divers, installed tanks between 180 and 240 feet, Sergio and Angel between 100 and 160 feet, Randy and

Dave between 50 and 80 feet, and Paul Smith helped me ferry in the bottles to shallower depths. (An Eastern Airlines strike prevented Tom and Nancy from being present for this part of the expedition.)

As usual, I made the final set-up dive myself, to install the four deepest decompression tanks and some extra weights. This dive, like all the other set-up dives, was made on compressed air, which enabled me to use considerably safer decompression tables than would have been necessary had I used a helium mixture. Needless to say, a decompression accident to any of us, requiring immediate evacuation to the nearest recompression chamber—600 miles away in San Antonio, Texas – would have forced us to cancel the expedition.

I verified the position of all the tanks, then attached the four bottles at 270 and 330 feet. I felt unusually clear-headed at 330 feet, probably due largely to the excellent visibility afforded by a 100–watt quartz-halogen lamp built by Lamar English, so I quickly dropped down to see if there were any spots that could be used for looping decompression tanks on future dives. When I stopped due to the onset of narcosis, I was surprised to see that I was at 381 feet, a new world record for an air dive in a cave.

At the motel that evening while making last minute adjustments to my dive gear and reviewing the dive plan, I suddenly broke out in a cold sweat and started shaking. Sure enough, I was running a fever and felt so weak that I had to lie down. I notified the others that our original plans to dive the next day might have to be postponed, a real disappointment to them, since they all wanted to get in some good dives of their own at Mante and Sabinas before it was time to head back to the States.

I had watched this kind of pressure stampede Archie Forfar, Ann Gunderson, and Jim Lockwood into making a fatal record attempt under adverse conditions in 1971. (See Chapter 5.) Their success at making practice dives to 440 and even

450 feet led them to believe that breaking Gruner and Watson's 437 foot record for diving on air in the sea would be easy. Unfortunately, the "official" attempt had to be made with a measured cable which arrived only the day before the dive, so there was no time to practice with it. The pressure on them came from having already scheduled and invested in media coverage and verification by Bahamian government officials. Even though the cable was too large for the markers that they had to clip on for verification, they elected to go ahead with the dive anyway. By the time they reached 350 feet, sliding the markers down the cable became so difficult that the only way to continue was to detach their safety system of drop-away weights, empty their buoyancy compensators, and attempt to swim the markers down. Postponing the dive would have meant trying to reschedule all the people that were waiting above them in the boats. They decided to keep going.

As one of three support divers hired to wait for them at 300 feet, I watched Jim Lockwood come floating up unconscious after blacking out at 400 feet from the exertion. Because of concern for the safety of the support divers (Randy Hylton and Bill Wiggins were two of the best deep divers in the world but I was the only one who had previously been to 400 feet) as well as because they were so confident of attaining their objective, they had made no provision for our having to descend below 300 feet and in fact requested that we did not go any deeper under any circumstances. Nevertheless, when Archie and Ann failed to appear, I attempted a rescue without any of the special preparation normally required. I made it to the unprecedented depth of 465 feet before I also started to black out and had to execute an emergency ascent.

Archie and Ann died at 480 feet, their bodies never recovered. Nearly two decades had passed but the lesson was not forgotten. There was no way that I would take any unnecessary risk such as diving while ill.

The next morning the fever was gone and I awoke somewhat weak but refreshed. Due to the elimination problems encountered on the 520–foot dive, I had gone on an all-liquid diet for 18 hours prior to the 660 and 780 footers. During my recent record distance dives at Chips Hole, which were as much as 14–hours long, I had not experienced any problems with a solid predive diet, so now ate my usual breakfast of shredded wheat and granola.

The early part of the dive was much like the 520–footer, with a long swim to the cave followed by a 10–minute period of rest and meditation. Then I submerged and carefully began working my way in and down against the current. My initial progress was slower than usual because of the increased drag from the three extra tanks on my back. The changeover to helium was right on schedule at 270 feet, then as the fissure belled out to a width of 15 feet below 300 feet, my practice dives to balance the quint set really began to pay off. My rate of descent actually exceeded that of previous dives with fewer tanks. A garter left by Mary Ellen at 400 feet seemed almost a blur when I passed it. I quickly arrived at my old tie-off at 515 feet, where I hooked a depth gauge, spare watch, and decompression tables, and switched from a stage tank to my quint set. My descent to the 660–foot tie–off was equally uneventful, as was the final leg to the end of the line at 780 feet.

On the previous dive, in 30-foot visibility with nitrogen narcosis equivalent to a 260–foot dive on air, I thought that the shaft—which we had jokingly named "Macho Pit" in 1979 —was flattening out to a descent angle of 60–75 degrees below 660 feet and 45 degrees below 780 feet. This could have meant that Macho Pit was bottomed out and that I was approaching the maximum depth of the spring. Now, with less nitrogen in my mix and the benefit of a second view, I could see that my earlier estimates had been wrong. The descent below 660 feet is very nearly vertical, probably more than 80 degrees from the horizontal. Beyond the large projection that I had tied off on at 780 feet, I could now see that the shaft was continuing to

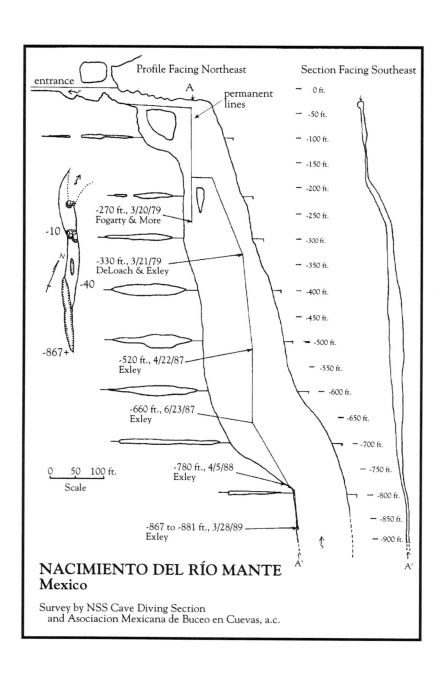

Profile Facing Northeast   Section Facing Southeast

entrance

A

permanent
lines

− 0 ft.

− -50 ft.

− -100 ft.

− -150 ft.

− -200 ft.

-270 ft., 3/20/79
Fogarty & More

− -250 ft.

-10

− -300 ft.

N

-330 ft., 3/21/79
DeLoach & Exley

− -350 ft.

-40

− -400 ft.

− -450 ft.

− -500 ft.

-867+

-520 ft., 4/22/87
Exley

− -550 ft.

− -600 ft.

-660 ft., 6/23/87
Exley

− -650 ft.

− -700 ft.

0   50   100 ft.

Scale

-780 ft., 4/5/88
Exley

− -750 ft.

− -800 ft.

− -850 ft.

-867 to -881 ft., 3/28/89
Exley

− -900 ft.

A'

A'

NACIMIENTO DEL RÍO MANTE
Mexico

Survey by NSS Cave Diving Section
and Asociacion Mexicana de Buceo en Cuevas, a.c.

plunge nearly straight down.

I glanced at the pressure gauge for my quint set, tied off a special Dive Rite reel containing my measured guideline, and continued my descent. No depth gauges were available for diving below 500 feet, so I had to rely entirely on the measured line and my estimates of the angle of descent to calculate my depth. This method had an advantage in that it was impossible for me to tell how deep I had gone while descending, so there would be no temptation to go a little deeper than my normal turnaround to attain "a nice round number", as I had done on the 520 foot dive. My turnaround would be established by my continuing evaluation of the safety factors or an audio alarm on my watch set to go off 22 minutes after submerging, whichever came first. The alarm would give me a minute to tie off and cut the guideline before I would have to begin my ascent. If I stayed longer, I would have to use a much longer decompression schedule than planned. Decompressing longer than 12 hours would subject me to increasing pulmonary oxygen toxicity, a problem that could cause pain and bleeding in the lungs, permanent damage, and even death as the alveoli lose their ability to exchange oxygen for carbon dioxide.

Meanwhile, it was becoming increasingly difficult to breathe as the gas in my regulator became more dense. It was like trying to breathe through a straw. Adding to this problem was my need to breathe more as I fought against an increasing current caused by a reduction in the size of the pit to only 30 by 15 feet. Finally the problem became sufficiently severe that I decided to call the dive, even though below me I could see another 30 feet before the walls of the pit vanished into the hazy, electric blue water.

As I prepared to tie off my line on a big rock, my watch alarm went off. Then the cave shook with a tremendous concussion as my battery pack, which I had not been able to flood properly, imploded. While the force of the implosion was not sufficient to stun me, it did destroy the base of the pack, causing the batteries to fall out and my 42-watt primary light to go out. It didn't matter, though. When I settled onto the rock, I had inadvertently disturbed an unusual amount of reddish-brown silt. The silt was fanned by the uprushing water into a dense cloud that completely obliterated visibility. I had to tie off the line blindly, at a depth that I knew had to be well in excess of 800 feet. Each minute at this depth I breathed a third of a tank of gas, so I couldn't afford to linger even if I had wanted to switch to the longer decompression schedule. Fortunately, I had cut line and tied knots underwater thousands of times, so there was no problem in getting the task done quickly by feel alone.

Since I could not see, I began my ascent by letting the line slide through my fingers. Soon the silt thinned sufficiently that I could see reasonably well with my five Pelican lights, and I was able to ascend close to the required rate of 120 feet per minute. Suddenly I saw something that made me feel good for our team: a large red stripe that I had put on the line for 820 feet (250 meters). This would be the depth at that point if the pit had continued nearly vertically, as it did.

My ascent was somewhat uncomfortable because the head-down balancing of my tanks made head-up ascent or even horizontal movement rather difficult. At 540 feet, I paused for the first of 54 decompression stops, an action that really drove home the seriousness of what we had accomplished: I was decompressing 100 feet deeper than the maximum depth ever attained by any diver in the world besides Jochen and myself. As I worked my way up through the myriad short stops below 330 feet, I also reflected that the maximum depth of this dive was more than twice that of the next deepest American (Mary Ellen) and nearly three times that of anyone else.

Above 330 feet my problem soon became too much gas, as I spent extra minutes beyond those required for decompression to ferry unused tanks up to shallower depths. Although several of our team members were hoping to make their own helium dives the next day, none of them had experience below 300 feet and would have enough problems without having to bring up my tanks. Experience had taught me that a deep tank recovery dive by myself, even on air, was also out of the question. Previous dives had left me so fatigued that I was almost too weak to walk for days afterward. For these reasons I wanted to bring all the tanks up with me to at least 200 feet.

Sergio, Angel, Paul, and the others started visiting me when I arrived at 140 feet. They took up most of the tanks that I didn't need. Finally, 13 hours and 30 minutes after submerging, I surfaced amid the floodlights and popping strobes of the photographers from the Mexican media. I felt stronger after this dive than I ever had before at Mante, which was a good thing. The newspaper reporters, radio interviewers, and politicians kept me answering questions in Spanish for two hours. I was glad to have the opportunity to give recognition and credit to all the members of my invaluable support team.

When we measured the remaining line on my reel the next day, we saw that I had attained a depth between 867 and 881 feet, depending on the angle of descent below 660 feet. As always, I went with the shallower number.

And Mante's Macho Pit? Add another name to Cathedral Canyon's when we speak of caverns measureless to man.

Sheck Exley was born on April 1, 1949.
He died on April 6, 1994, diving below
900 feet in Xacatún, Tamaulipas, Mexico.

Profile for 3/28/89 dive to 867-881 feet at Nacimiento del Río Mante, Tamaulipas, Mexico by Sheck Exley

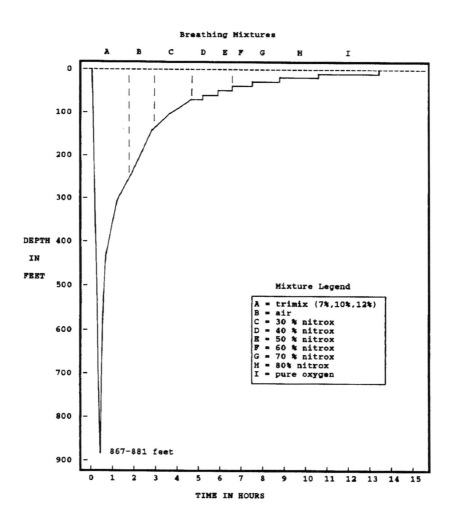

Breathing Mixtures

Mixture Legend

A = trimix (7%,10%,12%)
B = air
C = 30 % nitrox
D = 40 % nitrox
E = 50 % nitrox
F = 60 % nitrox
G = 70 % nitrox
H = 80% nitrox
I = pure oxygen

Actual DCP* of 3/28/89 dive at
Nacimiento del Río Mante, Mexico by Sheck Exley

Depth FSW	Stop Time	Run Time	Breathing Mix	Comments
0	0	0	Air	Descent to 270 fsw on air, rate 40 fpm
270	0	7	10% TMX	Switch to 10% O₂ TRIMIX
500	0	13	7% TMX	Switch to 7% O₂ TRIMIX
841-855**	1	23	"	Begin timing dcp, ascend at 85 fpm
520	1	23	"	First stop; ascent rate included in stop times from here tu surface.
510	1	30	"	
500	1	31	"	
490	1	32	"	
480	1	33	"	
470	1	34	"	
460	1	35	"	
450	1	36	"	
440	1	37	"	
430	1	28	"	
420	2	40	"	
410	3	43	"	
400	2	45	10% TMX	Switch to 10% TRIMIX
390	2	47	"	
380	3	50	"	
370	3	53	"	
360	3	56	"	
350	3	59	"	
340	4	63	"	
300	3	66	12% TMX	Swith to 12% TRIMIX
320	3	69	"	
310	3	72	"	
300	3	75	"	
290	7	8	"	
280	7	89	"	
270	7	96	"	
260	9	105	'	Unplanned extra 2 minute stop
250	10	115	"	Unplanned extra 2 minute stop
240	8	123	Air	Unplanned extra 2 minute stop
230	4	127	"	
220	4	131	"	
210	4	135	"	
200	6	141	"	
190	6	147	"	
180	8	155	"	
170	8	163	"	
160	9	172	"	
150	9	181	"	
140	10	191	30% NTX	Switch to 30% Nitrox
130	9	200	"	
120	14	214	"	
110	117	231	"	
100	18	249	"	
90	21	270	"	
80	23	293	40% NTX	Switch to 40% Nitrox
70	29	322	"	
60	40	362	"	
50	43	405	50% NTX	Switch to 50% Nitrox
40	58	463	60% NTX	Switch to 60% Nitrox
30	74	537	70% NTX	Switch to 70% Nitrox
20	113	650	80% NTX	Switch to 80% Nitrox
10	152	802	Oxygen	
0	30	832	Oxygen 30 minute	Oxygen at surface

* DCP = decompression profile
** Actual depth of dive was 867–881 feet by Sheck Exley 3/28/89

Appendix I: A Brief History of Organized Cave Diving in the United States

Organized cave diving began in the United States under the auspices of the National Speleological Society (NSS), the United States' only national caving organization, founded in 1941. In 1947, the NSS published the first information on cave diving in this country in the NSS *Bulletin*, and in 1952, members of the FSS, the Florida chapter of the NSS, were responsible for the first cave dives in America using scuba. In 1953, the FSS established the first cave diving training program in the United States, complete with formal written standards. Cave diving activity among FSS members reached such a peak that in 1955, the NSS chapter joined the Florida Skin Diver's Association (FSDA) of the Underwater Society of America as a scuba diving club.

The need for an organization exclusively devoted to cave diving as opposed to a caving or diving organization containing a cave diving branch prompted NSS divers to establish the Descenders Cave Diving Group in Georgia in the early 1960's, followed by FSS' Dave Desautels founding the Florida Cave Dwellers. In 1968, Sheck Exley founded the Dixie Cavern Kings, the first interstate cave diving organization. In 1969, Exley wrote America's first cave diving text, the *Dixie Cavern Kings Cave Diving Manual*.

In 1968, the Florida Cave Dwellers held a cave diving seminar in Florida. Encouraged by the interest shown, David Desautels and Larry Briel founded the National Association for Cave Diving (NACD) in 1969 with six other members. This was the first of three organization in Florida that have been called NACD.

In 1971, Exley and several other cave diving instructors replaced some inactive NACD directors, and a new organization was formed, although it was not formally chartered until 1973. Tom Mount, Bob Friedman, Rory Dickens, and Exley were probably the most productive of the new organization's charter directors. They served successive terms as president and were responsible for writing most of the contents of five cave diving books published during this period: *Cave Diving Manual* (Mount, 1972), *Mapping Underwater Caves* (Exley and Friedman, 1972), *Proceedings of the Fifth Annual Seminar On Cave Diving* (1972), *Safe Cave Diving* (1973), *Proceedings of the Sixth and Seventh Annual NACD Seminars* (1975). Exley was author or coauthor of all of these except Mount's *Cave Diving Manual*.

While Exley was president in 1975, NACD grew to its largest size ever with 87 members. Unfortunately, the membership of NACD had little voice in the organization since only five of the 15 directors were elected. (The other 10 were charter directors designated by the charter as "permanent" board members.)

The third version of NACD was started by Paul Meng in late 1978. The concept of permanent board members was abandoned in favor of a new democratic organization patterned after the immensely successful NSS Cave Diving Section. Under the leadership of Steve Gerrard, this latest edition of NACD is growing and is once more becoming a major voice in American cave diving.

In 1973, Exley chaired meetings in Missouri and Indiana at which the NSS Cave Diving Section (NSS CDS) was born. Instead of being primarily limited to Florida like the NACD, the NSS CDS is a democratic organization and has members from all over the country. The first executive committee of the NSS CDS was composed of Exley, Chairman; Jim Storey (Georgia), vice chairman; and Glenn Thompson (Arkansas), secretary-treasurer. Two other charter members who have made enormous contributions to American cave diving are Rick Rigg (Idaho), who wrote the cave diving portion of the *NSS Caver's Information Series*, and Stephen Maegerlein (Indiana), who served for many years as NSS CDS treasurer.

Besides Exley and Storey, NSS CDS chairmen have included Tom Cook, John Zumrick, India Fuller, Dennis Williams, Bill Fehring, Steve Ormeroid, Joe Prosser, Jeff Bozanic, and Mark Leonard. By 1976, the NSS CDS was the largest cave diving organization in the world, a position it has maintained ever since. There are now approximately 500 active members. All of the current cave diving texts have been produced by the NSS CDS: *Basic Cave Diving* (Exley, 1979), *NSS Cave Diving Manual* (Exley and Fuller, eds., 1982), *NSS CDS Instructors Training Manual* (Joe Prosser, ed., 1985), *Basic Underwater Cave Surveying* (John Burge, 1987), and *NSS Cavern Diving Manual* (Zumrick, Prosser, and H. V. Grey, 1988).

It is impossible to list all of the many NSS CDS members who have made important contributions to cave diving. In addition to the persons mentioned above, however, three divers have made a unique contribution to cave diving safety. The NSS CDS training officers, Forrest Wilson, Wes Skiles, and Joe Prosser, developed a program of certified cave diver training that not only has been used to train far more divers than all the other organizations combined, but also has the best safety record. Henry Nicholson has also made a tremendous contribution in heading up search and rescue operations.

For more information on the National Speleological Society, write: NSS, Cave Avenue, Huntsville, AL 35810.

For more information on the NSS Cave Diving Section, write: NSS CDS, P. O Box 950, Branford, FL 32008-0950.

Jochen Hasenmayer and Sheck Exley prepare for a 1981 dive in Blautopf, Germany. (Photo by Barbara Hasenmayer)

Appendix II: Progressive World Records for Underwater Cave Depth*

Depth (feet)	Date	Location, Participating Divers
75	3/27/1878	Vaucluse, France - Ottonelli (France)
90	9/27/1938	Vaucluse, France - Negri (France)
150	8/27/46	Vaucluse, France - Jacques Cousteau, Frederic Dumas (France)
197	8/31/47	Chartreaux Spring, France - Guy Morandiere (France)
210	?/?/55	Vaucluse, France - Jacques Cousteau (France)
250	?/?/56	Wakulla Spring, Florida, U.S.A. - Gary Salsman, Wally Jenkins (U.S.A.)
300	3/?/59	Sinoia Caves, Rhodesia - Sergio Crespi, Conrad Wilson (United Kingdom)
315	?/?/65	Devil's Hole, Nevada, U.S.A. - Jim Houtz (U.S.A.)
335	?/?/69	Sinoia Caves, Rhodesia - Rolly Nyman, Ian Robertson, Johnny van der Walt, Danny van der Walt (United Kingdom)
340	7/2/77	Boiling Hole, Andros, Bahamas - Frank Fogarty, Terry More, Sheck Exley (U.S.A.)
360	6/8/80	Die Polder Sink #2, Florida, U.S.A. - Dale Sweet (U.S.A.)
(tie) 360	3/29/81	Die Polder Sink #2, Florida, U.S.A. - Sheck Exley (assisted by Dale Sweet, Jamie Stone) (U.S.A.)
476	9/20/81	Vaucluse, France - Jochen Hasenmayer (Germany)
656	9/8/83	Vaucluse, France - Jochen Hasenmayer (Germany)
(tie) 660	6/23/87	Mante, Mexico - Sheck Exley (assisted by Dale Sweet, Jamie Stone) (U.S.A.)
780	4/5/88	Mante, Mexico - Sheck Exley (assisted by Sergio Zambrano, Angel Soto, Ned Deloach)(Mexico, U.S.A.)
867	3/28/89	Mante, Mexico - Sheck Exley (assisted by Sergio Zambrano, Angel Soto, Ned DeLoach, Paul Heinerth, Paul Smith, Randy Bohrer, Tom Bussell, Dave Hodgetts, Nancy Morris, Tom Morris)(Mexico, U.S.A.)

*Greatest vertical distance below the water surface in an underwater cave.
Note: Most of the later dives were accomplished with helium-oxygen mixtures. Diving below 130 feet on air is not recommended.

Appendix III: Progressive World Records for Underwater Cave Penetration*

Distance (feet)	Date	Location, Participating Divers
2099	6/29/70	Blue Springs Cave System, Florida, U.S.A. - Bob Rodgers, John Townes, Sheck Exley (U.S.A.)
2250	?/?/71	Devil's Eye Cave System, Florida, U.S.A. - John Harper, Randy Hylton, Jim Lockwood (U.S.A.)
2450	4/12/72	Devil's Eye Cave System, Florida, U.S.A. - Chuck Stevens, Sheck Exley (U.S.A.)
2886	10/?/72	Gouls de Tourne, France - Groupe d'Etudes et de Plongees Souterraines (France)
2952	10/20/73	Frais-Puits, France, - Jochen Hasenmayer (Germany)
3000	3/31/74	Devil's Eye Cave System, Florida, U.S.A. - Lewis Holtzendorff, Court Smith, Dana Turner, Sheck Exley (U.S.A.)
3105	4/13/75	Devil's Eye Cave System, Florida, U.S.A. - Lewis Holtzendorff, Court Smith, Sheck Exley (U.S.A.)
3305	4/20/75	Devil's Eye Cave System, Florida, U.S.A. - Lewis Holtzendorff, Court Smith, Sheck Exley (U.S.A.)
3956	5/4/75	Manatee Springs Cave System, Florida, U.S.A. - Lewis Holtzendorff, Court Smith, Sheck Exley (U.S.A.)
4110	5/11/75	Manatee Springs Cave System, Florida, U.S.A. - Lewis Holtzendorff, Court Smith, Sheck Exley (U.S.A.)
4457	3/19/78	Hole in the Wall Cave, Florida, U.S.A. - Dale Sweet, Sheck Exley (U.S.A.)
4527	3/26/78	Hole in the Wall Cave, Florida, U.S.A. - Dale Sweet, Sheck Exley (U.S.A.)
4802	10/14/78	Blue Springs Cave, Jackson Co., Florida, U.S.A. - Paul DeLoach, Sheck Exley (U.S.A.)
4816	11/4/78	Blue Springs Cave, Jackson Co., Florida, U.S.A. - Paul DeLoach, Sheck Exley (U.S.A.)

(continued)

(Appendix III cont.)

Distance (feet)	Date	Location, Participating Divers
5297	?/?/79	La Bourne, France - Bertrand Leger (France)
5326	?/?/79	Manatee Springs Cave System, Florida, U.S.A. - Lewis Henkel, Dave Manor (U.S.A.)
5740	?/?/80	Source du Ressel, France - Jochen Hasenmayer (Germany)
5847	6/21/81	Big Dismal Sink Cave, Florida, U.S.A. - Clark Pitcairn, Mary Ellen Eckhoff, Sheck Exley (U.S.A.)
5914	7/26/81	Manatee Springs Cave System, Florida, U.S.A. - Bill Main, Sheck Exley (U.S.A.)
6867	8/8/81	Manatee Springs Cave System, Florida, U.S.A. - Bill Main, Sheck Exley (U.S.A.)
7665	8/23/81	Manatee Springs Cave System, Florida, U.S.A. - Clark Pitcairn, Sheck Exley (U.S.A.)
8626	?/?/84	Doux de Coly, France - Olivier Isler (Switzerland)
10,168	?/?/84	Doux de Coly, France - Olivier Isler (Switzerland)
10,444	1/28/89	Chips Hole Cave System, Florida, U.S.A. - Sheck Exley (U.S.A.)
10,939	12/16/90	Cathedral Canyon, Florida, U.S.A. - Sheck Exley (U.S.A.)
12,595	7/29/91	Doux de Coly, France - Olivier Isler (Switzerland)

Appendix IV: Multiple Sumps or Traverses

Distance (feet)	Date	Location, Participating Divers
465	1/?/61**	Manatee Springs-Catfish Hotel, Florida, U.S.A. - unknown divers
2109	12/2/62**	Hornsby Sink-Hornsby Spring, Florida, U.S.A. - John Harper, Joe Fuller (U.S.A.)
4693	6/?/70	Orange Grove Sink-Peacock Spring I, Florida, U.S.A. - John Harper, Randy Hylton (U.S.A.)
5074	4/21/71	Orange Grove Sink-Cisteen Sink, Florida, U.S.A. - Chuck Stevens, Sheck Exley (U.S.A.)
7040	7/7/73	Orange Grove Sink-Waterhole #3, Florida, U.S.A. - John Harper, Randy Hylton (U.S.A.)
8032	5/?/79***	Cocklebiddy Cave, Australia - Hugh Morrison, Keith Dekkers, Simon Jones
9836	?/?/82***	Cocklebiddy Cave, Australia - Ron Allum, Hugh Morrison, Peter Rogers
14,756	9/15/83***	Cocklebiddy Cave, Australia - Francis LeGuen, Eric LeGuen
15,603	?/?/83***	Cocklebiddy Cave, Australia - Hugh Morrison

* Total one-way distance underwater in a cave on a single dive (air spaces not included)
** single sump or traverse
*** multiple dives were made instead of a single dive

Appendix V: Other Interesting Cave Dives

These so-called "minor" records are generally considered less important than those for absolute depth and distance given in the previous appendices. Nevertheless, this author believes that some of them are actually more difficult and all are worthy of mention.

Distance (feet)	Date	Location, Participating Divers

Current World Cave Diving Depth Records

Fresh water (mixed gas):

867	3/28/89	Mante, Mexico - Sheck Exley (U.S.A.)

Fresh water (air):

380	3/27/89	Mante, Mexico - Sheck Exley (U.S.A.)

Salt water (mixed gas):

320	7/–/87	Stargate, Andros, Bahamas - Rob Parker, Stuart Clough

Salt water (air):

340	7/2/77	Boiling Hole, Andros, Bahamas - Sheck Exley (U.S.A.)

Combination fresh and salt water (mixed gas):

420	8/3/90	Cenote Xkolak, Yucatan, Mexico - Paul DeLoach, Sheck Exley (U.S.A.)

Combination fresh and salt water (air):

386	7/6/89	Cenote Xkolak, Yucatan, Mexico - Paul DeLoach Sheck Exley (U.S.A.)

Water colder than 60° F:

656	9/8/83	Vaucluse, France - Jochen Hasenmayer (Germany)

Submarine vehicle (unmanned, fresh water):

1033	4/8/85	Vaucluse, France - Telenaute

Submarine vehicle (manned, salt water):

1500	early 1972	La Jolla Canyon, California - Deepstar (piloted by Harold D. Palmer)

(continued)

(Appendix V: Other Interesting Cave Dives cont.)

Current Cave Diving Penetration Records

Fresh water (scooter):
    10,939   12/16/90   Cathedral Canyon, Cathedral-Falmouth Cave System, Florida, U.S.A. - Sheck Exley (U.S.A.)

Fresh water (swimming):
    10,444   1/28/89   Cal's Cave, Chip's Hole Cave System, Florida, U.S.A. - Sheck Exley (U.S.A.)

Salt water (scooter):
    5308   –/–/–   Atlantida Tunnel, Lanzarote, Spain - Olivier Isler (Switzerland)

Salt water (swimming):
    4518   3/7/83   Atlantida Tunnel, Lanzarote, Spain - Ken Fulghum, Sheck Exley (U.S.A.)

Outflow cave:
    10,939   12/16/90   Cathedral Canyon, Cathedral-Falmouth Cave System, Florida, U.S.A. - Sheck Exley (U.S.A.)

Inflow cave:
    10,444   1/29/89   Cal's Cave, Chip's Hole Cave System, Florida, U.S.A. - Sheck Exley (U.S.A.)

Air cave sump (underwater part only):
    10,444   1/29/89   Cal's Cave, Chip's Hole Cave System, Florida, U.S.A. - Sheck Exley (U.S.A.)

Water colder than 60° F:
    10,168   –/–/85   Doux de Coly, France - Olivier Isler (Switzerland)

Average depth greater than 250 feet:
    4176   12/4/87   Wakulla Spring, Florida, U.S.A. - Paul Heinerth, Tom Morris, Wes Skiles (U.S.A.)

Maximum depth greater than 300 feet:
    4550   6/19/82   Indian Springs, Florida, U.S.A. - Jamie Stone, Sheck Exley (U.S.A.)

(continued)

(Appendix V: Other Interesting Cave Dives cont.)

Current Cave Diving Traverse Records
(one-way distance from one air space to another)

Single traverse:
8770   6/19/88   Sullivan Sink to Cheryl Sink, Florida, U.S.A. - Lamar
                   English, Bill Gavin, Bill Main, Parker Turner (U.S.A.)

Multiple traverse (underwater portions only):
19,221   9/-/83   Entrance Sump to Sump 1 to Rockpile Chamber to S2 to
                   Toad Hall to end of cave, Cocklebiddy Cave, Australia -
                   Hugh Morrison

Single traverse maximum depth:
230   6/19/88   Sullivan Sink to Cheryl Sink, Florida, U.S.A. - Lamar
                   English, Bill Gavin, Bill Main, Parker Turner (U.S.A.)

Single traverse maximum depth (side excursion):
300   3/10/84   Double Keyhole to Meng Spring, Florida, U.S.A. - Paul
                   DeLoach, Sheck Exley (U.S.A.)

Single traverse in water colder than 60° F:
6000   1/16/79   Kingsdale Master Cave to Keld Head, Yorkshire, United
                   Kingdom - Oliver Statham, Geoff Yeadon (U.K.)

Surveys

World's longest surveyed underwater cave:
38,398   Cathedral–Falmouth Cave System, Florida, U.S.A. –
                   National Speleological Society (U.S.A.)

World's longest surveyed underwater cave in salt water:
10,222   Giant Cave, Belize – National Speleological Society
                   (U.S.A.)

World's longest surveyed underwater cave containing both fresh and salt water:
30,124   Lucayan Caverns, Bahamas   – National Speleological
                   Society (U.S.A.)

World's largest underwater cave (volume):
28,723,500 cu. ft. Cathedral-Falmouth Cave System, Florida
                   U.S.A. – National Speleological Society (U.S.A.)

World's maximum topographical width (straight-line distance) for underwater
cave:
23,700   Cathedral–Falmouth Cave System, Florida, U.S.A. –
                   National Speleological Society (U.S.A.)

World's longest surveyed trunk passage:
36,300   Cathedral–Falmouth Cave System, Florida, U.S.A. –
                   National Speleological Society (U.S.A.)

Appendix VI: Sheck Exley's Dive Partners

Name	Year*	Number**	Name	Year*	Number**
Adams, J.	71	1	Burgess, Bob	71	1
Adams, Walt	71	6	Burney, Skip	79	14
Addy, Noel	79	9	Burton, Linda	79	7
Adkins, ?	70	2	Bussell, Tom	89	3
Allen, Jim	66	8	Butler, Bob	82	1
Allen, Rick	72	34	Byrd, Bill	71	14
Allen, Tom	71	17	Cameron, Dave	71	34
Anderson, Rick	71	1	Campoli, Bernie	87	1
Anderson, Rob	78	2	Carter, Bruce	71	5
Aut, David	79	5	Carter, Doug	77	3
Axelrod, Bob	66	15	Cass, Bill	75	11
Aydlett, Bill	71	2	Cate, Bill	72	11
Bailey, Roy	80	1	Cecil, Fred	84	13
Banbury, Jack	71	3	Cernik, L.	81	2
Barta, Alan	77	1	Chalkley, Mark	79	8
Barth, Charlie	85	7	Chalkley, Tex	72	30
Bastian, Bob	78	25	Chapman, Charles	79	1
Batten, Reggie	71	21	Chestnutt, Mark	75	2
Baumgardner, Ina	72	2	Chupka, Jim	75	3
Baxter, Jim	68	12	Clausen, Carl	71	8
Beard, Guy	78	1	Cockrell, Sonny	85	2
Belli, D.	77	1	Coke, Jim	89	1
Benz, Jim	80	1	Cole, Russell	79	12
Best, Bill	70	1	Collins, Larry	80	1
Bippes, Barbel	81	2	Collins, Rusty	66	1
Blalock, Marty	78	10	Cook, Tom	77	18
Blevins, Rusty	74	1	Cork, Bob	80	2
Blitch, Norm	80	4	Corns, Doug	85	9
Bohrer, Randy	89	3	Cottrill, Tom	69	3
Bolton, Margie	80	5	Cowart, Carl	77	19
Bond, Bill	75	3	Crain, Jeannie	84	4
Bortnyk, George	80	6	Crain, Jonie	84	4
Bostwick, Fred	71	3	Crawford, Jim	74	2
Bowden, Jim	89	2	Crosby, Jerry	72	1
Bozanic, Jeff	89	1	Culpepper, Jane	78	1
Bradshaw, Dany	80	3	Culpepper, Melton	78	1
Breland, Tom	78	13	Cummings, George	71	6
Brock, Ken	66	19	Curran, Dave	89	2
Brod, Don	74	1	Curry, Miles	72	8
Brodesser, Ed	75	12	Danciger, Dan	89	1
Brooks, John	78	6	Danyluk, Greg	80	11
Brooks, Mary	74	6	Darby, Rick	67	10
Brubaker, Larry	79	1	Darring, Hardy	66	1
Brumley, Kim	78	7	Davidson, Mike	89	1
Bryant, Guy	80	1	Davis, Hal	77	1
Bunch, Betty	69	27	Defraene, Alain	81	10
Burdiss, Barney	77	2	DeLoach, Ned	74	55
Burgess, ?	84	8	DeLoach, Paul	71	275

(Appendix VI: Sheck Exley's Dive Partners cont.)

Name	Year*	Number**	Name	Year*	Number**
Denny, James	69	13	Friend, J.	76	6
Desautels, Dave	72	5	Fulghum, Ken	78	7
Deurloo, Doug	69	2	Fuller, Bob	71	20
Dhoogee, Ted	80	9	Fuller, India	76	10
Dickens, Rory	71	51	Gaines, Sari	73	4
Dickinson, Leo	87	2	Garriga, A.	70	1
Dietrich, Paul	72	4	Garriga, Walter	70	1
Dillon, Bud	77	2	Gatling, Bob	66	22
Diperna, Sam	71	14	Gavin, Bill	78	4
Dixon, Ed	77	16	Glasser, Don	70	1
Donahoo, Bill	76	19	Glover, Tim	87	5
Donahoo, Mack	78	18	Godbee, Rawls	73	2
Dorian, Allen	71	1	Gomez, Bob	78	19
Dow, Don	71	1	Goodman, Bob	74	18
Dowdy, Mike	70	3	Greathouse, Zane	78	5
Duckworth, Alice	81	2	Green, Larry	87	1
Duckworth, Mike	81	2	Green, Rick	89	3
Dunn, Bill	82	1	Greene, Woody	80	1
Duvall, Steve	70	4	Grey, Jane	81	2
Eckhoff, Mary Ellen	77	289	Griffeth, Larry	69	16
Ekherd, George	70	1	Guglio, Jim	69	4
Emerson, Larry	71	4	Gunderson, Anne	71	5
English, Lamar	80	3	Hall, Ed	74	21
Euhus, Richard	79	2	Hall, Joe	79	2
Evans, Monte	78	19	Halliwell, Tom	73	9
Ewing, T.	85	1	Harber, Bobby	80	1
Exley, Edward	66	86	Harp, Bill	68	4
Eyring, Marc	89	3	Harper, John	69	12
Farabee, Butch	86	4	Harrack, Dick	67	1
Fehring, Bill	78	27	Harris, Len	71	1
Filsinger, Rick	89	3	Harris, Martha	79	3
Finando, Steve	72	1	Hart, Paul	85	2
Fisk, Dave	72	39	Hartman, Sherrie	72	1
Flanagan, Greg	79	13	Hartsfield, Brad	81	2
Fluty, Larry	80	9	Hasenmayer, Jochen	81	1
Fogarty, Frank	76	21	Haviland, Randy	69	1
Fordham, Elizabeth	70	1	Hawkins, Tommy	66	40
Forfar, Archie	71	5	Hayes, Maggie	77	3
Forman, Steve	78	11	Head, Eddi	76	7
Fortune, Bill	66	4	Heinerth, Paul	74	16
Fowler, Carl	69	139	Heinerth, Shannon	80	7
Fox, Dale	77	3	Hellwig, Gene	89	2
Franklin, Al	79	7	Hendley, India	71	18
Frazier, Bob	78	1	Hendley, Ron	71	21
Frehsee, Rick	70	22	Hendrickson, Leif	71	3
Friedberg, Alan	79	8	Hendry, Bill	83	2
Friedman, Bob	71	12	Henegar, Bobby	71	2
Friedman, Sue	71	4	Henkel, Lewis	77	3

(Appendix VI: Sheck Exley's Dive Partners cont.)

Name	Year*	Number**	Name	Year*	Number**
Hiebert, ?	72	2	Lloyd, Chuck	66	6
Hiler, Hilaire	89	4	Lloyd, Roger	71	2
Hillier, Ken	74	75	Lockwood, Jim	71	49
Hixon, Ray	72	1	Long, Mark	82	6
Hobbs, Paul	81	14	Maddox, Gary	87	5
Hodgetts, Dave	89	3	Maddox, Lori	87	5
Hoggard, Riley	79	2	Maegerlein, Steve	74	2
Hollingsworth, John	69	13	Main, Bill	79	22
Holtzendorff, Lewis	72	170	Malachowski, Jacek	75	1
Holub, Tom	78	6	Malcolm, Larry	73	1
Horne, Peter	80	1	Malloy, Dale	72	8
Howe, Fletcher	69	8	Manget, Bill	69	56
Hudson, Steve	81	10	Manget, Sandra	70	6
Hulon, Oral	79	4	Manor, Dave	77	2
Humphries, Kirby	78	1	Marshall, Wayne	80	5
Hylton, Randy	71	3	Martz, Frank	71	1
Ikehara, Ike	72	2	Mattox, John	80	9
Iliffe, Tom	83	1	Maufroy, Bob	80	9
Irwin, Lewis	66	3	Maxwell, Jinx	79	8
Isaacs, Darrell	79	17	McCormack, Greg	78	1
Jasper, Woody	80	6	McDonald, Bill	66	3
Johnson, Bob	74	16	McLean, David	70	1
Johnson, Breck	79	3	McMahon, Gary	77	2
Johnson, David L.	80	1	McMullen, Greg	79	4
Juarros, Thom	82	3	Melton, Gene	74	31
Kalakoskis, Ed	76	1	Meng, Paul	77	10
Kearns, Don	69	21	Millage, Bob	82	6
Kellar, Ed	75	1	Miller, Richard	71	2
Kemp, Polly	71	4	Miller, Roger	77	11
Kerley, Barry	72	23	Millott, Bob	72	1
Kight, Wayne	67	11	Monnot, Don	77	3
Kinard, Keith	89	2	More, Eric	87	1
Kipila, Terry	76	31	More, Terry	74	28
Klotz, Barbara	71	2	Morgan, Renee	87	5
Klotz, Dean	70	5	Morlock, Wolfgang	81	4
Koehler, Bill	71	1	Morris, Don	79	2
Krieg, Franzjorg	81	2	Morris, Nancy B.	89	2
Kuebler, Mark	71	5	Morris, Tom	89	3
Lackey, Jim	79	8	Morrison, Leon	69	1
Lancaster, Ken	72	2	Morrow, Dave	77	9
Landis, Don	89	3	Morse, Bill	76	18
Lecompt, Jim	79	21	Mossman, Rick	86	1
Leguen, Francis	84	3	Mount, Tom	72	20
Leifer, Greg	69	2	Mount, Zidi G.	72	10
Leitheuser, Terry	79	2	Munson, John	72	1
Lenihan, Dan	72	24	Murphy, Larry	75	7
Lewis, Ian	77	17	Nangle, Jim	72	10
Ley, Jim	74	5	Nicholson, Henry	80	48

(Appendix VI: Sheck Exley's Dive Partners cont.)

Name	Year*	Number**	Name	Year*	Number**
Oakland, Bernie	70	7	Russell, Michelle	80	7
Oigarten, Bill	77	4	Rutledge, John	83	5
Ormeroid, Judy	83	2	Rutledge, Nancy	83	3
Ormeroid, Steve	82	3	Ryschevitch, George	76	1
Oswald, Karl	70	3	Salas, Bernie	66	2
Overstreet, Willie	80	6	Saltus, Allen	71	1
Owens, Miles	72	2	Sandberg, Eric	74	3
Padgett, Lester	72	32	Sanders, Buddy	78	9
Palmer, Ed	69	5	Saunders, Mike	77	19
Palmer, Rob	89	1	Schane, Bill	75	1
Panter, Ben	78	2	Schelles, Alena	82	8
Paulsen, Beth Exley	78	5	Schelles, Dennis	82	8
Paulsen, David	82	4	Schenck, Bill	73	1
Pecell, Brad	87	1	Schmitz, Fred	70	6
Pepper, Sharee	73	2	Seeholzer, Rolf	81	3
Perez, George	73	1	Sendry, Alan	72	1
Perry, Jim	66	11	Shaftner, Alan	72	2
Phillips, Sunny	85	2	Shifflett, Tommy	80	1
Piskula, Michael	81	2	Sigmon, Rita	79	7
Piskula, Tom	74	4	Sinclair, Bill	80	9
Pitcairn, Clara	79	12	Skiles, Wes	77	29
Pitcairn, Clark	79	55	Sloan, Noel	87	1
Porterfield, Bill	78	15	Smith, B.	79	1
Powell, Judy	82	1	Smith, Court	72	178
Power, Rob	81	16	Smith, Gordon	86	1
Pribble, Karan	73	53	Smith, Paul	76	92
Prokopetz, Wayne	76	3	Soto, Angel	88	10
Prosser, Joe	66	115	Stace, Peter	80	2
Prust, Phil	78	8	Stelling, Dutch	80	2
Rail, Sandra	76	1	Stevens, Ben	71	5
Raven, Larry	79	2	Stevens, Chuck	70	70
Rawlings, Glen	78	1	Stillo, Jeff	80	6
Reed, Debe	84	9	Stone, Bill	80	25
Reeves, John E.	78	1	Stone, Jamie	78	17
Reeves, Steve	80	8	Stone, Pat	83	1
Reilly, R. Scott	80	4	Storrick, Gary	81	6
Reinholm, Paul	74	2	Straatsma, Steve	81	3
Reintz, Bill	77	2	Strickland, Greg	83	2
Rigg, Rick	87	3	Strickland, Irwin	72	1
Ripley, R.	80	3	Sturdivant, Charlie	71	47
Risk, Stan	88	1	Sullivan, Kirby	74	12
Roberts, Smokey	78	6	Swanger, Norm	71	2
Robinson, Lee	72	5	Sweeney, Jim	69	1
Rodgers, Bob	68	40	Sweet, Dale	76	64
Rodgers, Robert	83	1	Taggart, Dave	78	2
Rosanes, Mose	79	2	Talley, Charles	83	1
Royal, Larry	89	3	Tanaka, Tara	85	25
Rusk, Jeff	83	1	Tanis, Sue	73	2

Name	Year*	Number**	Name	Year*	Number**
Tarasovic, C.	76	2	White, Tom	83	1
Taylor, C. "Poppa"	79	1	Wicklund, Bob	73	1
Therien, Paul	71	1	Wiggins, Bill	71	9
Thompson, Coakley	66	6	Williams, Charlie	72	1
Thompson, Glen	73	2	Williams, Dennis	78	7
Toulomdjian, Claude	79	2	Williams, Dick	71	2
Townes, John	87	2	Williams, Larry	71	3
Troutner, John	87	2	Williamson, B. J.	79	4
Truitt, Joe	71	3	Willis, ?	70	2
Turner, Dana	72	92	Willis, R.	70	1
Uhrhammer, Chuck	69	7	Wilson, Forrest	76	24
Van Soeren, Mary	82	5	Wimberly, Steve	78	4
Vandenoord, Dutch	71	41	Wingate, Wayne	84	1
Vaughn, ?	70	3	Wingate, William	76	4
Vilece, Carol	78	6	Wong, Alex	73	1
Villeneuve, Les	66	5	Wood, Brian	78	2
Vinson, Dana	69	32	Wood, Skip	85	2
Vogt, Karen	76	36	Woods, Doug	78	2
Voynich, Mike	71	4	Woodward, Art	73	1
Wall, Tom	80	2	Woolf, Bob	71	13
Walten, Gary	89	2	Woolf, Danny	76	12
Walters, Will	75	24	Wright, Wayne	72	21
Wark, Karen	82	1	Wyatt, Jim	75	2
Warner, Barry	78	19	Yager, Jill	78	1
Warren, Carter	71	3	Yaklevich, Jay	71	7
Washington, Bill	82	1	Young, Billy	71	30
Watson, Pat	89	2	Young, Ken	79	1
Wattenbarger, Frank	72	3	Young, Ray	79	1
Watts, Gordon	71	10	Young, Tom	89	1
Watts, Hal	69	3	Young, Troy	76	9
Weiss, Ken	69	3	Youngblood, Robert	72	3
Werner, Roger	80	4	Zambrano, Sergio	81	15
Wetzel, Randy	79	21	Zepf, Brett	79	4
Whall, Dave	82	1	Zumrick, John	75	117

* approximate year of first dive together

** approximate number of dives made with that diver to date

Index

Bold numbers indicate photographs; bold numbers with an "m" indicate maps

A

Grand Bahama Island. *See* caves: Bahamas
Grand Cayman 73. *See also* caves
Greathouse, Zane 293
Green, Larry 293
Green, Rick 293
Greene, Woody 293
Grey, H. V. 284
Grey, Jane 184, 293
Griffeth, Larry 293
Groupe d'Etudes et de Plongées Souterraines 286
Gruener, John
  scuba diving depth record 69
Guglio, Jim 293
guideline. *See* diving Equipment
Gulf of Mexico 15
Gunderson, Anne 69-84, 271, 293
  diving accident 81

H

Habitrough 238
Hall, Ed 223, 293
Hall, Joe 293
Halliwell, Tom 293
halocline 110, 113, 119, 132
Hamilton, Bill 267
Harber, Bobby 293
Harp, Bill 293
Harper, John 42, **48**, 49, **51**, 56, 75, **92**, **100**, 105, 211, **213**, **224**, 234, 239, 267, 286, 288, 293
  cave diving penetration record 22
Harrack, Dick 293
Harris, Len 293
Harris, Martha 293
Hart, Paul 293
Hartman, Sherrie 293
Hartsfield, Brad 293
Hasenmayer, Jochen 161, 185, 238, 239, 249, 254, 255, 264, 267, 276, 285, 286, 287, 289, 293
  cave diving depth record 249, 264
Haviland, Randy 293
Hawkins, Tommy 25-36, **35**, 58, 81, 293
Hayes, Maggie 293
Head, Eddi 293
Heinerth, Paul 2, **4**, **5**, **88**, 266, 270, 277, 285, 290, 293
Heinerth, Shannon 2, **4**, **5**, **8**, **103**, 293
helium 68, 152, 184, 247, 248, 249, 255, 258, 259, 267, 277

Igoe, Jack 161
Ikehara, Ike 294
Iliffe, Tom 135, 139, 140, **141**, 294
Iliffe, Yolande 141
implosion, battery 275
Indian remains 89
International Union of Speleology Cave Diving Commision 93
Iowa. *See* caves
Irwin, Lewis 294
Isaacs, Darrell 294
Isler, Olivier 241, 287, 290
    scuba diving penetration record 238

J

Jagnow, Dave 166
Jasper, Woody 294
Jenkins, Wally 285
Johnson, Bob 97, 294
Johnson, Breck 294
Johnson, David L. 294
Johnson, Herb
    scuba diving depth record 68
Jones, Simon 288
Juarros, Thom 294

K

"Killer Lockwood". *See* Lockwood, Jim
Kalakoskis, Ed 294
karate 25, 57, 257
Kearns, Don 294
Kellar, Ed 294
Keller, Hannes 67, 72
Kemp, Polly 294
Kentucky 156. *See also* caves
Kerley, Barry 97, 294
Kight, Wayne 294
Kinard, Keith 294
Kipila, Terry 294
Klotz, Barbara 294
Klotz, Dean 294
knives, forearm. *See* diving equipment
Knowles, Bob 78
Koehler, Bill 294
Krasle, George 43
Krieg, Franzjorg **8**, 294

(nitrogen narcosis continued)
    258, 259, 261, 271, 273. *See also* cave diving sicknesses
    management techniques 68
    severe narcosis symptoms 72
nitrox 241, 261, 282
NOAA. *See* National Oceanic and Atmospheric Administration
Nonec. *See* Chakalal cenote
NSS. *See* National Speleological Society
NSS Bulletin. See National Speleological Society
NSS. *See* National Speleological Society
NSSCDS. *See* National Speleological Society
Nyman, Rolly 285

O

Oakland, Bernie 295
octopus regulators. *See* diving equipment
Oigarten, Bill 295
one-third rule. *See* third rule
Ormeroid, Judy 295
Ormeroid, Steve 284, 295
Oswald, Karl 295
Ottonelli 285
Overstreet, Willie 295
Owens, Miles 295
oxygen 184, 241, 259, 261, 282
oxygen toxicity 74, 79, 223, 255, 261. *See also* cave diving sicknesses
    pulmonary oxygen toxicity 275
    spinal oxygen toxicity 260
Ozark Mountains. *See* Missouri

P

Padgett, Lester 295
Palmer, Ed 295
Palmer, Harold D. 289
Palmer, Rob 295
Panter, Ben 295
panty hose 247
Parker, Rob 289
Parzefal , Jacob 140
Paulsen, Beth Exley 295
Paulsen, David 295
Pecell, Brad 295
Pelican light. *See* diving equipment
penetration record. *See* record dives
Pennsylvania 158. *See also* caves

S

Walters, Will 129, 296
Wark, Karen 161, 296
Warner, Barry 269, 296
Warren, Carter 296
Warshauer, Mike 154
Washington, Bill 296
watch 2, 269. *See also* diving equipment
water pollution 239
Watson, Bruce 269.
Watson, Neal
  scuba diving depth record 69
Watson, Pat 296
Wattenbarger, Frank 296
Watts, Gordon 90, 296
Watts, Hal 42, **48**, 49, 68, 71, 72, 247, 296
    scuba diving depth record 67, 68
Wefer, Fred 161
Weiss, Ken 296
Werner, Roger 296
West Virginia. See caves
wet suit. *See* diving equipment
Wetzel, Randy 296
Whall, David 161, 296
White, Tom 296
Wicklund, Bob 296
Wiggins, Bill 76, 82, 272, 296
Wilkens, Horst 140, 141,
Williams, Charlie 296
Williams, Dennis 111, 113, 118, 121, 140, **141**, **148**, **173**, 284, 296
Williams, Dick 58, 296
Williams, Larry 296
Williamson, B. J. 296
Willis, R. 296
Wilson, Conrad 285
Wilson, Forrest 152, 162-**163**, 296
  "The Wizard" 163
  NSS CDS training officer 284
Wimberly, Steve 296
Wingate, Wayne 296
Wingate, William 296
Wong, Alex 296
Wood, Brian 296
Wood, Skip 97, 296
Woods, Doug 296
Woodward, Art 296
Woolf, Bob 296
Woolf, Danny 296